WELLINGTON AGAINST MASSENA

WELLINGTON AGAINST MASSENA

The Third Invasion of Portugal

1810-1811

DAVID BUTTERY

Pen & Sword
MILITARY

First published in Great Britain in 2007 by
Pen & Sword Military
An imprint of
Pen & Sword Books Ltd
47 Church Street
Barnsley
South Yorkshire
S70 2AS

ISBN 978 1 84415 554 5

A CIP catalogue record for this book is
available from the British Library.

Printed and bound in England
By CPI UK

Pen & Sword Books Ltd incorporates the imprints of Pen & Sword Aviation,
Pen & Sword Maritime, Pen & Sword Military, Wharncliffe Local History,
Pen & Sword Select, Pen & Sword Military Classics and Leo Cooper.

For a complete list of Pen & Sword titles please contact
PEN & SWORD BOOKS LIMITED
47 Church Street, Barnsley, South Yorkshire, S70 2AS, England
E-mail: enquiries@pen-and-sword.co.uk
Website: www.pen-and-sword.co.uk

Contents

List of plates

(between pages 112 and 113)

List of maps

Map symbols

MAPS: key to military symbols

INFANTRY

- British
- French
- Portuguese

CAVALRY

- British
- French
- Portuguese

ARTILLERY

Chronology

1758	6 May	Birth of Andrea Massena
1769	1 May	Birth of Arthur Wesley
	15 August	Birth of Napoleon Buonaparte
1774	10 May	Death of Louis XV. Accession of Louis XVI
1775	18 August	Massena enlists in Régiment Royal-Italien
1777	18 April	Massena is promoted to sergeant
1781		Death of Lord Mornington. Wesley enters Eton
1784	4 September	Massena is promoted to Warrant Officer *(Adjutant)*
1787	7 March	Wesley enters the army as an Ensign
	25 December	Wesley promoted Lieutenant
1789	17 June	National Assembly assumes governmental powers
	14 July	The storming of the Bastille
	3 August	Massena discharged from Royal Army
	10 August	Massena marries Rosalie Lamarre
1790	30 June	Wesley becomes MP for County Trim, Ireland
1791	20 June	Flight of Louis XVI to Varennes
	30 June	Wesley promoted Captain
	17 September	Massena enlists in Volontaires du Var, 2nd Battalion
1792	1 February	Massena is elected to command his battalion
	20 April	France declares war on Austria and Sardinia
	19 August	Prussia invades France
	21 September	Establishment of the National Convention
	22 September	French monarchy abolished
1793	21 January	Louis XVI is executed
		The Committee of Public Safety is established
	31 May	The Reign of Terror begins
	25 June	Birth of Prosper Massena
	22 August	Massena is promoted to Brigadier-General
	27 August	Royalists in Toulon side with the British
	30 September	Wesley promoted Lieutenant-Colonel (Goes to command brigade in Flanders 1794–1795)
	15–16 October	Jourdan and Carnot defeat the Allies at Wattignies
	16 October	The execution of Marie-Antoinette
	18 December	Toulon falls to the French
	20 December	Massena is promoted to Divisional General
1794	15 January	Massena commands the right wing of the Army of Italy
	4 March	Buonaparte assumes command of the artillery in the Army of Italy

	25 June	Jourdan defeats the Austrians at Fleurus
	27 July	*Coup d'état* of 9 Thermidor sees the fall of Robespierre and the end of 'the Terror'
1795	5 April	Peace of Bâle between France and Prussia
	4 October	*Coup d'état* of 13 Vendémaire Buonaparte commands the army of the Interior
	1 November	The Directory replaces the Convention government
1796	2 March	Bonaparte (formerly Buonaparte) appointed commander of the Army of Italy
	9 March	Bonaparte marries Josephine Beauharnais
	12–21 April	Battles of Montenotte, Millésimo, Dego and Mondovi between Sardinia and France
	3 May	Wesley made full Colonel in the army
	10 May	Battle of Lodi
	15 May	Bonaparte enters Milan
	3 August	Battle of Lonato
	5 August	Battle of Castiglione
	8 September	Battle of Bassano
	15–17 Nov.	Battle of Árcola
1797	14 January	Battle of Rivoli
	2 February	Surrender of Mantua
	4 September	*Coup d'état* of 18 Fructidor
	17 October	Treaty of Campo-Formio between France and Austria
1798	19 February	Massena arrives in Rome to assume command
	15 March	Massena recalled in semi-disgrace
	19 May	Bonaparte sails for Egypt
	May to August	The Great Rebellion in Ireland
	21 July	Battle of the Pyramids
	1 August	French fleet destroyed at Aboukir Bay by Nelson
	10 December	Massena receives command of the Army of Helvetia
1799	1 March	The War of the Second Coalition
	25 March	Austrians defeat Jourdan at Stockach
	4 May	Seringapatam falls to Wellesley. Death of Tippoo Sultan. Wellesley (formerly Wesley) becomes Governor of Mysore
	20 May	Bonaparte abandons the siege of Acre
	4 June	Austrians force Massena back at the first battle of Zurich
	17-19 June	Battle of the Trebbia. Suvórov defeats MacDonald
	18 June	*Coup d'état* of 30 Prairial
	15 August	Battle of Novi. Joubert killed in Russian victory
	25 Sept.-10 Oct.	Second battle of Zurich. Massena defeats Austro-Russians

	9 October	Bonaparte lands at St. Raphaël, France
	9 November	*Coup d'état* of 18 Brumaire. Bonaparte becomes First Consul
	25 November	Massena commands the Army of Italy
1800	5 April	Austrians attack Massena at Genoa
	15 May	Bonaparte crosses the Great St. Bernard Pass into Italy
	4 June	Massena capitulates at Genoa
	14 June	Battle of Marengo. One of Bonaparte's greatest victories
	13 August	Massena is dismissed from command of the Army of Italy
	1 January	Act of Union in Ireland
	9 February	Peace of Lunéville between France and Austria
	14 March	William Pitt resigns after George III refuses Catholic emancipation. Addington subsequently becomes Prime Minister
	23 March	Tsar Paul I dies and is succeeded by Alexander I
	14 September	French evacuate Egypt
	14 September	Camp established at Boulogne for the Invasion of England
1802	25 March	Peace of Amiens between France and Great Britain
	4 August	Bonaparte made First Consul for life
1803	16 May	Great Britain declares war on France
	6 August	Second Mahratta War
	12 August	Ahmednuggur falls
	23 September	Battle of Assaye
	29 November	Battle of Argaum
	15 December	Gawilghur capitulates
1804	7 April	Execution of the duc d'Enghien
	10 May	Addington resigns as Prime Minister, replaced by Pitt
	18 May	Napoleon I declared Emperor of France
	19 May	Eighteen generals created marshals of France including Massena
	1 September	Wellesley awarded Order of the Bath
	2 December	Napoleon's Coronation as Emperor at Nôtre Dame
1805	10 March	Wellesley leaves India to return to Europe
	9 August	Third Coalition formed against France
	23 August	Massena commands Army of Italy
	19 October	Mack surrenders at Ulm
	21 October	Naval battle of Trafalgar
	28–31 October	Battle of Caldiero
	2 December	Battle of Austerlitz. Napoleon's greatest victory
	26 December	Treaty of Pressburg between Austria and France

1806	23 January	The death of William Pitt
	13 February	Massena enters Naples
	1 April	Joseph Bonaparte created King of Naples
	1 April	Wellesley becomes MP for Rye, Sussex
	10 April	Wellesley marries Kitty Pakenham
	18 July	Gaeta falls to Massena's army
	15 September	Prussia joins Anglo-Russian Coalition
	14 October	Battles of Jena and Auerstädt
	21 November	Napoleon issues Berlin Decrees to blockade Great Britain
1807	3 February	Birth of Arthur Richard Wellesley (firstborn)
	8 February	Battle of Eylau
	3 April	Wellesley made Chief Secretary of Ireland
	March–July	Massena commands V Corps of the Grande Armée in Poland
	14 June	Battle of Friedland
	7–9 July	Treaty of Tilsit between France, Russia and Prussia
	7 September	British capture Copenhagen and siege Danish fleet
	27 November	Portuguese Royal family sails for Brazil
	30 November	Junot occupies Lisbon
1808	March–July	Massena and eleven other generals are created Dukes
	25 April	Wellesley promoted Lieutenant-General
	2 May	Spanish rebel against Murat's occupying army
	10 May	Joseph Bonaparte created King of Spain
	12 July	Wellesley commands expeditionary force to Portugal
	20 July	Dupont surrenders at Bailén
	1 August	British land at Mondego Bay
	17 August	Battle of Roliça
	21 August	Battle of Vimeiro
	30 August	French evacuate Portugal after the Convention of Cintra. Wellesley recalled to England
	8 November	Napoleon invades Spain
	4 December	Napoleon enters Madrid
1809	16 January	Battle of Corunna
	9 March	Soult invades Portugal
	April	Wellesley resigns as Chief Secretary of Ireland. Sails for Portugal
	6 April	Archduke Charles invades Bavaria – war between France and Austria
	20–23 April	Battle of Eckmühl
	12 May	Battle of Oporto
	13 May	Napoleon enters Vienna
	17 May	Napoleon annexes the Papal States
	20–23 May	Battle of Aspern-Essling

	5–6 July	Battle of Wagram
	6 July	Pope Pius VII arrested by the French
	27–28 July	Battle of Talavera
	4 September	Wellesley created Viscount Wellington
	Sept–Oct	Wellesley orders the construction of the Lines of Torres Vedras
	July–September	British expedition to Walcheren
	4 October	Spencer Perceval becomes Prime Minister
	14 October	Treaty of Schönbrunn between France and Austria
1810	2 April	Napoleon marries Archduchess Marie-Louise of Austria
	17 April	Massena commands Army of Portugal
	9 July	Ciudad Rodrigo falls to Massena
	24 July	Combat on the Côa. Beginning of the Third Invasion
	27 August	Almeida capitulates to the French
	27 September	Battle of Busaço
	3 October	Massena enters Coimbra
	8 October	Wellington enters the Lines of Torres Vedras
	10–14 October	French halt before the Lines of Torres Vedras
	14 November	Massena withdraws to Santarém-Rio Maior
1811	5 March	Massena begins the retreat
	11 March	Badajoz falls to the French
	22 March	Massena dismisses Marshal Ney from command
	3 April	Battle of Sabugal. French army leaves Portugal
	3-5 May	Battle of Fuentes de Oñoro
	10 May	Massena relieved of command
	16 May	Battle of Albuera
1812	19 January	Ciudad Rodrigo falls to Wellington
	6 April	Badajoz falls to Wellington
	11 May	Perceval is assassinated in the House of Commons
	24 June	Napoleon's *Grande Armée* invades Russia
	22 July	Battle of Salamanca
	18 August	Wellington created Generalissimo of Spanish Army
	7 September	Battle of Borodino
	14 September	Napoleon enters Moscow
	27 November	French retreat across the Beresina
	14 December	Ney commands the rearguard crossing the Niemen

1813	16 March	Prussia declares war on France
	14 April	Massena appointed Governor of Toulon Military District
	3 May	Battle of Lützen
	21–22 May	Battle of Bautzen
	21 June	Battle of Vittoria
	20–30 July	Battle of the Pyrenees
	12 August	Austria declares war on France
	31 August	San Sebastian falls to Wellington
	16–19 October	Battle of Leipzig. Major defeat for Napoleon
1814	1 March	Treaty of Chaumont
	31 March	Allies enter Paris
	10 April	Battle of Toulouse
	11 April	Napoleon abdicates. Treaty of Fontainebleau
	26 April	Louis XVIII proclaimed King of France
	3 May	Wellington created Duke
	4 May	Napoleon reaches Elba in exile
	20 May	First Treaty of Paris
	5 July	Wellington made Ambassador to the French Court
	1 November	Congress of Vienna opens
1815	26 February	Napoleon escapes from Elba
	1 March	Napoleon lands at Golfe-Juan
	20 March	Napoleon enters Paris. Beginning of the 'Hundred Days'
	16 June	Battles of Ligny and Quatre Bras
	18 June	Battle of Waterloo – Napoleon's final defeat
	22 June	Napoleon abdicates
	7 July	Allies enter Paris
	5 October	Napoleon reaches St. Helena and final exile
	20 November	Second Treaty of Paris
	7 December	Execution of Marshal Ney
1816	1 January	Massena dismissed from command by Louis XVIII
1817	4 April	Death of Massena
	10 April	Massena's funeral
1821	5 May	Death of Napoleon on St. Helena
1852	14 September	Death of the Duke of Wellington

Preface

The Third Invasion of Portugal marked a turning point in the Peninsular War, a struggle that played a crucial part in the downfall of Napoleon Bonaparte and his Empire. Fought in an isolated and hostile region, it witnessed the clash of two of Europe's finest generals, with neither gaining the upper hand until the end of the campaign. Though Wellington's past is well known, this work examines the background of André Massena in some detail, whose origins and character are somewhat mysterious and controversial. It also examines their clash at Fuentes de Oñoro, the relevance of which is often overlooked, being one of the closest of Wellington's career. With the current level of interest in the Peninsular War, I feel that there is a place for a re-examination of this fascinating campaign, which played such a key role in the long Iberian conflict.

I have received considerable assistance in the research and production of this book and feel obliged to thank a number of organisations and individuals. The staff of the British Library were very helpful and many of the rare books I have used, particularly from the French side of the conflict, would have been unavailable without access to their collection. The archives of the National Army Museum have also proved useful, providing several primary sources from eyewitnesses. As a former student, the University of Leicester's library staff were extremely helpful, especially in providing access to newspaper and journal sources. I would particularly like to thank David Charlton, whose help and advice is much appreciated.

I would like to thank my colleagues Christopher Poole and Matt Coote for their advice on computer programmes when I designed the maps to accompany this work. Though I possess a fair knowledge of computers, their suggestions and comments were very useful during a long and occasionally frustrating task.

No thanks can be enough for Stuart Hadaway, a fellow historian whose views and opinions I have always valued and respected. We made a good team during our trip to the Peninsula and without his assistance I could never have found and visited as many sites as I did in what is still a remote and difficult region. His knowledge of the Napoleonic era has been invaluable during our many discussions, and he allowed me access to his personal collection of Peninsular War volumes.

I would like to thank Pauline Buttery for reading through the manuscript and picking up all those little typographical errors that hound every aspiring writer. Having worked in a provincial newspaper for many years, I appreciate the value of good proofreading and still consider such 'quality control' to be the most important job in the publishing industry. Even in the days of computerised spelling and grammar checks, no writer can do without a second pair of eyes that might catch embarrassing errors he has overlooked. I would also like to thank her for helping me with French translation, as her grasp of the language is considerably superior to my own.

Finally I would like to thank Rupert Harding and Pen and Sword Books for allowing me the chance to bring my work to a wider readership. After picking up a taste for writing at university it has been my dream to write a book and I am extremely grateful for the opportunity. I hope that all those I have mentioned will look over this work and consider it worthwhile.

David Buttery
June 2006

Chapter 1

The Peninsular War

In 1807 Napoleon Bonaparte had reached the zenith of his power in Europe. Born in relative obscurity on the isle of Corsica, the French Revolution enabled him to rise with stunning rapidity through military talent, political opportunism and unwavering ambition. During the Revolutionary Wars, France fought to maintain her borders and preserve the new republic and, as one of her foremost generals, Bonaparte's influence increased until he overthrew the Directorate in the *coup d'état* of 18 Brumaire 1799. Though initially sharing power, as First Consul he rapidly began to assume the status of a dictator. As his popularity grew, many Frenchmen were persuaded to accept a strong leader, fearing the old monarchies of Europe who despised the young republic and wishing to avoid the terror and corruption that typified the Revolution's seedy aftermath. By 1804 Napoleon felt confident enough to crown himself Emperor and his coronation took place at Nôtre Dame on 2 December.

France had been in a state of almost continual warfare since 1792, but the wars now took on a different character. Defending French interests alone was no longer enough for the ambitious new Emperor, who wished to make France the dominant European power. He believed that maintaining supremacy was closely inter-linked with imperialism and military success:

> *My power depends on my glory and my glory on the victories I have won. My power will fall if I do not feed it on new glories and new victories. Conquest has made me what I am and only conquest can enable me to hold my position.*[1]

With much of Europe opposed to France, Bonaparte had ample opportunity to put this theory to the test. Britain remained an implacable foe of French expansionism, so the invasion and subjugation of England became his first objective. However, the catastrophic defeat of the combined French and Spanish fleets at the battle of Trafalgar in 1805 saw this operation postponed indefinitely.

Over the next three years Napoleon demonstrated his military genius by inflicting a series of crushing defeats on the foremost land powers in Europe. In 1805 the French *Grande Armée* marched from their base at Boulogne, where they were massed for the abortive invasion of

England, and brought a new kind of warfare to Europe. Napoleon had restructured the army, dividing it into independent corps capable of rapid movement and yet strong enough to hold their own against considerable numbers until reinforced. His theories of war relied on swift marches and lightning strikes, intended to bring the enemy to a decisive battle as quickly as possible. The Austrians were caught off guard by the speed of French manoeuvres and General Mack was surrounded and forced to surrender with around 27,000 men in a relatively bloodless victory at Ulm in Bavaria.

On 2 December 1805, Napoleon won his greatest victory at Austerlitz, defeating the combined armies of Russia and Austria, who quickly sued for peace. In a tactical triumph, Napoleon lured the Allies into attacking him by abandoning the key strategic position of the Pratzen Heights. His carefully planned counter-attack enabled him to cut off his assailants' overextended assaults and inflict crippling losses, driving his enemies into headlong retreat. The political will to oppose Bonaparte crumbled, leaving the Third Coalition in tatters. The effect of the French victory was aptly summed up by British Prime Minister William Pitt's prophetic remark upon seeing a map of Europe: 'Roll up that map; it will not be wanted these ten years.'[2] Ten hours of bloodletting at Austerlitz had dashed his hopes of stopping the French and the terrible news reputedly hastened the great statesman's death.

The following year Napoleon shocked the Continent when he defeated the Prussians at Jena, since their army was thought to be amongst the finest in Europe after Frederick the Great's reforms. Frederick William III was eventually forced to concede humiliating terms to the French, with the Prussian army virtually destroyed. Russia had once again declared war against France and the costly battle of Eylau, fought in severe winter conditions, proved indecisive. However, the French won a conclusive victory at Friedland in 1807 and Tsar Alexander I made peace at Tilsit between 7–9 July 1807. Meeting on a raft in the middle of the River Niemen, the two monarchs agreed terms that saw France become the dominant power on the Continent. Prussia lost considerable territory and various states were divided between France and her allies. Most importantly, Alexander agreed to reverse his old allegiances and join France in a trade agreement against Britain, known as the Continental System. Britain's overwhelming naval superiority made a sea-borne invasion unlikely to succeed, so Napoleon hoped to close Continental ports to the British in an attempt to damage their economy.

However, Russia and France were still divided over several important issues and some clauses in the treaty were left deliberately vague. For example, although Napoleon promised some assistance against the Turkish Sultan, he would never allow Russia to seize Constantinople, thereby gaining strategic access to the Mediterranean. From the Russian point of view, French enthusiasm for an independent Poland was anathema to the Tsar, who wished to keep the recalcitrant Poles firmly under Russian control and feared a French client state so far to the east. Thus, despite some common interest, Russia was always a reluctant ally, brought to the negotiating table by force of arms. The longevity of the alliance was very much dependent upon future events. Nevertheless, this treaty made France the foremost state in Europe and only one significant foe remained – Great Britain.

Britain refused to make peace with France until the balance of power had been restored in Europe. Austria, Prussia and Russia had been subdued by the seemingly unstoppable French army and many small countries had become mere vassal states of France, Napoleon's influence being so great that he could impose members of his family as kings and queens over them.[3] Politically it was dangerous for the old order to allow upstarts like the Bonaparte clan to create a new royal dynasty, as it set an alarming precedent. Furthermore, allowing Napoleon to remain as the virtual master of Europe was unthinkable for the British.

In 1807 the two nations had reached a strategic stalemate. With the breadth of the English Channel and the dominance of the Royal Navy at sea, Britain was virtually impregnable. Yet her navy was incapable of defeating a land-based, largely self-sustaining empire by blockade, and the defeat of the formidable French army, totalling nearly a quarter of a million men, could only be achieved through direct military intervention on the Continent. Though the new Continental System would need time to take effect, many countries were hostile or at least ambivalent towards Britain, and her mercantile interests could be severely damaged if the war became a lengthy struggle. Although the French had suffered a crushing defeat at Trafalgar, given time Napoleon could rebuild the fleet and potentially cross the Channel. Prime Minister William Portland realised that the need for a swift conclusion was imperative and the current policy of conducting small sea-borne raids was proving ineffective. Lord Melville's reminiscences in 1814 are revealing in this regard, when he acknowledged that given sufficient time Napoleon would:

... have sent forth such powerful fleets that our navy must

*eventually have been destroyed since we could never have kept
pace with him in building ships or in equipping numbers sufficient
to cope with the tremendous power he could have brought against
us.'* [4]

This fact was well known to Napoleon, despite his general ignorance of
naval warfare. Though committed to economic warfare against Great
Britain, he never entirely relinquished the idea of crossing the twenty
miles of strait between France and England and inflicting a military
defeat on his oldest enemy. The British fleet possessed about 104 ships
of the line, but many of these were needed on the far side of the Atlantic
or in the Indian Ocean, protecting British colonies and interests. If the
French possessed odds of three to one, the Royal Navy could be
destroyed or at least kept occupied while troops were ferried across the
Channel. The combined French and Dutch fleet had around seventy-
five battleships in 1807. Allied Spain could contribute a further thirty
and Russia potentially had twenty-four to lend. Admittedly, a further
129 warships would be required for total superiority, but, in addition
to building further vessels, the Danish possessed seventeen battleships
and the Portuguese had ten. One of the secret clauses agreed in the
treaty in Tilsit permitted Napoleon to acquire these fleets from their
rightful owners.[5] Britain's bombardment of neutral Copenhagen in
August 1807 and the forcible seizure of the Danish fleet revealed that
the British were aware of the threat and made Portugal's navy even
more important.

Therefore, Napoleon had several motives for sending a military
expedition to the Peninsula. Portugal openly flouted the commercial
agreements France wished to impose on Europe, continuing a thriving
trade with Great Britain, and Napoleon coveted her navy. Furthermore,
as one of Britain's oldest Continental allies, the Portuguese might let the
English land troops on her shores, enabling them to secure a foothold
in Europe. Significantly, the country was already used as a stopping-off
point and unofficial base for British naval operations in the
Mediterranean. In political and strategic terms, Napoleon viewed
Portugal as a British colony in all but name and an invasion would be
a direct attack on British interests.

Prince Regent John of Portugal was soon made aware of French
designs on his country through the French and Spanish ambassadors,
and desperately tried to avert the forthcoming war. The Portuguese
royal house of Braganza was in an unenviable position when faced with
the threat of French expansionism. The Portuguese army was in a

deplorable state and certainly incapable of withstanding an invasion by the foremost army of Europe. However, Portugal relied heavily on trade by sea and could not afford to lose the revenue from British merchants or risk a blockade of her ports by the Royal Navy. Desperately trying to placate both sides, the Prince Regent offered to declare war on Britain, whilst assuring the English that this was in name only and that trade would continue despite any agreements he made with the French. However, neither side could be appeased and a British fleet appeared off the Portuguese coast to establish a blockade whilst Napoleon's threats, conveyed through French envoys, became increasingly vocal.

Meanwhile, France had entered into negotiations with Spain. King Charles IV was persuaded, largely through the efforts of his Prime Minister Manuel de Godoy, to allow a French army to march across Spain and invade Portugal. This was ratified at the treaty of Fontainebleau of 27 October 1807, in which the French agreed to divide Portugal into three sections. The north would fall under the Queen of Etruria's rule, central Portugal including Lisbon under France, and the duplicitous Godoy, who was deeply unpopular amongst his own people, would receive the south as a principality. The Emperor had made his decision to force Portugal to conform to his vision of Europe or be swallowed up by the growing French Empire. This was the first war since the Revolution to be fought without the pretext of a coalition of royalist states united against France. It would cost the blood of

The Iberian Peninsula
1808-1814

hundreds of thousands, inflict horrific damage in Iberia and eventually contribute to Napoleon's downfall.

Accordingly, General Andoche Junot, a particular favourite of the Emperor, marched into Iberia at the head of 28,000 men bound for Portugal. On the march the army was greeted by an exuberant Spanish population, excited at the prospect of war with their old enemy. However, the Spanish troops promised to assist Junot's invasion were ill prepared and he crossed the border without them. Having planned the campaign largely by map, Napoleon was aware of his lack of knowledge regarding Portugal's geography and had ordered Junot to make reports on the nature of the countryside, its population, fortifications and towns.[6] In future campaigns the lack of French knowledge about the Peninsula would prove crucial for the outcome of the war.

Napoleon had anticipated no opposition from the Portuguese forces and officially this proved to be the case. Nonetheless, Junot encountered great difficulties in traversing the mountainous terrain. Roads drawn on his maps proved to be mere tracks or occasionally non-existent, and the acquisition of sufficient food and shelter became a huge problem for his staff in a sparsely populated and inhospitable region. Although no military resistance was encountered, local peasants proved extremely hostile, fleeing at the sight of the French troops only to return in the night to cut the throats of sentries and stragglers, with banditry becoming commonplace. The fact that the invasion took place in winter added to the misery of the journey and when Junot's ragged army eventually reached Lisbon it was starving and much of his force was strung out along the route of the march. With his artillery more than a week behind his vanguard, he was lucky that the Portuguese had decided not to oppose him when he entered Lisbon on 30 November 1807.

Trying to forestall the invasion up until the end, the Prince Regent had declared war on Britain in an attempt to appease the French on 20 October, but decided to flee the capital five days prior to Junot's arrival. Napoleon thought so little of the Portuguese military that he had prematurely declared in Le Moniteur that the House of Braganza had ceased to reign. When the British gleefully showed the Regent the newspaper's claims, Prince Regent John fled into exile in Brazil, escorted by a British squadron, along with his court, the royal treasury and his fleet. As Junot's tired army marched into the capital they saw the massed sails on the horizon and realised that Napoleon's orders to seize the Portuguese navy at all costs were now impossible to obey.

General Junot now set about securing the country, as the rest of his army gradually limped into the capital, but he was forced to await the arrival of Spanish reinforcements before he could consider the nation under sufficient control. Most of the Portuguese sullenly accepted French rule, although there was some rioting and protests. Junot did his best to install a liberal regime but Napoleon, furious at the fleet's escape, ordered him to rule with a firm hand. The Regent, in his rush to set sail, abandoned fourteen cartloads of gold and silver on the quayside, but this was insufficient to placate the vengeful Emperor. An extraordinary tax of 100,000,000 francs was imposed on the Portuguese, Napoleon arguing that the war should pay for itself.

Napoleon had good reason to be satisfied with the outcome of the first invasion, despite the loss of the Portuguese fleet. Whilst it was true that Portugal was not wholly subjugated, it could now be forced to comply with the Continental System, which might eventually force Britain to capitulate. Britain now had to rely increasingly on Gibraltar to intervene in the Mediterranean and was denied a potential base in Europe. Nevertheless, Bonaparte's boundless ambition was both a blessing and a curse in his desire to achieve greatness. While his determination had driven him on to achieve great things, his success had blinded him to the limits of what was realistically possible.

Spain had always been a dubious ally for the French, partly because the ruling Bourbon family was related to the French royal family toppled by the Revolution. Once considered the foremost state in Europe, Spain's fortunes had dwindled, along with her crumbling empire. Her people were poor and discontent and the Spanish army was unreliable. The church and nobility possessed incredible power, oppressing the people while displaying little real loyalty to the state. The Government itself was corrupt and inefficient. There was political division, with many wishing to see Ferdinand, Prince of the Asturias, supplant his father Charles IV. The Spanish system was an ineffective relic of the past and Napoleon believed that the Spaniards would welcome its replacement with a more modern form of government.

In April 1808 Napoleon summoned the members of the Spanish royal family to a conference in Bayonne. He offered to mediate between the feuding factions in the royal family and, alternating between threats and bribery, the Emperor eventually persuaded Charles IV to abdicate in favour of Ferdinand, although Charles later reneged on this promise. The French had large numbers of troops stationed in Spain to support Junot's invasion, which would now be used to enforce the change in regime. Napoleon could have chosen to keep Ferdinand as a puppet ruler, especially as he felt grateful for French assistance in gaining his throne. It would have been easy for the French to influence the suggestible new monarch, who enjoyed considerable support from his people. However, even this was insufficient for Napoleon's grandiose schemes and he subsequently bullied Ferdinand into resigning his right to the throne and accepting exile in Valençay. A new ruler had to be imposed on Spain and Napoleon offered the throne to his brothers Louis and Lucien Bonaparte. Both had the sense to refuse, knowing that the difficulties encountered in any change of regime would be magnified by the unstable political situation in Iberia. Joseph Bonaparte reluctantly accepted the crown at his brother's insistence, relinquishing the throne of Naples in order to do so.

However, Napoleon's hopes that usurping the Spanish throne would be an easy process were unfounded. The Spanish had been restless under Charles and had detested his adviser Godoy, but although the enforced abdication of Ferdinand angered them, their insular society was outraged by the prospect of a foreign ruler. As more French troops entered the country to secure the transition of power the people became increasingly rebellious. This culminated in a large riot in May 1808, which became known as the *Dos de Mayo* in Madrid, when the crowds were infuriated at the sight of the remaining royal family being taken into exile. Individual and isolated groups of French soldiers were set upon and murdered in the most brutal fashion. Marshal Murat, a general known for extravagance and courage but lacking in restraint, ordered his cavalry to charge directly into the crowds, provoking hours of rioting and running fights with the mob. When the violence ended around 150 French soldiers had been killed, but around three times as many rioters had died.[7] The aftermath saw many Spaniards executed in scenes later immortalised by the Spanish artist Goya, and news of the massacre spread rapidly throughout the nation to widespread indignation. Local juntas were soon established across the country in opposition to Joseph's rule, many of which had militia or regular military support.

When Joseph entered Spain he had a genuine desire to institute lasting liberal reforms for Spain's benefit. Although Napoleon was younger, he was over-awed by him and possessed far more equanimity than his domineering brother. However, from the moment he arrived he perceived how discontented the people were and his official reception in the towns on his route to the capital was very muted. In Madrid, aghast at the sullen attitude of his new subjects and the growing acts of rebellion, he immediately wrote to Napoleon requesting further troops and huge financial support if he was to have any chance of ruling effectively.

Napoleon was dismayed by events in Spain, having hoped for a relatively peaceful annexation. Yet he still underestimated Spanish patriotism and was openly scornful of the martial qualities of Spain's armies and unafraid of the consequences of military action. As *The Times* later remarked with hindsight: 'The treaty of Tilsit, in which the destiny of the world seemed to be decided in his favour, was hardly concluded when he turned his eyes towards the West, and resolved on the ruin of Portugal and Spain...'[8] After the abdication, the Spanish nobility had divided into factions and was largely spread out across the country. Therefore Napoleon judged that mounting 'police actions' with flying columns against centres of resistance could conclude the war relatively swiftly. Although these expeditions met with some limited success, the Spanish generally refused to commit to battle and withdrew before them. Within a short time French troops were tied down in the siege of Saragoza and French columns were forced to pursue the Spanish far further south than expected, beyond the easy reach of supply and reinforcement. Though the Spanish forces were largely disunited and poorly led, Napoleon was reluctant to commit large numbers of troops and the French were therefore dangerously over-stretched.

General Dupont had been entrusted with the pacification of Andalusia and soon encountered far more resistance than anticipated. After the capture and sacking of the city of Cordoba, Dupont found the local peasantry raised against him and a large army approaching under General Reding. Although he possessed around 23,000 men with the promise of reinforcement, Dupont committed the worst of military sins by lingering indecisively on the plain of Andujar instead of making a strategic withdrawal. Hearing that the road to Madrid had been blocked, he sent General Vedel with 10,000 men to ensure that his line of retreat was clear. Dividing his force proved unwise, because a combined Spanish army under generals Reding and Castanos subsequently attacked him at Bailén. Repeated attempts to break out proved futile and the return of Vedel failed to extricate the French from the trap. On 21 July 1808 Dupont surrendered with at least 18,000 men.[9]

The defeat at Bailén was a disaster for the French campaign and had grave repercussions. King Joseph, already depressed by the enormity of his task, panicked at news of the reverse and fled the capital. The Spanish, who already dismissed him as a drunkard and a womaniser, viewed his overreaction as cowardice. Napoleon was furious at the debacle, making a scapegoat of Dupont, who after all had been allotted insufficient troops to subdue Andalusia, most of whom were conscripts and had been heavily outnumbered. Yet his brother's flight from the capital was even worse politically and, though he had stopped at the line of the River Ebro, it was almost as bad as having fled the country. The Spaniards were heartened by the scale of their victory and the Austrian war party made political headway on the strength of it. Even the Pope, previously cowed by Napoleon, felt confident enough to issue a public condemnation of French expansionism.

Meanwhile, General Junot was encountering severe problems in Portugal. Realising that the French conquest was far from secure, the British sent an expeditionary force under General Arthur Wellesley, later the Duke of Wellington, which landed at Mondego Bay in early August. Whilst Junot reacted quickly to repel the invasion, he underestimated the strength and resolve of British infantry and committed his forces piecemeal in poorly co-ordinated attacks. The French suffered three defeats within the month at Obidos, Roliça and Vimiero. At Vimiero the French sustained 2,000 casualties and lost thirteen guns, the capture of which was usually seen as representing the scale of a defeat, and Junot negotiated an armistice. The subsequent Convention of Cintra was poorly received in Britain as it gave extremely generous terms to the French. Not only were Junot and his army permitted to leave Iberia with all the plunder acquired in Portugal, but the Royal Navy was obliged to convey them back to France. Generals Dalrymple and Burrard, who had assumed command, were held accountable and re-called to answer for their actions along with Wellesley. A court of inquiry exonerated Wellesley and blamed his superiors, but nevertheless a notable victory had been won. The British Army had proved itself in three battles and the French had relinquished Portugal. The British political position was strengthened with the Regent in exile and, temporarily at least, they had regained their foothold in Europe.

With events in the Peninsula spiralling out of control, Napoleon was forced to admit that he had underestimated the strength of Iberian patriotism and that greater commitment would be necessary to accomplish his aims. Years of success had made the French army feared throughout Europe, but defeats on this scale would soon destroy their reputation and encourage resistance. He decided to intervene in person to restore French prestige. However, in central Europe Austria was making warlike preparations, eager to avenge former defeats and encouraged by the French preoccupation with the Peninsula. Knowing that he would have to weaken his forces in Germany to assemble enough men, Napoleon tried to ensure that Russia would support him in the event of Austria declaring war.

At a meeting with the Tsar at Erfurt, Napoleon requested Russian military aid against Austria. However, Alexander proved strangely intractable compared to his previous enthusiasm at Tilsit. He was under pressure from the Russian nobility to renege on his trade agreements against Britain and was wary of Napoleon's increasingly despotic actions. The Continental System showed little sign of weakening Britain, whilst its effects on the Russian economy were proving ruinous. For example, the Royal Navy bought large amounts of timber from Russia and the loss of such contracts was keenly felt, while the British had other sources they could rely on.

Well aware of French reluctance to fight on two fronts, Alexander won concessions from Napoleon, including an acceptance of Russian expansion into Wallachia and Moldavia and a pledge not to intervene in the Tsar's designs on Turkey. In return, Alexander promised to denounce any aggression on Austria's part, but the wording of the treaty was ambivalent regarding direct Russian intervention. This disappointment was a warning for Napoleon that his influence was diminishing and he might have been well advised to pull his troops back beyond the Ebro at this stage and postpone his Iberian conquests.

Napoleon, however, rarely abandoned a venture once he had embarked upon it. After all, his refusal to be discouraged had served him well in the past. As the most renowned soldier in Europe, the power of his reputation was a weapon in itself and he gave speeches proclaiming his intention to settle the Iberian struggle in person. The Bonapartist newspapers published contemptuous articles on the British Army in Portugal and speculated on how swiftly it would be ousted when the Emperor arrived. Bonaparte derided the British military and referred to them as 'leopards' in mockery of the thin British lions on their heraldic arms, remarking: 'The hideous leopard contaminates by its very presence the peninsula of Spain and Portugal. Let us carry our victorious eagles to the Pillars of Hercules...'[10] He promised that the Spanish rebellion would soon be crushed and the British driven into the sea.

The Spanish were now in a state of uneasy alliance with Great Britain, who had been their traditional enemy for centuries. The British presence in Portugal was being gradually consolidated, but it would take time for the army under Sir John Moore to march to Spain's assistance. In any case, the Spanish junta in Madrid hoped to resolve the war without foreign aid. They planned to envelop the French by attacking over the Ebro on their flanks, hoping to cut off their line of retreat to the Pyrenees. However, marshals Ney, Moncey and Bessières swiftly mounted attacks against Castano's forces in the Spanish centre and right, averting the Spanish offensive before it had even started.

When Napoleon arrived in the Peninsula French forces had been strengthened to around 190,000 men. He rapidly determined that his enemies were still set on their plan of encirclement, despite their recent reverse, and that this could be turned to his advantage. He decided to allow the Spaniards to attack his flanks and, as they moved forward, the French would attack their centre, pushing it back, thereby leaving the Spanish flank attacks exposed to a *manoeuvres sur les derrières*, whereby he would swing about on their rear and defeat them in detail. Once a clear victory was won Bonaparte would march on the capital.

Although the Spaniards were vulnerable to this strategy, Napoleon's plan relied on simultaneous movement and was marred by a premature attack mounted by Marshal Lefebvre on General Blake's forces. However, when the offensive began on 7 November the Spanish were outmanoeuvred and their forces scattered. Blake managed to save 10,000 men, roughly half his force, denying Napoleon a total victory, but the path to Madrid was open. The French 'Army of Spain' soon encountered great difficulties in finding supplies and troops resorted to looting on an alarming scale, forcing Napoleon to impose harsh measures to restore order.

Although their regular forces were in retreat, the peasantry began to ambush and murder isolated groups of French soldiers with increasing frequency. The pillaging of the country alienated the Spaniards, whose pride was already affronted by the invasion and many fled to the countryside to mount organised resistance. These groups came to be known as 'guerrillas', from the Spanish 'little war', and their raids became increasingly effective. Small garrisons, left in the wake of the advance, were attacked and couriers were forced to travel with large escorts. Napoleon soon became aware of this hazard when guerrillas began to intercept his dispatches. In later life, General Mattieu Dumas recalled his time in Spain as a young officer: 'I will always remember how I was afflicted with great anxieties. Each day saw the murder of several Frenchmen, and I travelled over this assassins' countryside as warily as if it were a volcano.'[11]

As Joseph rode back towards Madrid, Napoleon warned him of widespread banditry in the countryside, advising him to travel with a heavy escort. Though some were inspired by patriotic motives, Napoleon was correct in thinking that many guerrillas were nothing more than brigands. Often descending on Spanish villages with no warning, they would extort money, carry off provisions and press gang young men into 'enlisting' with them. Their attitude was aptly summed up by the Spanish jest: *'Viva Fernando y vamos robando!'* (Long live King Ferdinand and let us go robbing!') The land was devoid of supplies and full of roving bands of armed peasants, who threatened communications and harassed his troops. Having previously dismissed his generals' complaints, Napoleon began to appreciate the difficulties of war in Spain compared to the rest of Europe.

As the French approached the capital, the Spanish junta made preparations to flee to Cadiz, but a last-ditch defence was mounted just north of Madrid. General San Juan occupied a strong defensive position with around 12,000 men at the Pass of Samosierra and General Heredia took his troops to defend the defiles of Guadarramas to block the invaders' approach. Attacking San Juan, Napoleon encountered unexpected resistance and took some losses, but eventually dislodged the defenders, entering Madrid on 4 December. Joseph was restored to his throne but was received with indifference by his subjects. His rule, at least for the present, was entirely dependent on a large French military presence.

Napoleon, alerted to the presence of a British army under Moore marching towards him, determined to isolate and destroy this force. Moore was an experienced and capable general, having served in the Helder and Egypt campaigns in 1798 and 1800–1801. He was known for his great ability in training troops and his passion for military reform, but was a stern disciplinarian who expected a lot from his men. Having mounted an effective cavalry screen in front of his advancing army, he soon witnessed the defeat of his allies and the overwhelming superiority of the enemy and reluctantly decided to withdraw.

The British retreat was conducted in appalling weather conditions at the start of the Spanish winter. Napoleon was determined to catch the British force and defeat it, but the French pursuit was hampered by snowstorms and the lack of shelter and supply along the march. *The Times*, quoting from *Le Moniteur*, remarked on the pitiful scene left in the army's wake: 'The Emperor arrived at Astorga on the 1st of January. The road... to Astorga is covered with dead horses belonging to the English, with travelling carriages, artillery caissons and warlike stores.'[12] Yet Moore's skilful evasion won the Emperor's grudging respect, and he realised that, since the British appeared to be intent on

13

embarking as soon as they reached the coast, he would fail to inflict a decisive defeat. Alarming rumours had reached him that Austria was about to begin hostilities and he took his leave of the Army of Spain, leaving Marshal Soult in command to continue the pursuit.[13]

Napoleon's departure, with the Peninsula only half conquered, is cause for speculation. Whilst the Austrian threat was very real, some British contemporaries, including Wellesley, surmised that he was afraid to face British troops in open battle for the first time. Leaving aside patriotic bias, this was almost certainly untrue considering the calibre of Napoleon's previous enemies. After all, he had defeated the British at the siege of Toulon and had been eager to cross the Channel to invade their homeland. A more likely explanation is that, at least for this stage of the war, the Peninsula could no longer provide the decisive battle that the Emperor persistently sought. Most of his campaigns were dominated by this objective, though it would become progressively more elusive for him. The emphatic victories of Austerlitz, Jena and Friedland had all led to peace treaties shortly afterwards, providing a clear and unequivocal victory. In this case, with the Spanish throne usurped by his brother and Portuguese royalty having fled abroad, the defeat of forces under divided juntas or the Regency for an absentee monarch would yield limited military glory. Napoleon hoped that the following campaigns would be largely mopping up operations, best left to eager subordinates whose minor victories would not rival his achievements.

The British suffered terribly on the retreat towards Corunna in northern Spain. Hundreds died from the elements, with the camp followers and sick often being left in the snow to freeze or at the mercy of the pursuing French cavalry. The troops were discontent at being ordered to retreat without a fight and vented their frustrations on the locals, looting without restraint and occasionally committing acts of wanton destruction.[14] Moore's general order to the troops to desist from such indiscipline was sometimes ignored, with the officers sympathetic to their soldiers' plight. Rifleman Harris of the 95th Regiment recalled the men's feelings on the winter retreat:

> '...we now began to see more clearly the horrors of our situation, and the men to murmur at not being permitted to turn and stand at bay – cursing the French, and swearing they would rather die ten thousand deaths, with their rifles in their hands in opposition, than endure the present toil.'[15]

Rearguard skirmishes with the French vanguard failed to overawe the men, who yearned for the chance to prove their mettle in open battle once again. When the tattered force reached the port of La Corunna on 12 January, they discovered the ships that they expected had not arrived. Though a fleet arrived two days later to evacuate his army, Moore realised that he would have to turn and face the enemy in order to protect his withdrawal. Even so, with the docks crowded with cartloads of supplies, the priority was to save the artillery and many stores were fired and horses slaughtered to deny them to the enemy.[16]

Moore placed his forces on the heights surrounding Corunna, where Soult attacked on 16 January 1809. The British fought stubbornly, proving they had never feared to fight, and the French were only able to bring up enough men to roughly equal their force in terms of infantry. However, Moore's eagerness to embark his guns meant that the British were inferior in artillery, and a battery the French had dragged to the Penasquedo ridge was able to mount a very effective bombardment. As Soult's infantry assailed the centre, in an attempt to split the British force, the French superiority in artillery became apparent. It required steady infantrymen to withstand it: 'These regiments... suffered terribly from the fire of the great French battery, to which the British guns could make no reply. It needed Moore's presence to keep the men steady under so hard a trial...'[17]

The British counter-attacked effectively, contesting the village of Elvina in the centre, and the battle began to subside. However, whilst bringing up reinforcements, Sir John Moore was fatally wounded by a cannonball and died that evening. Casualties had been relatively light at around 2,000 for both sides, and the following morning French batteries fired on the harbour, causing some confusion and damage as the transports set out for sea. However, the British had escaped.

When the British troops landed back in southern England, people were dismayed at their ragged, filthy and half-starved appearance as they tramped back into barracks. Although they had fought their way out despite fearsome odds, significant losses had been sustained in men and material during the catastrophic retreat. In the House of Commons, Lord Grenville lamented that Britain's fortunes had sunk so low, remarking that within three years the country had lost two of her greatest statesmen, along with Britain's greatest admiral at Trafalgar. Now Britain had lost one of her best soldiers in a campaign ending in the army's unceremonious ejection from Spain.[18] As debates in Parliament raged on, Lords Moira and Grenville questioned whether Britain could afford to intervene directly on the Continent again, given the strength of the enemy, and some even proposed suing for peace.

Whilst many defended the performance of the army both in Parliament and the press, wild exaggerations were made over numbers of men and material lost and personal attacks were made on Sir John Moore's handling of the campaign and the inadvisability of continuing the war. As *The Times* dramatically proclaimed:

> '*Alas! Our victory is as useless as our retreat* (fortissima frustra pectora); *and neither in flying nor fighting, do we appear to have had any other object in view than that of saving ourselves and deserting the cause we sent troops to sustain. And this the country begins to feel now, and to feel it with shame and sorrow.*'[19]

Yet the very intensity of the attacks on the military worked against their critics and benefitted the cause of the war party with their obvious exaggerations. Moore had won a victory convincing enough to prevent serious interference in the evacuation, and had died achieving it, as an English hero.[20] Portugal was still in British hands and it was politically inconceivable to relinquish it without a struggle. With hindsight Moore's actions had achieved some significant results, forcing the French to abandon the siege of Saragoza, postpone another attempt on Portugal and inducing the enemy to march into a remote and inhospitable region of Spain where they incurred losses through disease and hardship.

Unsurprisingly, the French newspapers crowed over what they considered a clear British defeat, and made full use of the fact that they had been forced into the sea. As *Le Moniteur* gloated:

> *The English will learn what it is to make inconsiderate movement in the presence of the French army. The manner in which they have been driven from the kingdoms of Leon and Galicia and the destruction of a part of their army will, no doubt, teach them to be more circumspect of their operations on the Continent.*[21]

Such reportage served to harden the resolve of the British and the possibility of another expedition under the rising military star of Sir Arthur Wellesley was soon being discussed. Significantly, Wellesley never sought to deride Moore's achievements and acknowledged the debt he owed to him in training the army and from the lessons learned from the bitter retreat to Corunna.[22]

Napoleon's invasion of the Peninsula had many repercussions for the future of Europe. His mistreatment of the Spanish royal family and his political intrigues with Godoy had been viewed with distaste, and his attempt to annexe the country alarmed observers. His war had also been based on miscalculations from the beginning. Spain might have been an ineffectual ally, but it was certainly no threat to France, and the removal of the Bourbons was not only ruthless but also unnecessary. In thinking that the Spanish would accept a foreign puppet ruler, Napoleon had severely underestimated their sense of national pride, and in assuming he could overrun the country with minimal troops, he had overestimated his army's strength. This was clearly demonstrated in a string of defeats in Portugal and Spain and the sign that the French were overconfident and vulnerable hardened their enemies' resolve. The truth of the old adage that 'in Spain small armies are defeated and large armies starve' had been proved once again.

Britain had shown that her troops were capable of defeating the French in battle and had gained an important base in Europe, providing a rallying point for Iberian resistance. Though the Allies had indeed suffered defeats, Spain was still far from conquered, with large regions free from French influence and a rival government established in Cadiz. With many European states beginning to turn on him, Napoleon could ill afford the embarrassment that came from squandering large numbers of men and resources into a military quagmire. His personal presence had proved decisive, but the Austrian threat had forced him to leave the half-completed task of subduing the Peninsula in the hands of his marshals.

Chapter 2
Son of the Aristocracy

Arthur Wesley was born into an Anglo-Irish family in the region of Dublin in 1769. Ireland was in a state of uneasy peace at this time and, although the country had been under British rule for hundreds of years, the religious divide between Catholic and Protestant outweighed superficial cultural differences and the Anglo-Irish were never fully assimilated into the population. Arthur's father Garret Wesley, Lord Mornington, was a 'marginal Lord' with a relatively small estate by Ireland's standards. Nevertheless, maintaining aristocratic privilege was considered vital for an elite accepted neither as English nor Irish and governing a largely resentful population.[23]

Being born into such a background left an indelible mark on young Arthur's personality and beliefs. An upbringing in a society living in constant fear of violent rebellion goes some way to explaining his reactionary nature and fervent desire to oppose radical change in society.

However, Wesley's father was hardly a tyrannical landlord and was far more interested in pursuing musical interests, as Professor of Music at Trinity College Dublin, than the concerns of his seat in the Irish House of Commons. Lord Mornington spent prodigious amounts of money making the family mansion at Dangan the model of an eighteenth-century romantic retreat, and Arthur's early life was dominated by theatrical and musical pursuits. Indeed, he rapidly became a promising musician with the violin as his chosen instrument.

His father died when he was twelve, the same year that he was sent to study at Eton. He proved a capable if unremarkable student and was subsequently sent to Brussels for a year of private tutoring and then on to a French school in Angers. There he learnt the gentlemanly skills of riding, dancing and fencing, much to the relief of his mother, who had a rather poor opinion of him. He now spoke passable French, yet the violin was the only thing in which he excelled. Although more kindly disposed towards Arthur than before, Lady Mornington still worried about his prospects, perhaps because of the example set by his older brothers. Richard Wesley had embarked upon a notable political career and had a seat in the British House of Commons. William Wesley had also entered Irish politics, while Gerald was set for a career in the church. In common with many upper-class families with a troublesome son, it was decided that Arthur would enter the army. Many of Wellington's biographers have remarked upon his mother's exasperation, Buchan writing that: 'Her feeling towards him was "not far removed from aversion". She considered him the dunce of the family. He was her "ugly boy Arthur" – "food for powder and nothing more."'[24]

Wesley had experienced a difficult childhood, but his mother's coldness instilled a sense of independence along with a desire to match the achievements of his brothers.

Arthur received his first commission as an Ensign in the 73rd Regiment of Foot. In many ways this was a calling rather than a true profession, since an officer's pay was insufficient to live on. This was a deliberate product of the purchase system, in which commissions were bought and sold. Ever since the calamitous days of the English Civil War, the establishment had feared a professional officer class and decided that those who held military rank should have a stake in the country, the logic being that men of means made unlikely revolutionaries. For officers, the prospect of selling their commissions as they progressed, often at inflated prices, provided their financial incentive. Though the Wesleys were not wealthy by the standards of their class, they enjoyed great influence and Arthur found that his fellows of lower social standing resented the privileges his birth conferred on him.[25]

The nature of his position in Ireland had made the exercise of authority natural to him, whilst developing a certain cold superiority in his character. The highly structured nature of army life exacerbated this character trait and, though he gained respect, he was rarely well liked.

After eight months, Arthur became a lieutenant and his brother Richard obtained an appointment for him as aide de camp to Lord Buckingham in Ireland, along with a transfer into the 41st Regiment. Back in Dublin, liaison played a large part in his duties, accompanying Lord Buckingham's staff in society, enabling him to refine his social skills. During this period he developed a romantic attachment to Kitty Pakenham, daughter of Lord Longford. Although the attraction was mutual, the family disapproved of the match on the grounds that as a mere aide he had yet to make his way in the service and lacked sufficient means to provide for her. After all, as a younger son he could not expect to inherit the family estate and was obliged to rely on relatives for subsistence. His first marriage proposal was turned down on her brother's insistence following her father's death.

Arthur became a Member of Parliament for County Trim in 1790 aged only nineteen, and was uncertain whether to pursue a career in the army or politics. He was determined to marry Kitty and resolved to win her family's approval, giving up gambling and dedicating himself to mastering his profession to impress them. In any case, he had added to his considerable debts playing cards and he could ill afford so expensive a vice. Feeling that pleasure must now take second place to study, he burnt his beloved violin and never resumed his musical pursuits.[26]

He must have consoled himself that music had been the ruin of his father, but this act symbolised the death of the artist within him. By September 1793 he had risen to the rank of Lieutenant-Colonel in the 33rd Regiment. Although a capable officer, the rise from Ensign to Lieutenant-Colonel in seven years was a swift one, which owed as much to purchase and influence as martial ability. His attempts to rise within the government met with little success and Arthur realised that the war with France, declared in 1793, offered him the chance to make a name for himself.

In 1794 he took part in the British campaign in Flanders under the controversial leadership of the Duke of York. The campaign was a dismal failure, but Wesley learnt a great deal from his experiences. Britain maintained a small army in comparison with those on the Continent, but it was professional. In contrast, the French revolutionary forces relied heavily on conscription and, though they fielded large armies, were obliged to adapt their tactics for soldiers who lacked training and experience. The French refusal to conform to the linear tactics and strategic manoeuvring of the eighteenth century came as an unpleasant surprise. The old method of taking key strategic points to compel the enemy to negotiate became almost obsolete, replaced by the objective of destroying the enemy army.

The French began to rely on pressing dense columns of men against the enemy line, which initially proved devastatingly effective. Though a column lacked the firepower of a double or triple line of men with muskets, it would certainly punch through it by force of numbers if it reached them, exploiting their local superiority of numbers to destroy the line. Attacks were usually preceded by artillery fire and skirmishers headed the column, aiming to inflict casualties and weaken the resolve of enemy formations. An advancing column also looked and sounded very intimidating, with the pounding from the drummers within driving it onwards, along with the revolutionary slogans shouted by the men to inspire themselves. This tactic suited a conscript-based army since it was a relatively easy manoeuvre to perform for men unfamiliar with drilling yet instilled with revolutionary fervour.

Arthur Wesley saw action at the Battle of Boxtel on 15 September 1794 and witnessed the terrible effects the winter had on a poorly provisioned and badly led army. At the end of a horrific retreat, General Walmoden informed the Duke of York that: 'Your army is destroyed; the officers; their carriages, and a large train are safe, but the men are destroyed...'[27] Arthur realised that there was nothing wrong with the soldiers' fighting ability and he astutely judged the causes of defeat as poor leadership and logistical failure. The best troops in the world were not enough when they lacked clothing, food and ammunition. Reflecting on the campaign Arthur would say that he: '...learnt what one ought not to do, and that is always something.'[28]

He returned to England as a Colonel, but still lacked the money and status to achieve his ambitions. His attempts to win political appointments were rebuffed. After a position on the expedition to Manila fell through, he decided to accompany his regiment to India. Service in India could have a detrimental effect on an officer's career. While the east provided numerous chances for making a fortune, colonial service was looked down upon by elements within the military in comparison to campaigning in Europe. Soldiering on the Indian subcontinent was viewed differently due to the lack of respect afforded to Indian opponents, the rigours of the climate and the unjust view that native troops were inferior. Furthermore, an officer would be serving far away and lacked the opportunity of meeting the right people to influence his progress within the service.

Nevertheless, the appointment proved a godsend for Arthur, since his brother, Lord Mornington, was later appointed Governor General of India, arriving at Calcutta in 1798. On the voyage he enjoyed a stopover in Capetown, South Africa, and paid court to Jemima Smith. [29] Although his heart was still set on winning Kitty Pakenham, he was a free agent and showed considerable interest in women, finding time for the occasional mistress. However, his main intent was still to master his profession, which was reflected in the array of books he took to India. Though he read for pleasure, this was a functional collection including studies on the languages, geography and warfare of the Indian subcontinent and went far beyond what most British officers of the period would consider necessary.[30]

In 1798, Lord Mornington decided to change the family name from Wesley to Wellesley. It was considered more aristocratic, and Richard thought it would aid him in his designs to obtain a marquessate from the King George III, which he eventually achieved. Knowing the power of patronage, Arthur fully approved of improving the family's status by such means.[31]

The British held sway over parts of India at this time, with many states governed by independent rulers. Though the British wished to dominate the region, the fact that the French were trying to gain influence there lent urgency to their ambitions. The Tippoo Sultan, known as the Tiger of Mysore, was the main independent ruler in central India and actively opposed the British while intriguing with the French. Wellesley took part in the campaign against him, commanding a brigade under General Harris's leadership. Unable to resist the British in the field, the Sultan fell back to his capital Seringapatam, which was soon besieged. Here Wellesley suffered one of his few reverses during the actions to push enemy outposts back into the city. In a night assault on Sultanpettah Tope the 33rd Regiment, supported by two Madras battalions, was repulsed with some loss. Though he took the grove the following day he never forgot the minor defeat and determined never again to attack without better reconnaissance. The confusion encountered in the darkness also convinced him that night assaults were highly unreliable, a view he maintained throughout his career. The affair troubled him deeply and years afterwards he was capable of drawing a detailed map of the action from memory when discussing it.

Unlike many officers, Arthur took an active interest in logistics, knowing that supply and support was the key to successful campaigning. Militarily India was a logistical problem, with a huge train of transport wagons and camp followers required, carrying provisions and especially water in the humid climate. Rapid travel in the region was nearly impossible, with three camp followers required for every fighting man, but it could be made more efficient and Arthur's proposals regarding the commissariat were heeded. Writing to his brother Henry he claimed that his innovations at least meant that: '…Matters then will be brought into some shape, and we shall know what we are about, instead of trusting to the vague calculations of a parcel of blockheads, who know nothing, and have no data.'[32]

The Tippoo Sultan died defending the walls of his city when the British finally stormed Seringapatam and Wellesley was appointed military governor when the city fell. This was controversial, since he was appointed over the heads of senior officers such as David Baird, who had played a valiant part in the siege. However, he proved an able administrator, becoming popular with the locals due to his work on civil projects in addition to his military role. Nevertheless, it was widely believed that he had received the appointment largely on account of his brother's influence.

The end of the Tippoo Sultan made Britain's East India Company dominant in southern India, but his passing left a power vacuum that was exploited by Dhoondiah Waugh, a former mercenary. Dhoondiah formed a formidable force of around 40,000 men and began to ravage the countryside, the brigand terming himself the 'King of Two Worlds'. This was Wellesley's first campaign as an independent commander and he learned a great deal in the following campaign about fighting irregular forces. Living off the land meant the enemy was capable of swifter movement, but Wellesley accepted the limitation of a large baggage train, knowing that seizing provisions from the countryside would alienate the native population. After four months, he finally cornered Dhoondiah's forces at Conagul on 10 September 1800. The bandits proved no match for disciplined regulars in open battle and Dhoondiah was killed in the brief battle that followed.

Wellesley's next campaign was very influential for India's future. The Mahratta Princes ruled most of central India and constantly fought between themselves. The East India Company decided to intervene in one of these disputes, particularly since Scindia, Rajah of Gwalior, had French sympathies. By 1803 this had turned into a full-scale war, and two columns were sent against Scindia and his allies, General Lake invading from Cawnpore in the north with Wellesley advancing from the south west. He had been promoted to Major General in the East India Company Army in April 1802 and one of his first decisions was to divide his army, placing Stevenson in command of roughly half his force, knowing that it would aid supply and mobility.

However, the Mahrattas had modern weaponry and regular troops in addition to a host of militia. Wellesley encountered a huge army under the Princes of Scindia and Barar near the village of Assaye. Having expected to find only enemy infantry in the vicinity, he was surprised to find their entire army present, with an overwhelming force of cavalry. His own forces consisted of 13,500 men, whereas the Mahrattas' had 40,000 regular soldiers, around 50,000 levied militia and a substantial artillery train. They occupied a seven-mile frontage near the confluence of the rivers Kaitna and Juah. With the enemy present in such numbers a frontal attack was unthinkable, so Wellesley decided to attack their left by crossing the river Kaitna. Using his cavalry to cover the movement, he ordered the infantry to cross by a ford. The Mahrattas swiftly recovered from their surprise and fired on the troops as they crossed, inflicting some loss.

Between the two rivers, Wellesley knew that he was relatively safe from cavalry movement against his flanks. Yet this was not like facing Dhoondiah's ill-disciplined brigands. The regular Mahratta infantry swiftly redeployed to face the threat and the European-trained artillery took a heavy toll on the British as they advanced. Attacking the enemy right and centre, the guns were largely silenced, but an attack on the partially fortified village of Assaye was sharply repelled. Lieutenant-Colonel William Orrock had attacked prematurely and, since his troops therefore lacked support, they suffered heavy losses. Colonel Maxwell's cavalry met and defeated an attempt by Scindian cavalry on the British right flank, which tried to exploit this success, and the Indian army retreated to a new position with their backs to the River Juah. A determined general advance with Maxwell's horsemen in support finally broke the enemy infantry and the Mahrattas fled.

This was one of the hardest fought battles of Wellesley's career, but it made his reputation as a commander. Losses were severe at 1,600, and Wellesley had had two horses shot from under him. Eight of his ten staff officers sustained wounds or were unhorsed by enemy fire.[33] The Mahrattas lost approximately 6,000 casualties and suffered a severe defeat.

Though the victory won him acclaim both in India and back in England, Wellesley received some criticism for his handling of the battle. Stevenson's force had been too far away to intervene in time and he had not anticipated encountering such numbers. This was partially due to the huge numbers of enemy cavalry, which made effective reconnaissance virtually impossible. The flanking march of four miles across the front of a much larger army, combined with a river crossing, was also a serious risk. [34] It testifies to his incredible self-confidence. He had relied on surprise but his foe had been disobliging and nearly overcame his force. Nevertheless, he was generous towards Lieutenant-Colonel Orrock for his foolhardy attack on Assaye. Although he had endangered the army's right wing, Wellesley felt excessive zeal was to blame, feeling unable to castigate a man who had miscalculated but acted with good intentions.

Though the war dragged on, Assaye had broken the back of Mahratta resistance and by the end of 1803 they were suing for peace. Although a second conflict broke out, continuing for another two years, Wellesley felt that he had gained all he could in India. He left with his financial situation improved by several instances of prize money and the increased pay for his military governorship. More importantly, his reputation had been enhanced considerably and, though family influence had helped, he had ably demonstrated his skill as a commander.

Despite his successes, his prospects were relatively bleak on his return to England. He may have reached the rank of Major General, but, as an East India Company promotion, it did not have equal standing in the British army. In addition, the Duke of York had not confirmed his promotion and resented the fact that he had superseded Baird at Seringapatam. In any case Indian promotions were regarded with suspicion in Whitehall, the bureaucrats resenting anything outside their control. Richard had lost his position in India and the Wellesleys were suffering from a political smear campaign, Arthur being obliged to champion their cause within an increasingly factional House of Commons.

However, he had received the Order of the Bath for his services and his renewed advances to Kitty Pakenham were now received favourably by her family. They married on 10 April 1806. Naturally both were changed after a long separation and when he first caught sight of her again Arthur whispered: 'She has grown ugly, by Jove!'[35] to his brother Gerald, who conducted the service. Although she was to bear him two sons, they soon encountered problems. Arthur was accustomed to obedience, yet Kitty showed an alarming tendency to overlook his instructions, particularly with regard to household finances and maintaining appearances. It would not prove the romantic ideal that either had hoped for.

Arthur's first appointment, the command of a brigade in Hastings on the south coast, was a disappointment. By 1806 the invasion threat had receded and it was an unimportant posting. However, with over a hundred Major Generals on half pay awaiting commands, he was lucky to receive an active command. When friends expressed surprise on his acceptance of the post he replied: 'I am *nimmukwallah,* as we say in the East; that is, I have eaten of the King's salt, and, therefore, I conceive it to be my duty to serve with unhesitating zeal and cheerfulness, when and whenever the King or his Government may think it proper to employ me.'[36] This reply became famous during the Victorian era, encapsulating Wellesley's devotion to King and country.

His hard work on his political career also began to pay off, and he served as an MP for several districts in quick succession. Ireland was still a hotbed of dissent and hopes to relax the laws against religious dissenters were dashed when King George III refused to ratify them, with great insensitivity, on Saint Patrick's Day. The entire Cabinet resigned in protest and the King was obliged to ask Lord Portland to form a new Government. The position of Lord Lieutenant for Ireland was unpopular and it was with some difficulty that Lord Richmond was persuaded to accept it. However, this proved fortuitous for Wellesley, since Richmond offered him the post of Chief Secretary for Ireland. He was finally part of the Government.

Dublin had changed since Arthur's time as an ADC to Buckingham. The Act of Union with Great Britain in 1800 brought about the abolition of the Irish House of Commons and direct rule from London pleased neither Catholics nor Protestants. The country was in desperate need of reform, but Wellesley believed that attempted improvements only exacerbated the situation:

> No political measure which you could adopt would alter the people of this country. They are disaffected to the British Government; they don't feel the benefits of their situation; attempts to render it better either do not reach their minds, or they are represented to them as additional injuries; and in fact we have no strength here but our army.[37]

This reveals a great deal about Wellesley's character. Despite his heritage, he disassociated himself from his roots and considered himself an Englishman. Indeed, he regularly spoke of the Anglo-Irish as a force of occupation. Already a firm Tory, Ireland made him even more reactionary. The horrendous violence of the Great Rebellion of 1798 was a recent memory and the Government would do anything to avoid similar unrest. Consequently, he acted cautiously in Dublin, endeavouring to maintain the status quo and shunning change. Though he continued to enforce the religious laws he did so with as much sensitivity and moderation as possible, and his term of office was relatively peaceful but unremarkable.

The war with France had reached a stalemate. The French had been decisively beaten at sea in 1805, but naval battles alone could not win the war for Britain and it was difficult to determine where to challenge the French on land with any prospect of success. Furthermore, the naval struggle would recommence if the French could rebuild their fleet. The Danes possessed a sizeable navy and it seemed likely that they were about to submit to the French embargo against British trade. Reluctantly, the government decided that neutral Denmark could not be trusted and that their fleet must be secured. Wellesley was eager to win laurels in Europe and requested a leave of absence from Richmond to join the Danish expedition, commanding a brigade under Lord

Cathcart. Under orders to obtain the fleet without violence if possible, Cathcart negotiated with the Danes but they were justly outraged and refused to comply.

As the British set about investing Copenhagen, Wellesley's Brigade was sent to block an approaching Danish relief force at Kioge. This was one of the first occasions that the 95th Regiment saw action, and the riflemen mounted an effective skirmish line in front of the advancing redcoats that soon rousted the Danes out of their hurriedly improvised defences and drove them from the village. The largely militia-based force proved no match for regular troops and 1,700 Danes were captured, with 356 casualties, compared to minor British losses. Many Danes were taken prisoner due to their inability to run fast enough, since many were shod in wooden clogs.[38]

The British completed their siege works and offered the city a chance to reconsider its position. Cathcart was pleased to have Wellesley on hand during negotiations as a Government representative and attempts were made to lengthen the talks since he hoped to avoid unnecessary casualties.[39] However, the city possessed a strong garrison and they did not believe that the British would fire on a neutral city. Reluctantly, Cathcart opened fire on 2 September and, following a three-day bombardment, the Danes capitulated.

In Copenhagen, Rifleman Green was horrified at the damage British mortars and rockets had inflicted: 'I was astonished to see the havoc our bombardment had made. Whole streets lay in ruins; churches burnt down; and we had hard work to get through the streets to the dock-yard, to go on board, our road being blocked up with bricks, stones, tiles, and timber.'[40] Rockets were inaccurate and had negligible effect on battlefields, but their destructive power against towns and cities was awesome. In addition to military deaths, an estimated 1,600 Danish civilians had been killed with a further 1,000 wounded. Wellesley had opposed the bombardment and the memories of the destruction and civilian casualties it wrought led him to avoid similar tactics in future.

As a military action the operation had been stunningly effective, yet without an official declaration of war it violated the rules of war and shocked Europe. Though dictated by necessity, it was widely condemned and the previously neutral Denmark now sided uneasily with France. The British left Copenhagen without firing the docks, as some ministers had suggested, perhaps believing that: 'The principle of defence through offence may be carried too far...'[41] Wellesley gained another battlefield victory and considerable prize money from the captured shipping, but little glory. Significantly, no medals were struck for Copenhagen.

Although allowed to resume his office in Ireland on his return, Wellesley despaired at the prospects it offered and tried to gain another military appointment. With the local juntas in Spain and Portugal asking for assistance, the British Government decided to intervene in the Peninsula and Wellesley was offered a place in the expeditionary force sent there. He handed over his political responsibilities to John Wilson Croker, MP for County Downpatrick. Just before his departure, Croker noticed his friend in deep contemplation and enquired about his deliberations:

> ...I am thinking about of the French that I am going to fight. I have not seen them since the campaign in Flanders, when they were capital soldiers, and a dozen years of victory under Buonaparte must have made them better still. They have... a new system of strategy, which has out-manoeuvred and overwhelmed all the armies of Europe. 'Tis enough to make one thoughtful; but no matter: my die is cast, they may overwhelm me, but I don't think they will out-manoeuvre me. First, because I am not afraid of them, as everybody else seems to be; and secondly, because if what I hear of their system of manoeuvres be true, I think it a false one against steady troops. I suspect all the continental armies were more than half-beaten before the battle was begun. I, at least, will not be frightened beforehand.[42]

Arriving at Corunna, he received what he considered unreliable reports from the junta of Galicia but, sailing down the coastline, the Bishop of Oporto and representatives of the Supreme Junta provided better information. Though their troops and militia were poorly armed and trained, the majority of Portuguese were firmly opposed to the occupation: 'I am informed that there is no such thing as a French party; and indeed, from what I have seen... I should imagine that it could not be very safe for any man to declare himself in favour of the French.'[43]

Wellesley landed at Mondego Bay on 30 July 1808 and began disembarking troops the next day. It was a difficult coastline for such an operation and the thunderous surf claimed several lives as boats were upset bringing men ashore. His commissariat proved unequal to the task of organising the supplies, munitions and transport for 14,000 men and Wellesley had to intervene personally. It took eight days to unload the army and its equipment. Luckily the French made no attempt to oppose the landing, due to the fact that Junot's forces were spread out in garrisons across the country and he was having difficulty concentrating them.

Despite his logistical problems, Wellesley had a large force at his command, which he considered comparable with the French. He had received reports of 20,000 French soldiers in Portugal but considered this an over-estimate. In fact, the French possessed 26,000 men, but not all of these would be available to oppose him. In the knowledge that relieving the capital would inspire the growing insurgency, he decided to march upon Lisbon. Less creditably, he also hoped to defeat the French before the arrival of senior officers sent to assume command.

In order to give his commander time to gather his forces, General Delaborde tried to block Wellesley's progress at Roliça. He had only four battalions (around 4,000 men) to oppose the British but took up a strong position on the hills behind the village. Wellesley advanced steadily on his centre, but after some skirmishing and a brief exchange of artillery fire discovered the French had withdrawn to a fall back position above the Gorge of Columbiera. An entire morning had been wasted in these manoeuvres, but Wellesley decided to repeat the same tactics, hoping to defeat Delaborde before he could be reinforced.

The ridge the French stood on was broken by four gullies and the slopes were partially wooded and confusing for the advancing British. As the skirmishers engaged once more, Colonel Lake led the 29th Regiment up one of the gullies in an impetuous attack. As the 29th formed at the top of the gully they were fired upon from the front and both flanks. As if this were not bad enough, a French regiment below them on the slopes mounted a bayonet charge on their rear and the 29th broke and fled down the gully, leaving many dead behind them including Lake himself.

Wellesley felt obliged to order a general assault in an attempt to extricate the 29th, but the French resisted stubbornly. Though assailed from both flanks as well as his centre, Delaborde's regiments poured musket fire down upon the infantry toiling up the slopes and then charged them when they approached the summit. The broken ground confused and disrupted the advancing troops and three assaults were repulsed in this manner.[44] However, the British superiority in artillery began to tell and, knowing he would soon be overwhelmed, Delaborde withdrew. The retreat was well conducted, with French cavalry covering the infantry as their battalions retired in successive pairs, and the lack of British cavalry hampered the pursuit. However, when the road narrowed near the defile of Zambugeira the troops became disordered and the French lost three of their five guns to their pursuers.

Wellesley had won his first battle in the Peninsula. However, both sides had some cause to be pleased with the encounter. Delaborde had only suffered around 600 casualties and had managed to delay the British for an entire day. Had the British possessed more cavalry the French might have suffered greater losses. From the British point of view, they had overcome a strong defensive position and, though they outnumbered the French, only about four of their battalions had been engaged, amounting to a near parity of numbers. They had sustained 487 casualties, but admittedly they had a great advantage with Colonel Robe's eighteen cannons easily outgunning a mere five French artillery pieces.

As the British advanced southwards, news that ships had been sighted off the coast came through and Wellesley met with them at Maceira Bay and marched to cover their landing. He drew his army up on two ridges near the village of Vimeiro. Sir Harry Burrard had arrived to assume command and decided to proceed with caution, knowing the enemy's superiority in numbers. He ordered Wellesley to halt the march and await further reinforcements. Sir John Moore was expected within the week. Wellesley disagreed with his superior, but had no choice but to obey. Crucially for subsequent events, Burrard chose to stay aboard ship that night, leaving Wellesley in nominal command.[45]

General Junot had been in a quandary over how to proceed strategically against the British. Although they were growing stronger, he had little prospect of swift reinforcement from the Emperor, as troops would have to undertake a long and arduous march through Spain. Whilst he had the option of standing siege in Lisbon, the enemy's command of the seas would see that they received more supplies than he did, and relief might be long in coming. The only true way to secure the capital and Portugal itself was to defeat them in battle. Accordingly he marched on Vimeiro, arriving early on the morning of 21 August.

As the French attacked, Wellesley kept his forces on the reverse slopes of the ridgeline to limit the ricochet effect of enemy cannon fire. The French advanced in huge columns and were fired upon by British artillery and skirmishers as they climbed the slope. Rifleman Harris was one of these skirmishers and recalled the effect of cannon fire on the enemy: 'I saw regular lanes torn through their ranks as they advanced, which were immediately closed up again as they marched steadily on. Whenever we saw a round shot thus go through the mass, we raised a shout of delight.'[46] Yet it was not only round shot that flayed the oncoming columns. The newly invented shrapnel, fired from howitzers, was used in battle for the first time at Vimeiro, the projectiles inflicting many casualties as they exploded above their targets.

In his eagerness to engage the enemy, Junot pressed his columns forward recklessly and they advanced piecemeal up the slopes, virtually ignoring the British on their left. This allowed battalions to fire into the columns' flanks, making the resulting musket duel an almost foregone conclusion. The British could fire every musket and had sufficient width of formation to curve their line round the head of the column at both sides, partially enveloping their attackers, whereas only the first few ranks of the columns could fire. Outgunned, the French desperately tried to deploy into line to respond, but manoeuvring under heavy fire proved too much for men already shaken by cannon shot and skirmishers and they broke and fled. Generals Charlot and Delaborde were wounded and, when they fled downhill, the guns accompanying their attack were captured.

Junot now committed his reserve of four grenadier battalions, which met a similar fate. Although they endured the artillery barrage stolidly as they advanced, they were received by converging fire from at least three battalions. A private in the 71st Highland Regiment recalled how the line stood impassively while the French came on, shouting imperialist slogans as they toiled upwards. They fired a volley as they crested the ridge, cried out three distinct cheers and fell ominously silent as the French advanced with the bayonet:

> In our first charge I felt my mind waver; a breathless sensation came over me. The silence was appalling. I looked alongst (sic) the line. It was enough to assure me. The steady, determined scowl of my companions assured my heart and gave me determination. How unlike the noisy advance of the French![47]

The private believed that after what they had already endured, the unexpected silence after the cheers unnerved the French and, when they levelled their bayonets and rushed them, they broke and fled back down the slope rather than stand to meet the attack.

Wellesley ordered a charge by the 20th Light Dragoons at the enemy centre and, though it fared well initially, cutting down many infantrymen, they were counter charged by French cavalry when they pressed their advance too far. In the swirling mêlée of horsemen that followed, the regiment was badly cut up, losing forty-five casualties, including their colonel, and leaving at least ten prisoners in enemy hands as they withdrew in disorder. An attempt to outflank the British on the eastern ridge was also thwarted, although the village of Vimeiro itself was fiercely contested at the point of the bayonet.

After sustaining heavy losses, Junot pulled his army back and headed for Lisbon. Burrard had arrived halfway through the struggle and allowed Wellesley to continue in command, but objected to mounting a pursuit when the French began to withdraw. Wellesley would later complain that greater losses could have been inflicted on the enemy had he been permitted to do this despite the lack of cavalry.[48] The field of battle presented a grim sight:

> ...the birds of prey were devouring the slain. Here I beheld a sight, for the first time, even more horrible – the peasantry prowling about, more ferocious than the beasts and birds of prey, finishing the work of death, and carrying away whatever they thought worthy of their grasp. Avarice and revenge were the causes of these horrors. No fallen Frenchman that showed the least signs of life was spared. They even seemed pleased with mangling the dead bodies.[49]

Strategically, the French were now in a bad position. They had been soundly beaten and, though they could retire to Lisbon, their prospects during a protracted siege were poor. While the British were supplied by sea, the countryside was aroused against the French and any relief force would have to march through Spain to reach them. Junot sent General Kellerman to propose an armistice.

Lieutenant-General Sir Hew Dalrymple arrived the day after Vimeiro and assumed command, being senior to both Wellesley and Burrard. He and Burrard believed that the French were far from beaten and they managed to let this slip to Kellerman, who overheard Dalrymple whispering: 'We are not in a very good situation; let us hear him.'[50] In time the Convention of Cintra was drawn up and Dalrymple urged Wellesley to sign it, since he was officially a member of the Government. Reluctantly he assented, but the next morning he wrote to Viscount Castlereagh, Secretary for War, decrying his role in the affair and pointing out that his endorsement was his only real contribution.

The Convention of Cintra was indeed controversial and damaging to all concerned. Though Napoleon was furious at this setback, he could not have hoped for better terms. The French agreed to evacuate Portugal without becoming prisoners and were transported back to France by the Royal Navy. They retained their artillery, horses, baggage and personal possessions, and Portuguese collaborators were allowed to accompany them. In return captured Portuguese artillery and prisoners were given back and fortresses had to be left intact. British troops even escorted the garrisons of Elvas and Almeida through

Spanish and Portuguese forces that had massed to hem them in.

The Portuguese were incensed by the damage done to their country and the brutality of French methods. Furthermore, the departing enemy had an ambiguous interpretation of the 'personal possessions' referred to in the treaty, and took away large amounts of plunder looted from Portugal. Portuguese sympathisers, who did not leave with the French, were set upon and murdered, and British soldiers were required to escort their enemies to the quaysides. During the embarkation one officer witnessed the following:

> ...*General Kellerman had nigh fallen victim to the fury of the mob by his own imprudence, in venturing on shore, after the French troops were all embarked. Being recognised by some Portuguese, he was immediately attacked by the populace ...after receiving some severe blows, he fell into the boat... Our brave soldiers leaped in with him and parrying off the strokes of his justly enraged enemies, they rowed away and left him in safety – wondering at the magnanimity of our gallant and generous soldiers.*[51]

Public opinion was outraged by the perceived climbdown and Dalrymple, Burrard and Wellesley were called before a court of inquiry, while Sir John Moore took over in the Peninsula. Luckily, Wellesley had supporters in the Government, including Castlereagh, though his signature on the Convention nearly damned him. The inquiry did acknowledge the extraordinary circumstances he suffered in being relieved of command by two commanders in quick succession, and they eventually cleared him of any wrong-doing. Fortunately news of Napoleon's arrival in the Peninsula and Moore's disastrous retreat distracted the public and they lost interest in the investigation. Dalrymple received a severe reprimand and never received another active command, but Wellesley emerged from the scandal with his reputation only slightly tarnished.

Nevertheless, Britain had gained a great deal from the Convention of Cintra. It was true that harsher terms could have been imposed, but the primary objective of ejecting the enemy from Portugal had been achieved. The slight on Portuguese honour was forgotten in the rejoicing that followed Lisbon's liberation, and a new government was formed in the Portuguese Regent's absence, containing three members of the original council who had remained in the country, two members of the insurgency and the Bishop of Oporto. British forces were welcome to remain in the country, and Britain now had the Continental foothold she so desperately needed.

Unsurprisingly, Sir Arthur was ill tempered after the inquiry and back in Dublin Castle he did his best to contend with a role he disliked, along with his increasingly difficult marriage. Kitty seemed incapable or unwilling to comply with his instructions for running their household and complained to friends about her husband's remote and indifferent attitude. His unhappiness led him into the arms of the noted courtesan Harriette Wilson, whom he met through Mrs Porter's establishment in Berkeley Square. He visited her with increasing frequency and, though he endeavoured to be discreet, the affair would eventually lead to a minor scandal.[52]

Meanwhile, the situation in the Peninsula had deteriorated after Moore's army was evacuated at Corunna. Portugal still retained a British garrison under General Craddock, but he did not enjoy the confidence of the Government and a second French invasion was imminent. Writing to Castlereagh, Wellesley claimed that the geography of the Peninsula, along with the people's resistance, allowed Portugal to be defended by a relatively small army. 30,000 men would suffice he claimed, as long as they were well supplied with artillery and cavalry in which the Portuguese were deficient. If the Portuguese army could be reorganised along British lines, the prospects of not only retaining Portugal, but also of intervening in Spain, were excellent. Since he was one of the few generals with direct experience in the region, the establishment decided to give him a second chance.

Wellesley returned to Lisbon in April 1809. He had resigned from his Irish post, but this appointment was far from permanent and had restrictions. For example, he was expressly forbidden from entering Spain with his army without securing the Government's approval. Political expediency denied him a large army, so he would have to ensure he made the best of the meagre resources available and to avoid losses. He also received the rank of Marshal General in the Portuguese army, conveying supreme authority over their forces. The daunting task of modernising and improving the Portuguese army had been entrusted to Major-General William Beresford. Portugal's military had been poorly financed and neglected for over fifty years, the Regent having so little faith in his forces that he fled in 1807 without contemplating resistance.

The French were experiencing serious problems in Napoleon's absence. Fearing a potential rival, the Emperor refused to appoint a supreme military commander from amongst his marshals and, technically, King Joseph commanded French forces in Spain. However,

Napoleon constantly refused his brother's requests and regularly interfered, undermining his authority. Jealously abounded in the marshalate and these proud, ambitious men were united only in their contempt for Joseph. Though Napoleon had left a huge force of nearly 280,000 men, logistical problems and the vast scale of the Peninsula meant that these could not concentrate as a cohesive force and large numbers could only be united for short periods of time. Naturally, they had to be split up into smaller armies. Napoleon's attempts to direct Spanish operations from a distance also proved impracticable and damaging. Geographically, the region bore more similarity with Africa than Europe, and he often failed to consider local difficulties that were only apparent to those present.

Nevertheless, Marshal Jean Soult had invaded Northern Portugal hoping to seize Lisbon before the British could reinforce their position. He advanced as far as the city of Oporto, situated near the mouth of the River Douro. He had hoped for further support from Northern Spain, but Marshal Ney was having immense difficulties there attempting to pacify the Asturias and Galicia. Opposed by regulars and guerrilla bands, once one rising was put down, resistance would spring up elsewhere in an endless cycle. Napoleon had hoped for three French armies to converge on Lisbon, which looked feasible on the map but was proving impracticable on the ground. Marshal Victor had conducted a simultaneous advance through the Guadiana Valley, defeating the Spanish General Cuesta, but had been forced to stop through lack of supplies. Soult was considering withdrawal when he heard that Wellesley was marching against him.

Soult had the opportunity to attack the British as they marched towards Oporto, but decided to maintain his strong defensive position behind the river. Wellesley had garrisoned Lisbon and sent 12,000 men under General Mackenzie to watch Victor's forces in case he resumed his march. He also sent Beresford,with 6,000 men, to reinforce the Portuguese General Silveira at Lamego, hoping to cut Soult's line of retreat. After a fiercely fought action by his vanguard with advanced French units, he reached the Douro's southern bank.

Every boat in the area had been moored on the northern banks or destroyed and Soult felt confident that the Allies would attack near the estuary with naval assistance. However, after an extensive reconnaissance, Wellesley determined that a sunken ferry some miles upriver from the city could be salvaged and, with the assistance of locals, secured three wine barges. The river was 500 yards wide, so a crossing would be dangerous as enemy sentries were likely to detect it, but Wellesley decided to take a risk. Placing a battery in the highly placed Sierra Convent to cover the crossing, he ordered the 3rd Regiment to begin rowing across. Meanwhile, he despatched a brigade under General John Murray to cross by the salvaged ferry at Barca Alvintas.

The Douro's banks were extremely steep at this point and this, along with good fortune and sleepy French sentries, saw the British gain complete surprise. By the time General Foy had been alerted, the Buffs had established themselves in a large seminary on the northern bank and were knocking loopholes in the walls to defend it. Foy immediately ordered a counter-attack to dislodge them, sending three battalions of the 17th Line against them. However, the British infantry put up staunch resistance and the fire of the battery in the convent broke up the French attacks and silenced their artillery support. After an hour of heavy fighting, Soult feared his army might be cut in half, since the enemy were ferrying across more men all the time and ordered a retreat.

The French were forced to abandon their wounded, 1,700 men being taken prisoner, along with the loss of some artillery in the city, but Soult managed to evade Murray's outflanking move as he fled northwards. Unaccountably, Murray refused to attack the retreating French, whom he believed were too strong for his brigade. Though some brave efforts to impede them were made by Stewart with the 14th Light Dragoons, Soult's army continued to make an orderly withdrawal when a mere demonstration of force might have allowed Wellesley time to bring up more forces to trap the French between them.

Soult was forced to retreat through the mountains with the Allies at his heels. With British to the west and Portuguese forces under Silveira to the east, he was forced to withdraw northwards over narrow tracks, hoping he could endure the inevitable guerrilla ambushes and capture the bridges along his line of retreat intact. Most of the French horses and baggage were abandoned, and the cannon were placed muzzle to muzzle and destroyed. Soult's war chest was opened and the gold passed out to individual soldiers rather than left behind. Luckily for the French, Silveira lost his way and failed to block their retreat, and Wellesley abandoned his pursuit after inflicting some loss on their rearguard. The French lost 4,500 men on this hazardous retreat, leaving Soult's army a shadow of its former self.

Wellesley had triumphed and would have destroyed a French army, but for Soult's luck and the ineffeciency of some junior commanders. Yet the success was ill received in London, with no battle honours awarded to any of the regiments who took part, and Captain Stanhope, who carried the despatch, failed to receive the traditional promotion for heralding a victory. It had been Wellesley's biggest offensive gamble since the battle of Assaye, and some in Westminster considered it reckless. The troops had been desperately exposed while crossing the river, and could have been annihilated if Soult had placed sufficient men along the riverbank. Wellesley largely owed his victory to Soult's complacency, but it had been an awesome demonstration of nerve and decisiveness nonetheless.

Portugal was temporarily secure, and Wellesley felt confident enough to consider mounting an offensive into Spain. While Napoleon was occupied in central Europe, his forces in Spain had largely confined themselves to defensive operations. It took some time to secure Government approval for the venture, but eventually this was forthcoming. Meanwhile, Wellesley concentrated on improving the army and in June made the decision to divide the army into divisions. Initially only four divisions were created, varying between 3,000–4,000 men, except for the first division which possessed 6,000. The cavalry possessed its own division (eventually increased to two) and each had its own skirmishers and attached artillery. They would also contain specialised units such as engineers and provosts, and would eventually acquire their own individual identities in much the same way as pride and comradeship was generated at regiment level. These divisions were designed to be capable of independent action if necessary, and were partially inspired by the need to match the French corps system that had proved so effective in Europe.

When Wellesley crossed the border he hoped to locate and defeat Marshal Victor's forces, known to be in the region of Talavera. The plan was to combine with Spanish forces under General Cuesta and have General Francisco Venegas move to cut the French line of retreat. Negotiations with the Spanish went badly from the start. Cuesta objected to being pressured by a far younger general whom he knew was vying for the position of supreme Allied commander with London and Cadiz. Guedalla described him as being: 'Composed in equal parts of pride and failing health, he was the embodiment of Spain at its very worst – old, proud, incompetent and ailing…'[53]

The combined Anglo-Spanish forces outnumbered Victor's when they approached his base thirty miles west of Talavera. The operation opened well with the British advanced guard pushing French units back as Victor began to deploy his army to make a stand at the Alberche River. The enemy had left a trail of destruction behind them partly in reprisal for guerrilla activity, but also to denude the countryside of sustenance for the Allies:

> *...after skirmishing for a short time the enemy withdrew from Talavera to behind the Alberche and as usual in his retreat signalized himself by the most wanton acts of cruelty. All the detached houses and convents were burnt and whole fields of standing corn were set fire to by his order, which in this country, being without enclosures, extended many miles.*[54]

However, Cuesta refused to attack the next day, complaining his army was too tired to fight. The British, who were ready for the assault on the morning of 23 June, were outraged since their troops had marched over similar distances, yet appeared ready for the confrontation. They were forced to postpone their plans till the next day, by which time Victor had slipped away.

Now Cuesta wished to pursue the French, but it was Wellesley's turn to object. The area was devoid of supplies, having been swept recently by the French, and his men had been on half rations for days. Wellesley refused to join the advance, but the Spanish soon returned with the French in pursuit. An army under Sebastiani had reinforced Victor and King Joseph had arrived to assume overall command. The French now outnumbered the Allies and Wellesley drew up his men in a defensive position. The centre of the Allied position was on the plain but the right flank was anchored against the town on the Tagus River.

In his eagerness, Victor ordered a night attack without consulting his new commander-in-chief on 27 July. Ruffin's division was committed and several British units, preparing for the night, were taken unawares, sustaining severe losses and making a rapid retreat. However, the darkness also hindered the French and the entire 24th Léger went astray, taking little part in the struggle. Though some casualties were sustained, the Allies swiftly recovered from their surprise and drove back the assault. Wellesley was dismissive of the inconclusive affair. It confirmed his belief that night attacks were difficult to conduct and prone to mishap.

Victor easily overcame the inexperienced King Joseph and, despite the objections of Marshal Jourdan, decided to attack the Medellin hill sector of the British line. Jourdan pointed out that the British had reinforced that area after the failed night attack and suggested another point to no avail. A large artillery bombardment was mounted to prepare for the assault. Though most of men on the Medellin were partially protected on the reverse slopes, those on the plain had to endure heavy cannon fire:

...shots and shells were falling in every direction – but none of the enemy were to be seen – the men were all the while lying in the ranks, and except at the very spot where a shot or shell fell, there was not the least motion – I have seen men killed in the ranks by cannon shots – those immediately round the spot would remove the mutilated corpse to the rear, they would then lie down as if nothing had occurred and remain in the ranks, steady as before...[55]

Following a heavy cannonade, the French sent forward skirmishers to prepare a way for their attack columns, which advanced steadily through the valley as the British artillery played upon them. These huge columns, sixty men across and twenty-four deep, lost dozens of men as the British round shot ripped into their ranks, but they neared the Medellin's ridgeline. Here the British infantry, in lines two men deep, advanced to the crest to confront them. Every man could fire his musket when in line, while the French could reply only with their first few ranks. It would be a different matter if the column reached the line, but the Allied infantry was unbroken by the cannon fire or skirmishers and the British infantry were some of the best drilled in the world. Firing volleys by company or platoon, they inflicted devastating losses on the densely packed columns, firing at a rate of three or four times a minute. After a brief firefight the columns broke and were chased down the hillside.

Marshal Victor was amazed at their repulse, having expected the bombardment and skirmishers to weaken the Allied line sufficiently for the columns to break through. It took disciplined troops to stand the intimidating sight of an approaching French column and, believing that the British were weakened, he decided to attack again in greater force. Jourdan argued that they should now distract and occupy the troops on the Medellin and in the centre, whilst mounting an assault on the left, but Victor scorned such caution. Fearing his brother's anger if he failed to take decisive action, Joseph let the impetuous marshal have his way. However, these assaults met a similar fate and, though they suffered a fearful pounding from the artillery and the columns inflicted grievous losses, the British infantry stubbornly held their line. As the last attack was beaten off, a cavalry charge by the 23rd Dragoons and 1st KGL Hussars on the withdrawing French infantry effectively ended the battle. As the French pulled back across the Alberche River, the Allies were too exhausted to pursue them. Nevertheless, Talavera was a significant victory, with twenty French guns captured and 7,000 French casualties.

Wellesley had ridden from point to point throughout the battle, trying to supervise everything in person. Whilst this showed dedication, it also revealed a refusal to delegate responsibility. The final cavalry attack had been pressed too far, suffering losses when the French infantry assumed defensive square formations and their own cavalry counter-charged. This kind of incident renewed Wellesley's conviction that his subordinates could only be relied upon to an extent, and he must intervene at all levels to ensure his commands were carried out. It was both a strength and a weakness. Fearing his anger, his subordinates aspired to greater efforts but resented his constant checks and lack of trust. This style of leadership also meant that he was constantly on the move, increasing the physical and emotional burdens of command. Although there were obvious limits to what he could personally oversee, his method was largely effective.

Though Talavera was an undoubted victory, the campaign had lost its impetus. The Spanish had let their Allies down over supplies, and there were large numbers of wounded to care for. The British had lost a quarter of their fighting strength and Marshal Soult was approaching from the south with a fresh army. It was time to withdraw across the border and many wounded, placed in Cuesta's care, were left behind and captured. Wellesley ended the campaign with a poor view of the Spanish command: 'The Spaniards make excellent soldiers. What spoils them is that they have no confidence in their officers – this would ruin any soldiers – and how should the Spaniards have confidence in such officers as theirs?'[56]

Talavera was celebrated in England, and on his return to Portugal Wellesley received three new titles – Baron Douro, Viscount Wellington and Wellington. Though pleased by such recognition, by September 1809 he had become convinced that a third invasion of Portugal was inevitable. During the Talavera campaign the French had been occupied on two fronts, with Napoleon concentrating his efforts on central Europe rather than the Peninsula. After the Austrian defeat at Wagram the treaty of Schönbrunn was signed in October, leaving the French free to reinforce Spain. The British Government was aware of this, the Earl of Liverpool sharing Wellington's view that Austria's fall heralded a major new offensive:

> We know nothing as yet of the terms, but there can be very little ground to doubt of the fact, and we may presume that the conditions are as humiliating to Austria as Bonaparte could venture to make them. This event must have a powerful influence

upon our situation and policy in other quarters, and especially in the Peninsula of Spain and Portugal. The whole military efforts of France will probably in a short time be directed against Spain...[57]

London viewed events in the Peninsula with trepidation, and Perceval's Government was criticised on both sides of the House over its strategy. Some of the Whigs denounced the Talavera Campaign, claiming that while a battle had been won, Wellington had failed to exploit it and had been forced into retreat. They argued for a complete withdrawal, citing the cost of pursuing the war and the potential for a ruinous defeat. The Tories believed that Wellington was being starved of money and resources and was expected to achieve too much with such a small army. Opinions were deeply divided throughout Parliament and, although Wellington enjoyed some influential support, a serious reverse could have a catastrophic effect on British policy. Napoleon was aware of these divisions and did his best to foster them through propaganda in *Le Moniteur*, deriding Wellington as a 'Sepoy General' whose forces would crumble when the Emperor arrived to drive the British into the sea.

Contemplating these factors, Wellington decided to adopt a cautious strategy, planning a meticulous defence of Portugal. In communications with London, he reluctantly conceded that his Spanish allies were unreliable and argued that he could not protect both Lisbon and Seville with the troops at his disposal. Even if his army were raised to 40,000 men, he preferred to concentrate on the defence of Lisbon and leave the Spanish to maintain their tenuous hold in southern Spain with limited British support.[58] On the map Portugal appears to be a difficult country to defend, but, as numerous wars between the Portuguese and Spanish demonstrate, this is hardly the case. The border region is mountainous and four realistic invasion routes for a large army were available to the French. Spain never fell entirely to the French and the Spanish held the territories of Galicia and Seville, effectively blocking the northern and southern routes. Therefore the central routes into Portugal were preferable, though fortresses on both sides of the border would have to be reduced.

Three rivers flow through Spain into Portugal – the Douro, Tagus and Guadiana. Looking at these rivers from the map alone they appear to offer support for an invading force, but this impression is deceptive. All three flow through deep gorges and roads are not planned in conjunction with them, making them dubious supply routes. Additionally, roads were infrequent in the region, poorly constructed and of limited assistance to large armies with transport wagons and artillery. Incredibly, no major road existed between the Spanish capital of Madrid and Lisbon, due to age-old animosity between the two countries. Following numerous wars, the Portuguese increasingly came to rely on oceanic trade and commercially the state faced outwards towards the Atlantic rather than inward toward its Spanish neighbour.[59] This meant that wealth was concentrated along the coastal regions and inland the country was sparsely populated and poor.

Despite the difficulties facing the French, Wellington knew they were likely to seriously outnumber the Allies and believed they would eventually overcome his border defences and march into the interior:

> There are so many entrances into Portugal, the whole country being frontier, that it would be very difficult to prevent the enemy from penetrating; and it is very probable that we should be obliged to confine ourselves to the preservation of that which is most important – the capital.[60]

However, the region was perfect for fighting defensive actions and the enemy could be delayed in a barren country where living off the land would prove difficult. Wellington estimated that the French would need at least 100,000 men to totally subjugate Portugal, and the fortification of Lisbon would present them with severe difficulties. Wellington's main concern was preserving his army and if he could retain the capital he might outlast them. He had some difficulty in convincing the Government that his theories were sound. The views of his predecessor, Sir John Moore, were unhelpful since he had believed the country indefensible. Wellington tactfully pointed out that the situation that the late national hero had been familiar with had now changed drastically.[61]

Wellington's plan to defend Portugal divided into three main areas. Firstly, the fortification of Lisbon and improvement of existing strongholds. Secondly, the raising, training and efficient supply of a regular Portuguese army. Thirdly, starving the enemy of supplies by devastating the land before them. As Wellington began the hard work of implementing his plans, he knew there was little time before the French would be upon him.

Chapter 3
Child of Victory

Massena's upbringing was very different from that of his future rival. He was christened Andrea Massena at Sainte Réparte Cathedral two days after his birth in Nice on 6 May 1758.[62] At that time Nice lay within the Sardinian kingdom of Piedmont, a northern Italian state ruled by the House of Savoy. Therefore, in common with his future emperor, his heritage was more Italian than French. His father, Giulio-Cesare Massena, was a tradesman in Nice dealing in wine and olive oil. He died in 1764 leaving his wife Marguerite with five children and, when she swiftly remarried, Marguerite virtually abandoned her offspring. From the age of six André was brought up by a series of relatives.

He received very little formal education, but spoke Italian and French fluently and, though he disliked reading, became reasonably proficient in writing both languages. His relatives had great difficulty providing for André and his siblings and he had to start earning from an early age. His Uncle Agostino made him an apprentice in his soap-boiling business, but André disliked it so much that he ran away to sea, becoming a cabin boy on a merchant ship at the age of thirteen. Though used to hardship, life at sea proved arduous and on 18 August 1775 he enlisted in the Regiment Royal-Italien, in which his Uncle Marcel served as a warrant officer (adjutant). Though in French service, most of the soldiery were Piedmontese and the seventeen-year-old André found the military to his liking, his tough and varied upbringing having been an ideal preparation for army life. He soon gained his sergeant's stripes and his ability at infantry drill and tactics marked him out, leading to his promotion to warrant officer. However, lacking gentle birth and the money to buy a commission, he was very unlikely to rise any further in the army and after fourteen years of service he obtained a discharge.

Only a week after leaving the army, Massena married Marie-Rosalie Lamarre, the daughter of a surgeon from Antibes. Despite her father's profession, the family was not wealthy and André opened a grocery business on the ground floor of the Lamarres' residence. The business was unprofitable and it was rumoured that he engaged in smuggling to supplement his income. However, little evidence exists to support these rumours and they probably arose from his investment in a ship that regularly ran cargoes through the British blockade under French licence. His shares in this venture also failed to make much profit. In 1789 the start of the French Revolution made for radical change in society and Massena, who had experienced hardship and squalor, was determined to take advantage of any opportunities it offered.

With the old order swept away, wealth and privilege were no longer required to rise within the military and Massena re-enlisted in the Garde Nationale as an instructor. This was a kind of volunteer militia and both pay and prospects were poor. In January 1791, with war looming, the revolutionary National Assembly desperately needed soldiers and called for 100,000 volunteers to defend France. Massena was able to transfer into the Volontaires du Var as a junior officer and was sent to defend the frontier. The army had become very politicised, with government commissars wielding considerable influence, but this was no obstacle to Massena, whose humble background made him an enthusiastic revolutionary. His fourteen years' experience in the former Royal Army was a tremendous advantage and when, in true revolutionary style, the regiment elected their officers, he was made Lieutenant-Colonel on 1 February 1792. No longer obliged to rely on the charity of relatives, he had progressed rapidly in the army and with the new system there were no limits to his aspirations.

The execution of Louis XVI in January 1793 along with the brutal reign of terror against 'enemies of the people' meant that there was no turning back for the revolutionaries. Europe was alarmed at events in France and a period of perpetual warfare ensued, providing Massena with ample opportunity to hone his military skills. For the next six years he fought with the Army of Italy,[63] becoming a Général de Brigade by August 1793. France had declared war against Austria and Sardinia in 1792 and the Italian sector was regarded as a sideshow by the National Convention, which regarded Germany as the main theatre of the war, consequently allocating the bulk of their resources there.

Mountain warfare dominated the early years of the Italian campaigns and fighting in such difficult terrain, with ragged and poorly supplied troops, was a great test of a commander's ability. Massena played a major role in the fighting and distinguished himself at the Battle of Loano in 1795. His task was a difficult one, beginning with an assault on prepared Austrian positions on the summits of Monte Guardolia and Monte Lingo. Careful reconnaissance revealed that the Austrian troops in these positions left their trenches at night for the shelter of nearby villages and Massena took advantage of this by ordering a night march and attack, which achieved partial surprise. Stiff resistance and terrible conditions held up the advance, but Massena took personal command when Charlet (one of his brigade commanders) was killed. He also managed to persuade mutinous troops to move, with a mixture of threats and cajoling, when the advance faltered due to the soldiers' tiredness in the deep snow impeding their march. He managed to reach all his objectives and captured ninety-two guns, which magnified the scale of his success.

The Army of Italy had endured a succession of lacklustre commanders-in-chief and when Schérer resigned in disgust at Paris's refusal to provide adequate provisions, Massena seemed a likely successor. However, to the surprise of many, Napoleon Buonaparte was given the command. At twenty-seven Buonaparte was ten years Massena's junior, and though he had some experience of campaigning with the army his main achievements were a remarkable contribution to the siege of Toulon and putting down a royalist revolt in Paris. Very much a political soldier, Buonaparte had won allies in the Directory (which had recently replaced the National Convention) by his ruthless suppression of the royalists. Massena resented being passed over, but was astute enough to welcome this young commander and await events.

However, Buonaparte's youth belied his ability, and he quickly proved himself an exceptional commander-in-chief and, though relations were never easy between them, Massena soon acknowledged his remarkable talent. The young commander also changed the spelling of his name to make it sound less Italian. From 1796 Bonaparte's energy and drive helped the French break the impasse they had reached. He successfully invaded Piedmont, where he induced the Austrians and Sardinians to divide, allowing him to concentrate his might on the Sardinian Army and defeat it. Once the King of Sardinia had capitulated, the French redirected their main efforts into ousting the Austrians from the Italian states. Bonaparte had turned the sideshow into the main theatre of the war.

Massena played a key role in much of the fighting, taking part in virtually all the major battles, with his division often spearheading the advance. He fought at Montenotte, Lodi, Castiglione, Bassano, Caldiero, Arcola and Rivoli, amongst others, amassing a wealth of experience. Knowing the power of personal example in the French Army, he was unafraid of taking part in the fighting when necessary and personally led attacks in many engagements, notably at the Bridge of Lodi, where the French pressed the Austrian rearguard. Accompanied by other high-ranking officers, he led the second assault over the bridge into a storm of musketry and cannon fire and two of his aides de camp were wounded in the struggle around the guns the Austrians had placed to command the bridge.

Massena secured the French left flank at Arcola when Bonaparte tried to outflank General D'Alvintzy's army in the marshes, and held the village of Porcile against repeated counter-attacks on the first day of the battle. On the third day he lured the Croatian troops defending Arcola village into the marsh by placing a weak force before them to invite attack. When they pushed this unit back along the causeway, the enemy fell into Massena's ambush, concealed in the ditches on their flanks, and was crushed. Following up this success, Massena personally led a rush over the bridge before Arcola, where so many men had been cut down in the previous two days. Flourishing his bicorne hat on the point of his sword, he led his troops into the village, which was taken at the point of the bayonet. Though a cautious strategist and tactician, Massena was physically tough despite his small stature and knew when to inspire the men by personal example. ADC Paul Thiebault recalled his impression of his commander:

> *Massena had no education nor primary instruction, but his face bespoke sagacity and energy; his glance was that of the eagle; in the attitude of his head, always raised and slightly thrown to the left; there was an imposing dignity... his gesture was commanding, his ardour and activity indescribable; his speech, curt in the extreme, testified to the lucidity of his thought... he was a man made for authority and command...*[64]

It was the Battle of Rivoli on 14 January 1797 that decided the first Italian campaign and enabled the French to take the war into Austria itself. This was a great victory for Bonaparte, but Massena's contribution was crucial for its success. In order to defeat the Austrians, Bonaparte had to determine which of their two assaults was the stronger so that he could counter-attack, isolate and destroy this force. Once it was determined that Joubert's division was under attack by the stronger of the two Austrian armies, Bonaparte rushed to support Joubert, ordering Massena to reinforce them. Massena's division had already fought off a serious attack at Verona and, leaving adequate men for the city's defence, he conducted a forced night march. Covering fifteen miles with remarkable swiftness, he arrived just in time to swing the battle in favour of the French. The Austrians were decisively beaten, suffering 3,376 casualties, losing nine guns and leaving 7,000 prisoners, with D'Alvintzy himself narrowly evading capture.

Yet Massena and his battered division were not permitted a rest after two days marching and fighting. General Provera was wreaking havoc in the south and set on relieving the besieged fortress city of Mantua, crucial for the domination of northern Italy. Embarking on another forced march, the tired division covered a further thirty miles to meet the threat. Provera's force was trapped between Massena and the troops besieging the city and 7,000 men were forced to surrender. Mantua capitulated a few weeks later. It was a glorious end to the campaign, with the Austrians in full retreat. Bonaparte knew how close he had come to defeat at Rivoli and was duly grateful for Massena's lightning marches. In the presence of the troops he praised his conduct, acclaiming him: '*l'Enfant chéri de la Victoire.*'[65]

Massena's actions during the whole campaign encapsulated the new style of warfare that Bonaparte was introducing to Europe. In brief, this was mobility and endurance with an emphasis on attack. In many ways the Austrians had been outmanoeuvred and frightened out of the Italian states by the speed of French marches and constant, unexpected attacks on their flanks or rear, inducing them to withdraw. Though a decisive victory, Rivoli was not on the scale of later battles, which would appal Europe with the extent of their slaughter.

Massena spent some time in Paris in the wake of the military triumph. Bonaparte, ever mindful of advertising his victories, sent him as part of a delegation to present Austrian standards and captured arms to the Directory, and the general was showered with honours including a ceremonial sword of honour. Here he was persuaded by Barras to stand for political office. Although far from being the only soldier to do so (Schérer, Kleber and Augereau also stood) his attempt proved a near farce, ending in a shattering electoral defeat.[66] He achieved little beyond proving his political naiveté in allowing himself to be drawn into Barras's schemes and irritating his political opponents, among whom was Carnot, who would later prove obstructive towards him as War Minister. It seems that Bonaparte did not resent his ill-advised venture into politics, probably deriving some amusement from it.

1799 brought disaster for the French Republic. Though initially welcomed as liberators, the French confiscated and stole vast sums, hoping to restore their depleted treasury, rapidly alienating the northern Italian states. Levies were even demanded from neutral states and the Vatican itself, the Republic having little respect for Papal authority with the Pope's opposition to their new order. Smarting at the humiliations inflicted upon Austria by the treaty of Campo-Formio, the Aulic Council of Vienna pressed their sovereign to avenge their losses and a second coalition was formed against France with Britain and Russia. War was declared on 1 March 1799 and, though the French initially made progress, they were soon in retreat.

Previously, Massena had received his first independent command with the leadership of the Army of Helvetia (Switzerland). The Swiss Confederation, having refused the offer of French 'protection', had been invaded and occupied after brief resistance and Massena had established himself at Zurich. It was a vital strategic point, being at an important road junction, but Massena had constructed fortifications to the north, which dominated the town rather than improving its defences. Lake Zurich, twenty-three miles long, protected his flank and the mountainous nature of the area was ideal for defence. This was just as well, since the Allies rapidly defeated the French armies to the north and south. General Jourdan was defeated by the Archduke Charles, the Emperor's brother and the foremost general of Austria, and retreated through the Black Forest to add the remnants of his force to Massena's.

In the south the French suffered a string of reverses, culminating in a major defeat at Austro-Russian hands at the Battle of Novi on 15 August, in which General Joubert was killed. The redoubtable General Alexander Suvórov commanded the Russian contingent and was considered one of the greatest generals of the eighteenth century. As a stern disciplinarian he pushed his men to their limits, demanding frequent forced marches and relying on massed formations to overwhelm his opponents. Though no great strategist, he had succeeded against the Poles, Persians, Tartars and Turks and had a reputation for brutality after ordering the sacking of Ismail in Bessarabia.

With the treasury exhausted once more, the Directory had failed to supply Massena's army with enough supplies and he therefore refused the order to invade the Austrian Tyrol, offering his resignation if they objected. Having withdrawn into Switzerland his army was now the only intact force standing between the Allies and an invasion of France. Bonaparte had left France the previous year on a military expedition to Egypt, so the Republic had only Massena to rely upon.

Though France could now be invaded through Germany or Italy, it was strategically unsound for the Allies to leave Massena in the geographical bastion formed by Switzerland, since he could fall on their flanks or rear as they marched. Soon Switzerland was invaded from the north and an army under the Archduke Charles met the French at the first Battle of Zurich on 4 June. Massena had abandoned Zurich itself and withdrawn to the entrenched camp above on the Zurichberg. In the struggle that followed, Massena hurried from one threatened sector to another as the Austrian assault threatened to overwhelm them. The Austrians lost over 2,000 casualties and failed to carry the defences, but the action had been a close one. Torrential rain discouraged the Austrians from attempting a second assault the following day, the wet not only hampering musketry but also making the precipitous slopes extremely treacherous to climb. Massena used this pause to withdraw to the stronger position of the Albis Ridge centred on the Ütilberg. Having possession of the town, the Austrians could claim a victory, but the French still dominated the northern approach and they could not advance beyond it.

The Austrians now considered Massena virtually defeated. The Archduke marched elements of his army north towards the Netherlands as a Russian army under General Rimski Korsákov reinforced Zurich. For an entire month Massena dispassionately surveyed his enemies massing below him, the Russians in the town and the Austrians at the eastern end of Lake Zurich. In Paris the Government was unhappy at his immobility and pressed him to act. He responded angrily:

> Since I am informed that my detractors are trying to criticise my military operations and what they call my inaction, I must point out to you that during the past two months I have repeatedly called attention to the terrible lack of supplies provided for this army... If I had fertile country ahead of me, there might be some point in advancing. But the further I move forward, the further I should be removed from my sources of supply... and if I am too firmly convinced that the movement which you order me to make is premature and would lead to disaster, then, Citizen Directors, you need only approve my renewed request that you will appoint a successor to relieve me in command...[67]

In recent years generals had been executed for failing the Republic so this defiance required some courage, but Massena was backed up by military common sense and though the Directors considered removing him, they relented.

Suvórov, now appointed commander-in-chief of the Allied forces, had decided to dislodge Massena by a circuitous march on his rear which, when combined with attacks from Korsákov and the Austrians, would trap Massena in a pincer movement. Advancing through the St. Gotthard Pass Russian progress was slowed by narrow tracks, gorges and rushing mountain streams. Snow and mist, along with French resistance, made surmounting such obstacles even more difficult, with General Lecourbe's division, experienced in Alpine fighting, mounting ambushes and destroying bridges, to impede their march. On 28 September Suvórov was appalled to learn that the forces at Zurich had been defeated.

Massena had played the waiting game long enough and, following careful observation of enemy positions, came down from the mountains to mount a twin assault. Massena led the attack on the Russians deployed outside the town and forced them back within Zurich's walls after fierce fighting. Meanwhile, a second force under General Soult crossed the lake and attacked the Austrians under General Hotze, positioned around the town of Uznach. Hotze and his chief-of-staff were both shot down by French skirmishers as they brought up reinforcements and the Austrians were in full retreat after two days' fighting. Bottled up within the town, Korsákov realised that he stood little chance of defending it with the heights in enemy possession and ordered a full retreat. However, the French mounted a swift pursuit and the Russians were routed, leaving 7,000 men as prisoners along with all their guns and baggage.

The unexpected move on his rear caught Massena off guard, but he reacted calmly and turned upon Suvórov, coming very close to trapping the Russians in the passes. Although Suvórov managed to fight his way out, he did so at the loss of around half his force, eventually limping back over the Rhine with only 14,000 men. The second battle of Zurich from 25 September–10 October 1799 was a triumph for Massena and his crowning achievement. He held out against superior forces and timed his counter-attack to perfection, defeating one of the foremost generals of the era. He achieved this through patience and refusing to be bullied by his political masters. In contrast, Bonaparte's Egyptian campaign had faltered and, sensing impending defeat, he returned with the excuse that France was under grave threat. Embarrassingly, he was informed in Paris that Massena had saved France in his absence. The *coup d'état* of 18 *Brumaire* made Bonaparte one of three consuls ruling France. He would rapidly outmanoeuvre his fellows and take power, these events largely overshadowing Massena's victory. However, it is unlikely they could have taken place without it.

Bonaparte's seizure of power brought Massena command of the Army of Italy, an appointment he had long coveted. Yet the army was a shadow of its former self, following a succession of defeats and neglect. He was obliged to resort to stern measures to deter desertion and restore order amongst the mutinous ranks. His main task was to preserve what was left of French territory in Italy and maintain communications with France. However, on 5 April 1800 a major Austrian offensive began under the command of Baron Michael von Melas, eventually obliging Massena to fall back on the city of Genoa.

The Genoese Republic was kept in a state of 'enforced neutrality' by the French and the people were only kept in order by force of arms. Its defences were strong enough to withstand siege, the city being walled and surrounded by a ring of hills surmounted by a stone rampart. Aware of this likelihood, Massena had already started improving these defences. Though the city was a port, the harbour was virtually useless to the French, with the British Navy dominating the Gulf of Genoa.

Admiral Lord Keith offered the French terms on 24 April, but Massena replied that he intended to resist and the Austrians began major siege operations in conjunction with the British naval blockade. One of the first Austrian moves was to sever the city's main water supply via their aqueduct. The bread mills relied on water for power and, since the Genoese Government maintained a monopoly on production, supplies soon dwindled. Soldiers took priority for food supplies, but they had to be content with a quarter pound of horseflesh and a ration of rancid bread, the composition of which contained more hair powder and sawdust than flour. Soon all the dogs and cats in the city were caught and eaten and citizens would brave enemy fire by following in the wake of French sorties to cut grass and nettles for sustenance. Jean-Baptiste Marbot, one of Massena's new aides, left a harrowing account of the siege:

> My courage fails me to describe what the garrison and population of Genoa had to suffer during the two months... The ravages of famine, war, typhus were enormous... every day seven or eight hundred corpses of the inhabitants, of every age, sex and class, were picked up in the streets and buried in an immense trench filled with quicklime behind the church of Carignan. The number of victims reached 30,000, nearly all starved to death.[68]

In order to get their guns close enough to bombard the city walls; the Austrians made constant attempts to capture the outlying forts. Some changed hands several times, with the garrison obliged to mount regular sorties in their support. During one of these sallies General Soult was wounded and captured. Massena had difficulty maintaining morale amidst squalid conditions and the townsfolk were on the edge of rebellion.

Several attempts were made to contact France, and on 2 May Colonel Reille managed to run the British blockade and bring dispatches from Paris. He learned that Bonaparte was preparing to cross the Alps and invade Italy, so there was a chance of relief. It took an iron will to endure, but Massena's determination alone could not make the city stand. On 29 May a revolt by the Genoese was suppressed with difficulty and desertion was widespread. Massena knew that Bonaparte was weeks or even days away, but had to yield to the inevitable when the food supplies ran out. To the end he tried to prolong the negotiations, and managed to win favourable terms. The troops were permitted to leave with their arms and baggage, with Lord Keith repeatedly saying: '...General, your defence has been so heroic that we can refuse you nothing.'[69]

The garrison evacuated Genoa on 6 June, yet even these generous concessions were not enough for Massena and he gained a safe conduct for two aides to ride and inform Bonaparte of the city's capitulation. On 14 June 1800 Napoleon won his celebrated victory at Marengo, a major step towards gaining his crown. Yet it was a very close victory, and the presence of the Austrian troops surrounding Genoa may have made all the difference. Commiserating with an Austrian delegate during the peace talks Berthier remarked: 'It must be a consolation to have been beaten only by a fine army under the greatest general in the world.' The Austrian officer replied briskly, 'The battle of Marengo was not lost here, but before Genoa.'[70]

Following the siege Massena was physically drained and suffering from severe emotional strain. On 13 August 1800 he was relieved of command and allowed to go into temporary retirement on full pay. He spent most of the next five years at his château in Reuil near Paris and was grateful to be able to spend time with his wife and children. The First Consul became increasingly powerful during this period and on 18 May 1804 was crowned Emperor Napoleon I of France. Mindful of the debt he owed to the great captains who had placed him on the throne, the new Emperor created fourteen active and four honorary marshals of the empire, Massena being among the first to receive the marshal's baton.

Membership of the marshalate was as much a civil honour as a military one and the Emperor intended to allow the army some political influence through its creation and increase his power base. However, the military and political capabilities of his appointees varied considerably. As a dictator, the Emperor wished to maintain strict control of his subordinates and feared to raise anyone capable of outshining him to prominence. After all, a king had recently been deposed because of the people's dissatisfaction and it could easily happen again. The Republic had taught France that merit alone was sufficient for success, and if Bonaparte's talent waned then so would his power if they had a viable alternative. Out of the twenty-six marshals eventually appointed only Massena, Davout and Suchet could be classed as great commanders, and Bonaparte was consequently wary of them. Likewise, he was not going to allow them to unite against him and he deliberately fostered jealousy and mistrust between them.[71]

1805 saw Massena return to the Army of Italy and fight once again in the north. He eventually won the three-day Battle of Caldiero of 28–31 October, but there is reason to believe that the Austrians only withdrew due to their losses in Germany, as Bonaparte simultaneously pursued his great campaign that terminated at Austerlitz. The fighting continued into 1806, Massena entering Naples in February and capturing the city of Gaeta on 18 July after a prolonged siege. In 1807, although Massena commanded a Corps of Napoleon's Grand Army, he saw relatively little action, but the rigours of the campaign in Poland had a crippling effect on his health and he was compelled to take nearly a year off due to sickness. He was now forty-nine, beginning to feel his age and convinced that his days of active campaigning were numbered.

In March 1808 the Emperor created him Duke of Rivoli in acknowledgement of his outstanding performance during that campaign, but his health was not improved by a hunting injury he sustained later that year. Attending a shooting party at Fontainebleau, Massena was struck in the face by birdshot fired by the Emperor. Reputedly a poor shot, Napoleon characteristically made Berthier take the blame for the incident, which blinded Massena in his left eye.[72] Publicly he accepted this explanation, no doubt encouraged by his dislike for Berthier, but it could not have improved an already strained relationship.

Massena was now beginning to slow down, but showed some signs of his former brilliance in the Danube campaign of 1809. Though the French dominated Europe, the Austrians decided to challenge the supposedly invincible Napoleon yet again, the Archduke Charles leading an invasion of Bavaria on 6 April without a formal declaration of war. In spite of the reforms Charles had imposed on the Austrian army, the Austrians were soon in retreat, being defeated at Abensberg and Eckmühl. Massena's Corps was heavily committed and the enemy was obliged to retire across the vast Danube River and abandon their capital. Violating one of his own principles, Napoleon then captured Vienna before inflicting a conclusive defeat upon the enemy, which made it vital to bring the Archduke to battle as swiftly as possible.

The French entered Vienna on 14 May to find that the city garrison had crossed the Danube and destroyed the bridges behind them. Undeterred, Napoleon ordered an extensive reconnaissance to find other crossing points and decided to bridge the river at the island of Lobau, a few miles south of the capital. A pontoon bridge to Lobau and a second from the island to the eastern bank were constructed but, although pains were taken to conceal their preparations, the Austrians were soon aware of the move. As the French began to cross and occupy the villages of Aspern and Essling, Austrian pioneers began to float tree trunks and stone-filled boats downriver to damage the bridges. Massena's force garrisoned the village of Aspern but no preparations were made to fortify it. At that night's council of war, Napoleon argued that the Austrian army would have to be sought out beyond the Marchfeld plain and the one dissenting voice was Massena's, who alone suspected that the enemy was closer than they thought.

The following day Archduke Charles sprang his trap, mounting a huge attack on the two villages. Only 24,000 French had crossed and the Austrians strongly outnumbered them with around 83,000 men. The two sides fought over the villages throughout the day and Aspern changed hands several times, with Massena in the thick of the fighting. That night, following petty disagreements during the battle, marshals Lannes and Bessières nearly came to blows:

> ...old Massena, interposing between the adversaries, sought to calm them, and not succeeding, he took the high tone in his turn. 'I am your senior, gentlemen; you are in my camp, and I shall not permit you to give my troops the scandalous spectacle of seeing two marshals draw on each other, and in the presence of the enemy. I summon you, therefore, in the name of the Emperor, to separate at once.' Then adopting a gentler manner, he took Marshal Lannes by the arm, and he led him to the further end of the bivouac...[73]

The role of peacemaker was unusual for Massena, but the French had other foes to fight and the following day Marshal Lannes was mortally wounded, becoming the first of Napoleon's marshals to die in action.

In an aggressive counter-attack, Massena completely ousted the Austrians from Aspern and his troops fought hard for it during the desperate fighting that ensued. However, Bonaparte had made the key mistake of relying on a single line of supply and, when a huge burning hulk crashed into the first bridge, it was severed for hours, shattering any hopes of reinforcements. Although the French had managed to reinforce their bridgehead they were still vastly outnumbered and the disaster meant that they had to adopt a defensive strategy. Great losses were inflicted on both sides, the Austrians having over 292 guns from which they amassed a huge battery to enfilade the French centre. Eventually Aspern fell and the way to the bridge was open. Potentially the French could be cut off at Essling and the rest of the army pressed against the river and annihilated. Yet Charles was cautious and unwilling to risk losses against a cornered enemy and the French were able to withdraw in the night. Massena organised the rearguard and retreat and made some show of being the last man to cross the bridge to Lobau island.

Aspern-Essling was one of the bloodiest battles of the Napoleonic wars up to 1809, each side sustaining around 20,000 casualties. It was Bonaparte's first clear defeat and the Austrians expected him to sue for peace. However, Bonaparte was an inveterate warmonger and thirsted to avenge the stain on his military reputation. Learning from previous errors, he constructed multiple bridges to span the Danube at Lobau and crossed the Marchfeld to meet the Archduke's army on the hills edging the plain.

The Battle of Wagram was fought on 4–5 July and was an even greater slaughter than its predecessor. Massena had suffered a severe fall from his horse shortly before the battle and was unable to ride. Unwilling to relinquish command, he had himself driven in an open-topped carriage over the field: 'The marshal was in his carriage and the enemy, noting it with its four horses in the middle of the line, guessed that its occupant must be a person of importance, and poured a storm of shot upon it.'[74]

The Austrians had been surprised at the speed of the French manoeuvre, having expected a renewed attack at the former crossing point. Nevertheless, Charles did not panic but made a determined attempt to turn his enemy's left flank on the second day, coming close to cutting the French off from Lobau. Despite his handicap, Massena performed the complicated move of disengaging from the enemy and marching to support the threatened flank. In conjunction with artillery support from the island he secured the French left. Wagram was Napoleon's last truly decisive victory and Massena hoped this would be his last campaign. The Austrians eventually agreed a peace with the Treaty of Schönbrunn on 14 October and shortly afterwards Massena was created Prince of Essling for his efforts.[75]

The highlights of Massena's military career only give a partial insight into his personality. To gain some understanding of his true character it is necessary to examine how others viewed him, particularly as he left no memoirs and was considered mysterious even by some contemporaries. Napoleon had a chequered relationship with this man who, it must be admitted, he saw as a potential rival. In the early Italian campaigns he wrote: 'He had a strong constitution and would ride tirelessly, night and day, over rocks and through the mountains; that was the kind of war he specialised in and understood thoroughly. He was decided, tough, fearless, full of ambition and self-esteem; his outstanding quality was doggedness, he was never discouraged.'[76] Perhaps thinking this overly generous, Napoleon qualified this remark by denigrating his ability for instilling discipline and organising attacks, but admitted that his talents shone brighter than ever when under fire. Indeed the Directory removed Massena from command of the garrison of Rome in 1798 due to his inability to deal with mutinous troops. Nevertheless, his expertise in mountain warfare was unmatched in the French army and Thiebault recalled Massena's reaction when a captive officer informed him that the mountains ahead were virtually impassable: 'Tell General Lusignan from me that, after having shown him, the day before yesterday, how to attack a village, I shall show him, today, how to cross the mountains.'[77]

However, Bonaparte never gave Massena due recognition for his achievement at Zurich, probably due to jealousy and the fact that it rivalled his own achievements. His controversial abandonment of his army in Egypt also appeared in a worse light since Massena had saved the Republic in his absence, the ostensible reason for his return. A dukedom or principality for Zurich would have been appropriate for Massena, but the Emperor only awarded him titles for actions associated with his own campaigns, thereby sharing the glory. Napoleon alternated between praise and derision with bewildering frequency regarding his marshals, no doubt by design. In 1800 Massena was at the pinnacle of his career and therefore more dangerous to his master's imperial ambitions, so it came as no surprise that he scarcely acknowledged his tenacity in Genoa and actively criticised his performance. He claimed that he should have concentrated on defending the city instead of trying to keep the road to Nice open simultaneously, could have held out for longer and should have marched to his aid at Marengo after the capitulation.[78]

This was grossly unfair. Genoa was incapable of supporting a larger garrison and the troops guarding communications with France were performing an important task. The garrison resisted as long as humanly possible, with considerable loss of life, and Massena won better terms from the besiegers than could have been predicted. Furthermore, the addition of a half-starved and mutinous garrison would have provided dubious assistance to Bonaparte had the tattered force been able to march to reach him. In direct contrast, Thiebault observed:

> Words cannot express the electric influence and almost
> supernatural power which he exercised on the troops by the
> quickness of his decisions... and by the lightning speed with which
> he imposed their execution. General Massena was everywhere,
> and took charge personally, even in minor operations; he usually
> left nothing to be done by his subordinates...[79]

It is claimed that Massena's hair turned grey at Genoa and, had the garrison capitulated earlier, Bonaparte might have suffered a disaster at Marengo.

Staff officers often gain valuable insight into their commanding officers, being constantly in their company and observing them under most circumstances. Clearly Massena stood very high in Thiebault's estimation, but Marbot's memoirs, as another aide de camp, are more ambiguous. Initially in awe of Massena as a young officer and grateful for his support in various matters, he gradually turned against him. At Wagram he assumed that his chief had overlooked the fact that Prosper Massena (also an aide) was next in line when he asked him to carry a dispatch across the battlefield: 'But Massena soon destroyed my illusion by saying, in a wheedling tone, "You understand, my friend, why I do not send my son, although it's his turn; I am afraid of getting him killed. You understand? You understand?"'[80] This drew an angry response from Marbot and Prosper was so ashamed that he accompanied him on the hazardous ride, both surviving to tell the tale. According to Marbot the Emperor personally admonished Massena for his breach of military protocol when he heard of it.[81]

Marbot had other grudges against his commander. For example, at Genoa when Massena banned funerals, their frequency having ruinous effects on morale, he personally distracted the seventeen-year-old Marbot while his father's body was smuggled out of the back of the house for secret burial. Though he acknowledged the military necessity of this act, amongst others it led Marbot to refer to Massena as '...the wiliest of Italians'[82] in later life.

Yet Massena often stood up for his subordinates when he saw them slighted or undervalued. In Italy when he read Bonaparte's inaccurate dispatch allotting credit to two of his own aides, he wrote angrily to him claiming:

> It was Chabran, and no one else, who marched at the head of
> the grenadiers, and he was there the whole time; Marmont and
> Leclerc only arrived at the end of the action... I also have cause to

complain about your despatches on Lonato and Rovereto, in which you did not give me the credit which I deserved. This neglect is most heart-breaking and discouraging to me. [83]

Perhaps the differing accounts that reached him, along with the confusion of battle, may have been to blame rather than any intent to deceive, but Napoleon never took criticism lightly. Yet Massena was no sycophant and was always prepared to contradict him even when he became Emperor. Throughout the army he had a reputation as a capable general whose tenacity and cunning had brought victory to many a desperate field. He was no diplomat, being inclined to speak his mind, which won him few friends, but his ability won him respect.

However, Massena's reputation was founded on more than his generalship alone. His long career had made him notorious for two vices – an excessive passion for money and sex. During the Napoleonic wars the French Army gained an unenviable reputation for looting and pillaging. During the Italian campaigns, successive revolutionary governments advocated the principle that war should pay for itself and monetary 'contributions' were officially extorted, along with art treasures that were shipped back to Paris.[84] Along with the unofficial 'taxes', the soldiery frequently committed excesses against property and people, leaving a lasting resentment. Napoleon's famous address to his troops at the start of the campaign in Piedmont is often quoted as an invitation to pillage:

'Soldiers', he said, 'you are hungry and nearly naked. The Government owes you much; it can do nothing for you. Your patience and courage do you honour, but cannot procure you either profit or glory. I am come to lead you into the most fertile plains in the world. There you will find rich provinces and great towns. There you will find glory, honour and riches.' [85]

This attitude continued into the Imperial period and, with such a background, Massena's reputation for unbridled looting is difficult to reconcile. There are a number of reasons for this. In the early Italian campaigns his chief-of-staff, Jean-Baptiste Solignac, was notorious for extorting 'contributions' in occupied territory and not above using threats and blackmail. He was an inveterate gambler and, having risen from a poor background, possessed an unquenchable thirst for money. Thiebault was astonished when Solignac told his companions that his trunk contained 400,000 francs when they travelled by coach back to Paris.[86] Many assumed that Massena endorsed Solignac's actions and blame was therefore attached to him.

There is also some evidence to suggest that Massena's enemies used allegations of corruption against him. For example, when both Berthier and Massena wished to gain command in Italy, General Kilmaine wrote to Bonaparte as part of a campaign to discredit him:

> *The people of Padua claim that at various times they have given Massena three millions of Venetian currency for the use of his division; the division say that only 300,000 francs have been spent on their behalf and that the remainder must have been employed in winning popularity for himself and in stirring people up against you.*[87]

Such malicious hearsay almost certainly denied him the command, though it has to be admitted that he lacked Berthier's skill in what had become more of an administrative post under the occupation.

Throughout his career Massena was accused of embezzlement and corruption, though the allegations usually lacked any conclusive proof. Solignac was eventually cashiered for his crimes and Massena was certainly at fault for tolerating his excesses. He displayed an uncanny ability to acquire money, but he was far from being the only culprit in the marshalate. Augereau, Brune and Victor were all incorrigible looters and Napoleon considered Soult the worst offender of all, holding entire towns and provinces to ransom.[88] Though his associations may have damned him, the fact that Bonaparte increasingly came to suspect him of irregularities implies that there was some substance to the allegations. He wrote several times to Massena questioning his financial practices and eventually warned his brother Joseph:

> *Massena is no use in a civil administration; and besides it is not easy to secure his devotion. He is a good soldier, but entirely dominated by his greed for money; it is the one thing that influences his conduct, and it is only that which has spurred him on... It began with small amounts; now millions are not enough for him.*[89]

At one time Napoleon took the almost unparalleled step of confiscating three million francs, which Massena had deposited in a Genoese bank, and the fact that he failed to protest implies that their origins were illicit. During his time in Italy, it was even rumoured that he sold trading licences allowing wealthy merchants to contravene Napoleon's Continental System. Though he may not have been the robber baron that many claimed, to win a reputation for corruption in a regime which had practically stripped Europe bare was a dubious distinction.

Massena certainly gained a reputation as a miser in the army and Marbot recorded one amusing incident to support this. The staff argued that the civilian coach drivers who had risked their lives at Wagram driving Massena over the battlefield deserved a reward. Though he eventually complied, he reacted badly when Marbot asked if this constituted an annual payment:

> *The eyes of a tigress who sees her young attacked by the hunter are not more terrible than were Massena's on hearing me speak thus. He leapt from his chair, exclaiming: 'Wretch! Do you want to ruin me? What! An annuity of 400 francs? No, no, no; 400 francs once for all!'*[90]

However, Marbot had grown to dislike his commander and somewhat overplayed his hand, claiming that during the following arguments the marshal careered about the room in a rage, knocking furniture about and screaming abuse. Notwithstanding, Massena's reputation for meanness appears to have had some foundation.

Massena's second weakness is less ambiguous. Though devoted to his wife and family, he was unable to endure long periods of campaigning without female company. This was certainly not unusual in the French army and Napoleon said of his future brother-in-law: 'What faults Murat committed in order to set up his headquarters in *châteaux* where there were women! He needed one every day so I have always allowed my generals to take a strumpet along with them in order to avoid this trouble.' [91] Nevertheless, this was at the time of Marengo and, when the old revolutionaries became marshals, dukes and princes during the imperial period, many assumed airs compatible with their new status in society. With his background, Massena saw no need to change his ways and remained true to his principles, or lack of them, his appetite for women remaining as insatiable as his indiscretion. During the Piedmont campaign, Massena openly maintained a mistress in the form of Silvia Cepolini, the widow of an Austrian Consul, their liaison lasting five years. Hundreds of prostitutes followed in the wake of the army and were frequently the cause of indiscipline. Knowing this, Bonaparte prohibited high-ranking officers from keeping mistresses, believing it set a bad example, but met with limited success, especially with Massena. Massena viewed his career as a means of continuing his vices in direct contrast to Wellington's attitude. Wellington gave up his interests in music and gambling, fearing the disapproval of others, but it is difficult to imagine Massena giving up anything in the hope of improving his image.

In 1809 Massena was over fifty and in failing health. He wished to retire to his estates and enjoy his wealth, but the Emperor still needed his services in the Peninsula. Here his abilities and experience would be pitted against Britain's foremost general. They shared some character traits, but hailed from very different backgrounds. On one side was Wellington – meticulous in preparation, prepared to adapt to circumstances and with one eye fixed on his political future. Very much a product of the upper classes, he hoped to fend off encroaching change and protect the old order. On the other side, Massena had risen from humble origins but probably set glory and personal gain above his Republican ideals. Unlike Wellington his baggage contained no case of books detailing the country and its culture, but he was an old campaigner with a wealth of experience. Cautious, patient and always on the lookout for anything he could turn to his advantage, he hoped that Portugal would provide a great victory to end a distinguished career.

Chapter 4
The Key to Portugal

Austria had been defeated, but Napoleon knew the Continent was seething with resentment and that many states were biding their time, waiting for a chance to challenge his Empire. He hoped to end the long series of wars by allying with the Austrian royal family and, having divorced the Empress Josephine, he married Marie-Louise, daughter of Francis I, in 1810 to cement the alliance. Following so much bloodshed, it would still require skilled diplomacy to win the Austrians over, along with the more pleasurable task of providing the Empire with an heir. Therefore Napoleon felt unable to return to Iberia and complete its subjugation. He needed someone to send in his stead and in any case believed the Spanish were on the verge of defeat and would crumble if the British were forced out.

With twenty-two marshals of France on the active list, finding a replacement should have been easy, but this was not the case. Whilst some were too old, the majority had been chosen more for their political compliance than their military capability, and had little experience of commanding a force beyond the level of a single army corps. Davout would have been perfect, but he was needed in northern Europe, where Russia's intentions were still unclear. Soult and Junot had both failed in Portugal and Ney was too impetuous for an independent command. Massena appeared to be the only real choice but, when offered command of the Army of Portugal, he protested bitterly, citing his recent injury and sicknesses. Having sneered at Massena's achievements over the years, there was little affection between them but now Napoleon managed to win him over with charm and patriotic appeals.

Massena arrived to assume command at Valladolid on 10 May 1810. Determined not to exert himself, he had brought a large staff with fourteen aides de camp. Among these was Captain Renique, whose sister Henriette Leberton (*née* Renique) was Massena's current mistress. He was surprised when Junot and a party of other generals met him on the road in their eagerness to greet the new commander. As Junot's wife recalled, this led to some embarrassment:

> *Massena rode first in a small uncovered* Calèche, *and at his side was seated a very boyish officer of dragoons, decorated with the*

Cross of the Legion of Honour. As this badge of distinction was then very sparingly distributed, its appearance on the breast of so very young an officer attracted general remark.[92]

Observing their approach he tried to draw up the carriage's hood, but was not quick enough as the generals rode up. Junot was puzzled that both men appeared ill at ease during the ensuing pleasantries but then: '...could scarcely refrain from laughing outright, for at that moment someone whispered in his ear that the Marshal's military companion was a young lady!'[93] Knowing that Junot had brought his wife with him, Massena was reluctant to share the *Palacio Real* at Valladolid with them, but eventually consented. Madam Junot came to know Massena fairly well during his stay but the arrival of his travelling companion was something of a social slight. She recorded: 'As to the lady, she immediately retired to her own apartment, and during the three months which the Prince d'Essling passed at Valladolid, I never caught a glimpse of her but once. She had strict orders to keep herself concealed.'[94] The arrival of a mistress was not a major scandal, though her uniform and medal were highly irregular, but to commit a social *faux pas* as soon as he arrived did not portray the new commander-in-chief in a good light.

When Massena addressed his new command they were dismayed by his first speech to them that betrayed his discontent:

Gentlemen, I am here contrary to my own wish; I begin to feel myself too old and too weary to go on active service. The Emperor says that I must, and replied to the reasons for declining this post which I gave him, by saying that my reputation would suffice to end the war. It was very flattering no doubt, but no man has two lives to live on this earth – the soldier least of all.[95]

Although obviously resentful of being forced into the role, and perhaps doubtful over what could be achieved in Iberia, it was extremely unwise of Massena to share his doubts so openly. This was hardly an inspiring beginning for what promised to be a difficult campaign. His two foremost commanders both believed they should have been appointed in his stead and it was folly to provide them with such information. He gave a poor first impression at this meeting, as General Maximilien Foy, who had served under him in Switzerland, recalled:

He is no longer the Massena of the flashing eyes, the mobile face, and the alert figure whom I knew in 1799... He is only fifty-two but looks more like sixty; he has got thin, he is beginning to stoop; his look, since the accident when he lost his eye by the Emperor's hand, has lost its vivacity. The tone of his voice alone remains unchanged.[96]

Though he had a force of at least 50,000 men, the army required some attention with sickness and low morale. Massena once again offended Ney by interfering with his staff and his inspections and changes caused some consternation. However, though this was his role and he made some progress regarding the troops, Ney resented it. The way the Emperor handled his marshals was the root cause of such problems. He had deliberately left his authority ill defined, fearing to create a potential rival. The trouble was that few of the generals viewed Massena as a true commander-in-chief and regarded the Emperor as their only real superior. This was particularly true of Ney, who never really obeyed anyone's orders except Bonaparte's. Furthermore, Major General Fririon, Massena's chief-of-staff, was highly competent, but Massena largely ignored his advice in favour of Major Pelet. As a member of the engineer-topographer's corps, Pelet was highly skilled though lacked experience in staff work. He would prove a great help to him, but the corps commanders, feeling that Massena disregarded their views, resented his influence.

Though he had made a poor start with his subordinates, the Army of Portugal was a cohesive force and much could be achieved if the campaign was approached with vigour and forethought. Napoleon's general instructions to Massena were as follows:

The Prince of Essling will have 40,000 infantry and 9,000 to 10,000 cavalry… which will give him an army of 50,000 men, with which he will besiege first Ciudad Rodrigo and then Almeida, and will then prepare to march methodically into Portugal, which I do not wish to invade until September, after the hot weather and in particular after the harvest.[97]

The Army of Portugal comprised II Corps under General Jean Reynier, VI Corps under Marshal Ney and VIII Corps under General Junot. Ney approached Massena with a plan to mask the two fortresses and seek battle with the British, but Massena rejected his suggestions in favour of the Emperor's instructions. After experiencing both sides of siege warfare at Genoa and Gaeta, he was well versed in this kind of conflict and felt confident of reducing the town. Indeed, he immediately set about the investment of Ciudad Rodrigo, allowing Ney and VI Corps to continue with operations there. Ney would repay his confidence with obstinacy and disrespect.

The importance of fortresses had lessened during the Napoleonic wars, with far greater emphasis placed on seeking and destroying the main enemy army in a decisive battle. However, their relevance was increased in the Peninsula with the pressing need to dominate wide swathes of the country to gain supplies and guard communication routes. Both Ciudad Rodrigo and Almeida were modelled along eighteenth-century lines and fell into the generic term 'star fortresses'. This design followed the principles set out by the famous military engineer Sebastien Vauban (1653–1707), who matched modern developments in artillery by creating low set forts capable of matching a besieger's firepower.

In brief, a star fortress comprised a low curtain wall with artillery *bastions* established at various points and preceded by a deep stone-lined ditch. Placed at intervals within the ditch lay *ravelins*, triangular-shaped artillery platforms, usually backed by a wall known as a *tenaille* providing further protection for the inner defences. Before the ditch lay a long slope known as a *glacis*, the purpose of which was to deflect enemy cannon shot over the walls. The angular design of the structure allowed the converging fire of artillery batteries to be concentrated against a force attempting to storm the structure. In order to break these defences the besiegers would have to dig trenches very close to the fortification, placing batteries within range, and batter a breach in the walls to allow an assault. This was difficult, time consuming and placed the besiegers in great danger both from the fort's guns and the possibility of sallies by the garrison to interfere with their operations. Huge amounts of powder and shot were required to effect this, along with heavy calibre artillery, digging equipment and copious amounts of manpower. Such fortresses could be reduced with persistence but they were costly and time consuming to overcome.

The fortress and town of Ciudad Rodrigo were built on an eminence adjacent to the Agueda River. The town was dominated by two hills – the great and little Teso of San Francisco. Suburbs had been built fairly close to the walls of the fortress and the French considered its defences relatively weak. The garrison comprised around 6,000 men and though many were militia they were bolstered by the presence of regular Spanish troops and irregulars under the famed guerrilla chief Don Julian. The town was well armed with at least a hundred cannon of various calibres, eighteen howitzers and large quantities of muskets and ammunition.

Addressing the town junta in January, the sixty-nine-year-old Governor, Andrés Perez de Herrasti, proclaimed: 'The Supreme Junta, the Council of War and I have decided to defend this place to the death... The strength of the fortress and the thickness of its walls are all prepared for the defence. Providence and fortune will serve us.'[98] The garrison and the townsfolk were confident of withstanding a siege, at least until the Allied army came to their assistance. In constant communication with Wellington, Herrasti believed that the British would eventually march to his support rather than let the fortress fall.

On 31 May, French reconnaissance determined that the most vulnerable sector of the defences was a stretch of the north-western wall near the cathedral, which looked down over much of the town. The French soon surrounded Ciudad Rodrigo, taking the two Teso hills and fighting off sorties from the garrison. Herrasti was determined to resist and tried to interfere with every stage of their operations but gradually the ring around the town drew in tighter and by June siege trenches were being sapped towards the walls. On the first night of these operations, Ney set troops lying down in formation to cover his sappers as they dug the first parallel trench. These were to stand and fight off any sally made by the garrison when they realised what was going on. Meanwhile, distraction attacks were made on the outlying suburbs and the trench was two and a half feet deep before the defenders realised what the French were attempting and turned their cannon against them. By 20 June trenches were gradually snaking towards the intended point of attack and artillery was being established in the works.

However, Massena was encountering serious logistical problems at his base in Salamanca. General Michaux, the army Quartermaster-General, experienced great difficulties finding sufficient wagons and caissons to transport the vast amounts of siege equipment and food that VI Corps required. In addition, the roads from Salamanca to Ciudad Rodrigo were extremely poor and required improvement to bear heavy artillery. Michaux complained to Massena when food magazines were raided by troops from VIII Corps and both Junot and Ney exacerbated the problem by issuing extra rations to their troops while loudly bemoaning the scarcity of provisions. Foragers had to search for supplies over a much larger area because there was little to steal or confiscate after years of fighting in the area. General Joseph Daultane was so worried at the lack of supplies and the methods used to acquire them that he wrote to Massena: 'Confidentially, if Michaux continues to operate the same system he did in Aragon... the province of Avila will soon be abandoned by its people and become a nest of insurrection.'[99]

The British were keeping an eye on French progress and frequently sent patrols to interfere with their operations, but Wellington was unwilling to make any serious relief attempt. He had over 20,000 men in the border region but nearly half of these were Portuguese and Spanish troops who were relatively untested in battle. By 9 June Massena had allowed Junot to bring up VIII Corps to support and cover Ney's siege operation and, though Massena deliberately dispersed them over a wide area, Wellington wisely refused to be tempted out, knowing Massena hoped to lure him into an uneven battle. Ney still entertained hopes of going in search of the Allied army and destroying it. He wrote to Junot on 6 June, questioning his commander's inaction and proposing that they unite their two corps and march on Portugal, claiming the Emperor would back his decision. The plan had some merit in theory, since a serious blow to the Allied

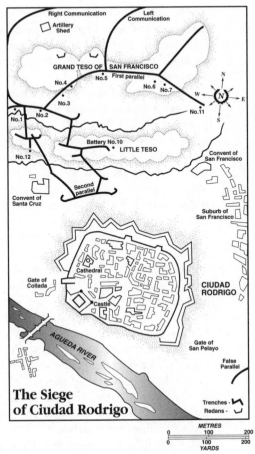

The Siege of Ciudad Rodrigo

army might see the British withdraw entirely from the Peninsula and end the campaign. However, the troops were too poorly supplied to embark on such a bold venture this early, and Junot wisely ignored the suggestion.

Massena was beset by acts of disobedience from high-ranking officers. Some were even insubordinate enough to post orders signing themselves as 'General in Chief,' an implied challenge to his authority. Ney was far from the only officer to write to the Emperor with details of Massena's orders and hint at ways of improving the situation. Consequently, Napoleon wrote to Massena with unhelpful suggestions. The English were the only force to be feared, he argued, and, even with rumours of the Allies fielding nearly 49,000 men, he refused to permit Massena a force of more than 70,000. He dismissed Portuguese soldiers and irregulars as militarily ineffective and refused to include them in his assessment of Allied strength. At first he wavered between ordering an advance into Portugal and continuing the siege, but eventually decided to stick to the methodical approach and delay the invasion until September.

The roads had now dried out sufficiently to allow heavy cannon to be transported to Ciudad Rodrigo and a bombardment would soon be possible. By 24 June Massena decided to assume command of the operation, feeling confident that the siege would soon be over. He wrote to Berthier: 'We could hope to be masters of this place soon if it were abandoned to its own forces; but the movements made by the English army appears to announce its intentions to defend or delay its reduction.'[100] Following weeks of intermittent firing, a serious bombardment was opened on Ciudad Rodrigo at 3am on 25 June. The fire of forty-six guns was trained upon the north-western wall, whilst howitzers lobbed shells into the town and its suburbs, setting large areas alight. The Spanish gunners mounted effective counter-fire and several guns on both sides were dismounted, but on the first day alone around 150 townspeople were killed with 500 wounded. Massena personally inspected some of the damage the next day and ordered heavier guns of sixteen and twenty-four calibres brought up to gain superior firepower and increase the damage inflicted. The glacis was highly effective in deflecting shot over the defences, but the fact that the French had possession of the two hills overlooking the town went some way to negating this. Serious damage was being inflicted and Herrasti was offered terms on 28 June, but rejected them on the grounds that his walls remained unbreached.

By 29 June a serious breach was beginning to appear near the cathedral but the Spanish kept repairing the damage, despite the heavy fire raining down upon them. Major Couche, Ney's principal engineer officer, advised him that heavy calibre shot was running low and smaller artillery pieces must be used until a fissure large enough to be exploited was made. Ney approved his plan and sent a report to Massena before consulting him. Massena, furious at being passed over, ordered that Colonel Valazé be appointed to take charge of the engineers. Angry at this interference, Ney sent a strongly worded and insubordinate letter, refusing to comply. Once again the two marshals clashed over a relatively trivial matter, which ended with Massena inviting the insolent Ney's resignation unless he obeyed orders. Reluctantly, Ney backed down.[101]

Massena's disapproval of Couche's proposals was largely founded on the fact that it would take longer to breach the defences. He was dismayed when, after making a careful appraisal, Valazé submitted a report stating that it would take at least eight days to batter a wide enough breach and crown the counterscarp, permitting the assaulting infantry easier access. It was all taking too long, and Massena had placed too much faith in tales told by Spanish deserters of low morale within the town. He had hoped that Herrasti would submit after the sufferings of the town and the beginnings of a breach developed. His letters to Berthier revealed his increasing frustration and a desire to make an example to discourage such resistance when he went on to besiege Almeida: 'I will make another summons and if they refuse a capitulation, I will take it by force and put the garrison to the sword without sparing the inhabitants who are the most stubborn.'[102]

Massena also suffered a lucky escape around this time. Marbot was bringing the marshal important news and had fallen from his horse into the Agueda when it slipped crossing the ford. Already feeling ill, the cold water accelerated his fever and Marbot was ailing when he delivered the dispatch. Massena, in the company of General Fririon, then returned to observing the fortress. To Marbot's horror, a howitzer shell exploded right next to them. Both were covered in earth and badly bruised. Massena's remaining eye was also so filled with sand that he was practically blinded. Luckily Marbot managed to get him out of range: '...as he was small and thin, I managed, ill though I was, to take him on my shoulders and carry him out of reach of the enemy's shot.'[103] The marshal's injuries proved slight, but the garrison had come very close to killing two high-ranking officers purely by chance.

Massena believed that a handful of fanatics, largely amongst the priesthood, were compelling the garrison to hold out against their own wishes. By the rules of war a garrison risked their right to quarter if they resisted an assault after rejecting terms. It was rare that an attacking force would massacre everyone inside a besieged city, but not unheard of, and many soldiers viewed the orgy of looting, drunkenness and rape that followed a storming as their just reward. In addition, enraged after enduring the concentrated fire poured into the confined breach, their officers would be powerless to restrain them.

Many of the buildings within Ciudad Rodrigo had been reduced to piles of rubble and ash and Herrasti knew that the town could not resist much longer. It was still possible to send word to Wellington with increasingly desperate pleas for aid. Initially Wellington had been sceptical over how long the town could withstand, but their tenacity had impressed him. However, he would not hazard his army to gain what could only be a temporary respite for the town, the chances of defeating the French on the plain while outnumbered two to one being poor. Wellington tried to compromise by sending stronger probes against them to harass their operations. Several clashes occurred, notably at Gallegos and Villar de Puerco, but these had little real effect on French operations.

The siege was now progressing more swiftly. Valazé's engineers successfully undermined the counterscarp and placed barrels containing 800lb of gunpowder beneath it. The resulting explosion brought a large section of earth and rubble into the ditch for the storming party to cross and blasted a twenty-five foot gap in the wall. Forty Spanish workmen were killed whilst trying to repair previous damage. Sustained cannon fire was concentrated on the breach and it was soon considered practicable for an assault. On 9 July men were massed in the trenches preparing to storm the breach. For days the soldiers had talked of little other than exacting their revenge on the stubborn defenders who had caused them so much hardship, fatigue and privation. As Pelet recalled, even Ney thought sacking the town might prove beneficial: 'The Marshal said he had learned to know the Spaniards and the war could be ended only with the most terrible examples. I replied by indicating that Europe and France would react with abhorrence to such brutality.'[104]

However, when an advanced party of volunteers ascended the breach they met with no resistance and, as more troops clambered up, a white flag was raised. Herrasti had finally accepted the inevitable after a seventy-two day defence and surrendered rather than see the town sacked. Though he had threatened dire consequences during weeks of uncertainty, Massena permitted the garrison the honours of war and congratulated the Governor on his gallant resistance. At least 1,800 people had died within the town, most of them civilians, and Herrasti believed he had been betrayed: 'The valour, the fortitude, and the sacrifices of the garrison and the inhabitants deserved a better fate. They have had the misfortune of not being supported by the armies of our allies.'[105] Indeed, Wellington received criticism from many quarters for not doing more to relieve Ciudad Rodrigo, not least from the officers in his own command. How much could have been achieved by risking the Allied army is questionable, and a reverse would have been catastrophic, but the Spanish were slow to forgive his inaction. Yet he violated no promises and preserved his army while the garrison had won valuable time for the Allies.

Though the town was not sacked, many soldiers indulged in looting the evening after its fall and were even joined by Spanish prisoners. Pelet recalled how difficult it was to restore order:

> When I entered the city, I realised there was no way of imposing restraint except by sabre thrusts. A few other officers and I struck right and left at the pillagers, no matter who they were – my eyes were impervious to distinctions of rank, and if I recognised anybody I only hit harder.[106]

Massena did his best to stop the looting and the situation was only serious for one night. After the tension building up to the assault, it was not surprising that the troops needed to vent their frustrations and the townspeople later credited Massena with having spared them from the full horrors that could have resulted. Even so, the town was ruined:

> I went into the fortress to take a look. It was dreadful. We entered by the breach. Everything adjoining it had been crushed, pounded and destroyed. The ruins and devastation extended to the middle of the city. At every step one could see collapsed or burned houses.[107]

Massena ordered the silver from the churches to be confiscated, but very little of any worth was found within the town. He also ordered a levy of 500,000 francs imposed on the town to pay for its repair. Disappointingly the garrison's food stocks were low and would not go far to support the advance into Portugal. However, a substantial amount of munitions had been captured and a symbolically important fortress had fallen. Strategically, its possession was more useful for an army invading or defending Spain, but the way to Portugal was now open.

While the French garrisoned Ciudad Rodrigo and brought up supplies, both sides expected a rapid advance into Portugal. Wellington had placed the Light Division under General Robert Craufurd between the Côa and Turones rivers to monitor the frontier, prevent French incursions and to maintain communications with the fortress of Almeida for as long as possible. Craufurd was a lowland Scot with a fiery temper and a deserved reputation as a martinet. Unpopular with many of his officers for his fanatical imposition of discipline, he was nonetheless respected for his competence and determination. The Light Division had carried out the bulk of outpost duties during the recent siege and were now based in the region of Almeida.

After the fall of Ciudad Rodrigo, the French had increased the strength and frequency of their patrols and the British gradually fell back across the frontier. Though the Light Division had performed an invaluable service, its position was now untenable and Wellington decided to withdraw them to the western side of the Côa. In preparation, Craufurd slighted Fort Concepcion near Almeida to deny its use to the enemy, but was uncertain over the timing of his withdrawal. Wellington had forbidden him to fight a serious engagement, but nevertheless it would be folly to leave Almeida to be besieged until the enemy made their appearance in great strength. He finally received clear orders from Wellington:

> I order two battalions to support your flanks; but I am not desirous of engaging in an affair beyond the Coa. Under the circumstances, if you are not covered where you are, would it not be better that you should come to this side with your infantry at least?[108]

However, although this letter was dated 22 July, it is uncertain whether Craufurd received it before the following night and in the meantime the French had been making plans of their own. French reconnaissance had revealed the position of the Light Division and, knowing of the defile that lay in their rear, Ney hoped that he could trap the force against the river and annihilate it.

According to the invasion plan, it was important to take Almeida before September and Ney was ordered to mount a reconnaissance with a view to securing the area around the town. The Light Division occupied rising ground on the edge of the plain south of Almeida, their left flank nearly reaching the town where the 95th and the 43rd Regiments were positioned and their right anchored on the Côa itself where the 52nd were placed. The Portuguese 1st and 3rd Caçadores lay in the centre with cavalry and artillery in support. The ground was broken, covered in many places with stone walls, and sloped sharply down towards the river. The river was in spate and contained in a deep gorge, a single stone bridge being the only easy means of crossing.

It had rained heavily in the night and the early dawn found the men mustering in the expectation of pulling back across the river when firing broke out on the advanced picket line. The cavalry vedettes briefly exchanged pistol and carbine fire with the French, but soon fell back, with fifteen squadrons of French cavalry approaching rapidly. These were elements of the 15th Chassseurs and the 3rd Hussars. Large numbers of infantry were observed crossing the plain towards them and Craufurd could have chosen to retire across the Côa with little risk at this point. Uncertain of the French strength, Craufurd now made the fateful decision to stand and fight. Ney was advancing with 24,000 men against only 4,000–5,000 Allied troops.

It took an hour for the French to deploy, during which time they sent swarms of voltigeurs against the Allied light infantry skirmish line, which was hard pressed. As their infantry marched forward in column, the Allies met them with well-disciplined volley fire, but the sheer weight of French numbers soon began to tell, along with the French superiority in artillery. As the fighting raged, the French 3rd Hussars made a determined attempt to turn the British left, charging within range of the guns of Almeida, who fired upon them. A Company of the 95th was caught in the open, many being cut down or captured:

> ... a cry of 'The French cavalry are upon us,' came too late as
> they charged in amongst us. Taken thus unprepared... our men
> were trampled down and sabred, on every side. A French dragoon
> had seized me by the collar, while several others, as they passed,
> cut at me with their swords. The man who had collared me had
> his sabre's point at my breast, when a volley was fired from our
> rear... which tumbled the horse of my captor. He fell heavily with
> the animal on his leg, dragging me down with him.[109]

The dark uniforms of the 95th led the gunners in the town to mistake them for Frenchmen as they fired into the confused mêlée. The charge was highly successful and only the stone walls impeding their path

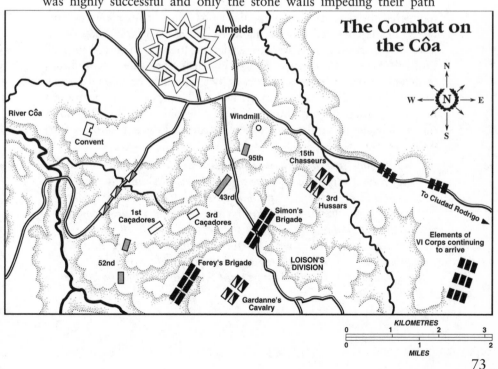

The Combat on the Côa

prevented the horsemen from riding up the line and threatening its entirety. It was now plain how badly outnumbered the Allies were. When William Napier approached his commander he appeared:

> ... overwhelmed with anguish at his own rashness in fighting on that side of the river. I have always thought he was going to ride in amongst the enemy, who were close to us, but that, finding me with a considerable body of men in hand whom he had given up for lost, he changed his design; at all events he was confused and agitated, and very wild in his appearance and manner.[110]

This was of course pure speculation on Napier's part, but the situation was desperate and Craufurd was yet to live down his surrender at Buenos Aires in 1807. Doubtless he feared that a repetition would destroy his reputation, but he kept his head and tried to retrieve the situation. He ordered his cavalry and artillery across the bridge while the infantry fell back in echelon in a fighting withdrawal. The road the horsemen used ran parallel with the river before executing a sharp turn back towards the bridge, providing the necessary gradient for wagons to climb the steep hillside. This meant their route was longer than the infantry's and the 1st Caçadores made the bridge before them, choking the bridge with their numbers. An artillery caisson also overturned in the road and chaos ensued as men struggled to cross.

The broken ground and walls slowed the French advance, but also hampered the retreat, and companies from different regiments became mixed in the confused running fight. At one stage a large body of the 43rd was trapped in a high stone-walled enclosure and forced to push down the rear wall to escape. Every few yards British units would turn to defend a wall or rocky outcrop as they fell back, desperately trying to stem the French advance. On the western bank, Craufurd positioned his guns to cover the withdrawal and set riflemen of the 3rd Caçadores on the hillside above the bridge. He instructed Ensign Brunton of the 43rd to stand there:

> On being forced back in some disorder on the narrow and rocky road leading down to the bridge, General Craufurd came up to me, and the other Ensign and desired us to cross the bridge, take up a conspicuous position on the opposite side as near the bridge as possible, and display the colours for the Regiment to rally on. This was done and we remained standing under a tremendous fire of musketry from the opposite side which was ferocious and well within range until the Regiment had passed the bridge and rallied.[111]

A rocky knoll overlooked the bridge on the French side and here elements of the 95th and 43rd made a stand until ordered across. As the French took possession of this feature, five companies of the 52nd were observed running frantically along the riverbank towards the bridge. These men had fought on the right flank and were now cut off.

The French maintained a heavy fire from the knoll but it had to be retaken if the stranded men on the east bank were to be saved. Colonel Beckwith of the Rifles and Major MacLeod of the 43rd made a hurried attack back across the bridge with elements from both regiments. Though the French took a heavy toll as they rushed over the bridge, they recaptured the knoll in a bayonet charge, redcoats fighting side by side with the green jackets:

> No one present can fail to remember the gallantry of Major MacLeod. How either he or his horse escaped being blown to atoms... I am at a loss to imagine. It was one of those extraordinary escapes which tend to implant in the mind some faith in the doctrine of fatality.[112]

Though hard pressed, they held the position until the stranded companies could dash across. Supported by fire from the far bank, the attackers now sprinted back across the bridge, though many were shot down as they did so.

As the battle dwindled to desultory firing over the Côa, Ney rode up and decided to press the enemy's retreat. So far the Allies had sustained greater losses, but Ney believed that he could turn their withdrawal into a rout if he could carry the bridge. He instructed the 66th regiment to attack and they charged across under heavy fire from the light infantrymen ranged on the hillside above it. The bridge is a three-spanned structure and, crossing the river diagonally, denied the attackers a straight path across, slowing their charge. Totally dominated by the heights, a tremendous volume of rifle fire and musketry rained down upon the leading Grenadier Company, felling dozens of men. Though some made it across to take cover on the western bank, they were effectively pinned down and could make little headway against the men above them on the hillside.

Unwilling to sacrifice his chance to inflict a crippling blow on the enemy, Ney then ordered the *Chasseurs de la Siège* across, a new unit of picked men who had distinguished themselves at Ciudad Rodrigo. This assault met the same fate, reportedly suffering 237 casualties in only ten minutes and choking the bridge with bodies. Undeterred, Ney ordered a third attack, but having seen the fate of their predecessors, the men faltered and withdrew when the 66th's colonel was killed. Seeing that further slaughter was futile, the French agreed to a truce to collect the wounded and those who had made it across the Côa slipped back across the bridge in the night.

The French had achieved their objective and settled down to besiege Almeida, but what later became known as 'The Combat on the Côa' proved to be one of the most controversial actions of the war. Wellington was justly outraged by Craufurd's decision, writing to his brother: '...I had expressed my wish that he should withdraw his infantry to the left of the river; and I repeated my injunction that he should not engage in an affair on the right of the river.'[113] However, though he had fought an unnecessary action, Wellington knew Craufurd's worth, continuing:

> I had positively forbidden the foolish affairs in which Craufurd involved his outposts... and repeated my injunction that he should not engage in affair on the right of the river... You will say, if this be the case, why not accuse Craufurd? I answer, because, if I am to be hanged for it, I cannot accuse a man who I believe has meant well, and whose error is one of judgement, and not of intention.[114]

This is reminiscent of his attitude towards Lieutenant-Colonel William Orrock at the battle of Assaye years before. Wellington had a fearsome temper and was implacable when faced with wilful disobedience, but honest mistakes he could tolerate. Many accounts testify to his formidable anger when fully roused against unfortunate subordinates. Luckily Craufurd was popular with the Duke since, had it been anyone else, they would probably have received the full extent of his wrath. However, this view was far from universal within the army and Craufurd's ability to command was called into question by many officers. For example, Napier scorned his performance:

> He occupied a position a mile in front of a bridge: thus voluntarily imposing on himself the most difficult operation in war, viz passing a defile in the face of a superior enemy, and in the confusion of a retreat! The result might have been destruction – it was great loss.[115]

As if such backbiting was not bad enough, Massena's account of the action was damning, appearing in the French newspapers and relayed in *The Times*. Praising the actions of Ney, his brigade commanders and the performance of the troops he concluded:

> The English sustained a considerable loss in this action. Their

estafette *man, or chief courier, has been taken, with all his dispatches; several of which... represent the English army as in full rout; that it is impossible to form an idea of its deplorable condition; that the English never were engaged in so brisk an affair; and, in short, that they had lost 60 Officers, 24 of whom have been interred in the field of battle; 400 rank and file killed, and 700 wounded... We have taken from them one standard of colours, 400 men, and two pieces of cannon; our loss amounted to nearly 300 killed and wounded.*[116]

The casualty figures were almost certainly exaggerated and Oman records how papers in the *Archives du Ministère de la Guerre* reveal Massena caught in the very act of falsifying the records, crossing out Ney's honest report of 500 French casualties and substituting his own figures.[117] Furthermore, no colours were taken and the two guns captured were dismounted and belonged to the garrison of Almeida rather than Craufurd's force. Yet it must be borne in mind that the French were fighting a deeply unpopular war in the depths of a very hostile country, and such propaganda had to be expected.

Angered by Massena's claims, Craufurd wrote to *The Times* to refute them:

Marshal Massena, not content with the gross mis-representations which were contained in his first official account of the action of the 24th of July, near Almeida, has, in a subsequent despatch, reverted to it in a tone of boasting wholly unjustified by the circumstances; assuring the war-minister that his whole army is burning with impatience to teach the English army what they taught the division of Craufurd in the affair of the Coa.[118]

He went on to challenge Massena's figures, commenting on how well his troops had performed such a difficult manoeuvre and claiming that it was: '...indisputable that they had the best of it.' British reports recorded remarkably slight casualty figures for the action, claiming slightly over 330 killed, wounded or missing compared to Ney's 500. However, these should not be accepted without question, those present testifying to the ferocity of the action and how lucky they were that losses had not been far higher considering the difficult ground they had to retreat over.

Whilst it could be claimed that Craufurd won a 'moral victory' during his rearguard action, the British had really sustained a defeat in a wholly unnecessary clash. Had it not been for the outstanding quality of Craufurd's troops, many more of the 52nd would have been killed or captured in the flight to the bridge. Furthermore, if they had not contested possession of the span so fiercely, it is possible that Ney could have turned their retreat into the rout that Massena subsequently claimed. Fortescue summed up Craufurd's performance thus:

> *Beyond any question he lost all control of the flight very early, and was saved from disaster only by his regimental officers. It was a pity, for while holding the line of outposts he had done superlative service; but there is no contesting the fact that Craufurd was rarely at his best in action.*[119]

Allowing for exaggerations on both sides, the casualty figures were fairly even and Craufurd had achieved nothing by his stand. Forced into a precipitous retreat, the Light Division had narrowly averted taking serious losses, but had neither delayed the enemy significantly nor inflicted serious losses upon them. While it was true that the French had probably suffered greater casualties, their larger army meant they could afford to lose them, while the loss of even a hundred men was a serious matter for Wellington if nothing were gained by the sacrifice.

In contrast, the French were very pleased with the outcome of the clash. The Allies had been forced to withdraw following a well-fought engagement, and they were now free to set about the reduction of Almeida. It was true that Ney's attempts to take the bridge had incurred losses, but his attempts to cross the defile could have seen the total destruction of the enemy and was thwarted only by the famous tenacity of the British infantry and their Allies. The numbers of the troops actually engaged had also been similar, bolstering morale in the army and making the affair an inspiring start to the invasion. However, privately the Prince of Essling was once again exasperated with Ney's conduct, his instructions having been merely to reconnoitre the area around Almeida. At his next meeting with his commander-in-chief, Ney proudly boasted of his achievement, but was embarrassed when Pelet tactfully reminded him that he had exceeded his orders, advancing with his entire corps without warning the Prince.[120] Unusually, both Wellington and Massena had good reason to criticise their subordinates over the same incident.

Chapter 5
The Third Invasion

With Almeida isolated, Ney set about securing both banks of the Côa, guarding bridges and fords in its vicinity. The bulk of the Allied army was based at Guarda and Celorico and Massena knew that the river was his best line of defence should the Allies march against them. General Ferey was placed in command of the advanced guard, with orders to retire across the Côa and hold the bridge near Almeida if hard pressed. Ferey mounted regular cavalry patrols to keep an eye on the British and was surprised at the extent of resistance they encountered from the peasantry. The French soon discovered that this was part of Wellington's plan to deny them the least refuge or assistance. They faced not only guerrilla bands but also *Ordenanza* militiamen who shot at them from the hills and forests and attempted to hinder them whenever possible.

When the Marquis d'Alorna, a Portuguese renegade in French service, returned to Pinhel in search of supporters, he was appalled by what he found. Not only were the French extremely unpopular after previous invasions, but the countryside was also virtually barren. In accordance with Wellington's 'Proclamation to the People' livestock had been driven off, farmsteads laid waste and shelter destroyed. The people had been instructed to flee to the hills or seek refuge either in Lisbon or to the south. Those who refused to leave, destroy their property or join the *Ordenanza* were deemed traitors and treated as such. D'Alorna recorded that the English: '... have committed horrors...'[121] to enforce this. Though British and Portuguese actions had alienated the peasantry, he found little sympathy for the French cause. The peasantry was in a terrible position, facing the destruction of their lands and liable to persecution by either side if they protested.

Massena was eager to win Portuguese support and was heartened to hear, from Ney and d'Alorna, that the British placed little confidence in the regular Portuguese troops and that the depredations of the *Ordenanza* were a hindrance rather than a real threat. It was true that they interfered with foraging parties and sprang ambushes on small units, but they were inexperienced, poorly armed and not yet effective. Massena wrote that the British:

> ... *employ a means of defence that results in the greatest*

misfortune to the nation. They have ordered the inhabitants to leave their homes; the women, the children, and the old are to put themselves behind the army; the men, between seventeen and fifty years of age, are to arm themselves with guns, pikes, axes, fire etc, in order to act as partisans.[122]

Many were pressed unwillingly into the new militia and the devastation of the countryside denied them their only means of livelihood. Few of the *Ordenanza* possessed uniforms and were likely to be treated as guerrillas if captured and dealt with summarily under the rules of war. It is quite possible that the Allies hoped to provoke French reprisals by their strategy in order to alienate the people even further. Massena believed that it was still possible to win support and issued a proclamation claiming: 'We enter your territory not as conquerors. We do not come to make war on you, but to fight those who force you to make it.'[123] However, the actions of his troops, hardened by the resistance they had encountered in Spain, belied this. He constantly received reports of looting, murder and rape and, despite making examples and threatening to hold officers accountable, he failed to prevent such outrages.

French attempts to besiege Almeida proceeded slowly, with food in short supply throughout Spain and transportation hard to find. The countryside had been stripped of oxen, mules and wagons, with the result that those who had them guarded them jealously. Lambert, now Quartermaster-General, encountered great difficulties in acquiring provisions for the Army of Portugal, exacerbated by corruption and intransigence. For example, General Kellerman claimed to have sole authority over the districts of Zamora and León, initially refusing Lambert's requests. Massena had to intervene personally before Kellerman would submit to his orders and even then with a poor grace. Napoleon had established a bad precedent by allowing military governors in parts of Spain virtual autonomy over their regions and precious time was squandered in persuading them.

Salamanca was the region's main centre for food production but was too distant for the easy supply of Almeida, guerrilla raids on supply columns between the city and Ciudad Rodrigo magnifying this problem. Massena knew that a good commissariat was vital for the invasion to succeed and decided that Ciudad Rodrigo must start baking bread en masse, ordering the repair or construction of sixteen large ovens for the purpose. This was an additional burden to the garrison, who already had the mammoth task of filling in the siege trenches, repairing the town and restoring its defences. Though food was brought in 'on the hoof' in the form of sheep and cattle, the best rations for the campaign were bread and biscuit, due to their longevity. However, grain supplies were minimal and the local corn had not yet ripened. Shortages, profiteering and logistical problems all conspired against the French, making the swift fall of Almeida a priority. Yet by 27 July the lack of French activity around the town had almost convinced Wellington that they intended to mask the town and march against his army.

For months Colonel William Cox, the military governor of Almeida, had been improving his defences and putting his Portuguese troops through intensive training. He had one complete Portuguese regiment in the form of the 24th Line and elements of the 23rd to support him. He had continually requested reinforcements but

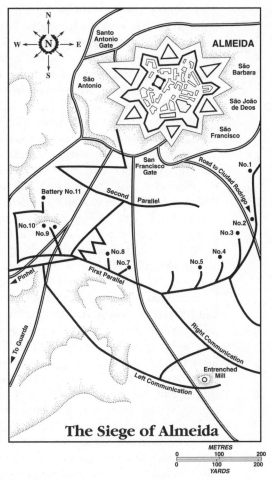

The Siege of Almeida

had been denied British regulars or artillerymen. His gunners were Portuguese regulars of the 4th artillery and he was eventually sent some companies of the 11th Cavalry to supplement a garrison mainly comprised of militia. In all, he had just under 4,000 men under arms. Cox felt that the policy of devastation was doing enormous damage to the region and had great difficulty in restraining his militia from returning to their farms, suffering constant desertions. Placing little faith in his militia, he discounted the *Ordenanza* knowing that their arms were even poorer than his own militia's, most having fowling pieces rather than muskets. Since the guns of the fortress could not cover the bridge on the Côa he knew that any relief attempt from

Wellington's army would be difficult. In common with many British officers familiar with the region, he lamented the fact that Almeida had not been built a few miles to the west across the river, which would have increased its effectiveness. When light troops from Simon's brigade established a presence around the town they offered terms that Cox rejected contemptuously, seeing their lack of artillery. In letters to General Beresford, commander in chief of the Portuguese Army, he speculated that the slow pace of French operations indicated an intention to blockade the town rather than besiege it.[124]

However, French troops continued to arrive around the town and General Jean-Baptiste Eblé was ordered to make a thorough reconnaissance of the fortress. Almeida was smaller than Ciudad Rodrigo, but this was a benefit in defensive terms since troops could be concentrated with greater ease to reinforce threatened sectors. Unlike its Spanish counterpart, the town had no suburbs outside the walls that could potentially shield approaching troops. The fortress presented a low silhouette and there were no nearby hills or features that could dominate it. Eblé submitted an eleven-page report describing it as a formidable work, superior to its neighbour yet far from impregnable. It had six bastions supported by ravelins, though Eblé considered four of these inadequate to protect the bastions fully. The ditch was wide, being over a hundred feet across in many places, and the walls were all dressed with faced stone in a good state of repair. The glacis was effective but so steep in places that it would conceal attackers from view for some of their approach if the fortress were stormed. The British had improved the structure, building and repairing several bombproof casemates and enlarging the barracks. A large medieval castle lay in the centre of the town, which was used as the powder magazine.

Eblé considered the bastion of São Pedro near the main gatehouse of São Francisco to be the best point to attack as it was more vulnerable to artillery than its counterparts due to the positioning of its supporting ravelins. A slight depression in the land to the south would provide some protection for the early stages of digging at this point. In addition the ground here appeared more favourable than elsewhere, which was the main strength of the fortress. The whole town lay upon a granite plateau and the soil was exceedingly stony, with rocky outcrops jutting out of the ground in places. Even worse from the attackers' point of view was the presence of hard rock lying under only two feet of topsoil in many places. This meant that the trenches would have to be bolstered with hundreds of wicker gabions and fascines to raise the trench to a practical defensive height.[125] Not only would this be dangerous and time consuming, but the materials for their construction would also have to be carted in along with the huge amount of material that the siege already required. Eblé expressed concern about the rocky terrain and the questionable safety that wicker defences would provide for their trench workers, but following his experiences at Genoa, Gaeta and Ciudad, Massena felt capable of handling these difficulties.

Trench works were started on 14 August by 2,500 volunteers of the 6th Léger, who were promised full rations in return for their labour. Distraction attacks were made against the São João de Deos Bastion to cover the workers who began digging the first parallel trench less than 1,500 feet from the fortress. An unexpectedly accurate and well-sustained bombardment was mounted by the Portuguese gunners for three hours. This night's work revealed the ground was harder than feared and in some areas the workers dug down only a foot before reaching solid rock. The following morning the engineers brought canvas bags filled with gunpowder and took the unusual step of blasting several outcrops of rock getting in the way of the excavations.

The engineers suggested eleven batteries to fire on Almeida using sixty-four guns, but there was some disagreement over their placement based on the nature of the ground and the strength of the granite walls. As former Lieutenant-General in the Portuguese Army, d'Alorna had not only been based at Almeida but had also worked on improving its defences. However, though he was eager to be helpful his information proved inaccurate compared to Eblé's studies and Pelet disregarded his counsel. The hard work the siege was entailing, along with the logistical nightmare encountered in bringing up materials from Spain, demoralised the French engineers. The operation had only just begun but an exasperated Pelet felt compelled to remind them that: '…we were dealing only with a rather poor fortress and a Portuguese garrison, commanded by a foreign general.'[126] By 15 August the town was closely invested as the heavy cannon began to arrive. Guns of high calibre were needed to penetrate the granite walls and the siege train was comprised mainly of twenty-four and twelve-pound cannons with a few ten-inch mortars for use against personnel.

Massena and his staff were now based at Fort La Concepción. Though rendered almost indefensible by Craufurd's engineers, the structure still possessed adequate living quarters and three companies of Taupin's brigade were delegated as guards for the Prince. In an effort to make the place more congenial, amusements were provided for the staff there including horse racing, gambling and even a café. However, Massena was pessimistic about meeting his timetable for reducing

Almeida with the daunting amount of work required and the mammoth logistical tasks. His letters to Berthier revealed that he was hard pressed to meet the demands of his office and had little chance to avail himself of the distractions he had set up for his officers.

Work on the trenches progressed slowly due to the strenuous nature of the task, but when the first parallel trench was completed, approach trenches were dug, zig-zagging towards Almeida. Portuguese gunnery was proving far more accurate than anticipated and inflicted numerous casualties among the trench workers, despite the marksmen set to protect them. Major Fortunato José Barreiros commanded the artillery and under his direction the gunners pounded the trenches on the night of 19 August, inflicting six dead and thirty-five wounded in a heavy bombardment. The stony soil magnified the effect of Portuguese round shot as it ploughed into the ground, often showering the trenches with chips of stone. However, the sappers had already established batteries and French counter-fire was beginning to take effect. The earth-filled gabions, sandbags and fascines were providing better protection than the French had hoped and every night the trenches crept closer.

Signal fires observed in the direction of Celorico and Guarda, along with extensive use of the British semaphore communications, caused some consternation in the French camp and Massena called a council of war. He speculated that Wellington might be contemplating a relief attempt for the beleaguered town. Rumours were rife that the Patriarch of Libson had arrived at Guarda and, in his capacity as a council member, was pressing Wellington to act. Massena was sufficiently concerned to order Reynier and Junot to bring their corps closer to Almeida to be within two hours' march of the fortress. Massena would have been overjoyed if Wellington had attempted a relief across the Côa, as the precipitous area was easily defensible. Yet he suspected that Wellington would resist such foolish counsels and refuse to hazard his army in such a venture.

At five o'clock on the morning of 26 August the French began bombarding Almeida. Initially their fire was unimpressive, with the artillery finding the range difficult. Some of the rear batteries even dropped shells into the second parallel trench, killing some of their own sappers, but after a few hours shot was slamming into the São Pedro bastion. General Lazowski, directing the siege operation, reported that the besieged were directing very effective counter fire against them and several guns on both sides were dismounted and put out of action. Howitzers and mortars fired over the defences into the town, hoping to kill artillerymen bringing up more ammunition, and soon many buildings were set ablaze in Almeida.

The bombardment continued over the next day. The intensity of the fire was so great that workers digging an approach trench towards the São Pedro bastion had to be withdrawn, several of them being killed in the attempt. As the guns thundered on a massive explosion rent the evening sky. The French gunners paused as debris showered down, with masonry falling into the trench works, killing some of the besiegers. Several Portuguese guns had been swept from the walls into the ditch and a large fire could be seen raging in the town. Pelet recalled how he felt when he heard the explosion:

> 'It is the fortress,' I shouted with a feeling of horror and joy. 'It is certainly ours!' My thoughts passed quickly to our army. Now it would be able to concentrate against Wellington's army, which was scattered weakly in cantonments. I said to myself, 'Fortune has given us Almeida, but it has also given us Wellington and his army.'[127]

Pelet's confidence concerning the British army was premature, but it was plain that a major disaster had befallen Almeida and it could not hold out much longer. Cox ordered the garrison to man the walls and maintain a heavy fire, fearing that the French might immediately storm the town as he hurried to discover what had occurred. The exchange continued but the French noted that the Portuguese cannonade had slackened to be replaced largely with musketry as infantrymen fired on their trenches.

Dawn revealed the extent of the disaster, with numerous fires burning in the town and the top storeys of nearly every building blown off. As Massena and his staff surveyed the damage by telescope Pelet recorded: 'We could not see the tower, the church, or the castle. Everything appeared turned upside down.'[128] Cox had hurried to the scene of the explosion that night, which had confirmed his worst fears. The garrison powder magazine, stored in the castle, had ignited, detonating 150,000 pounds of gunpowder and over a million musket cartridges. The castle had been destroyed down to its foundations along with the cathedral. The majority of the town was ruined with the roofs and upper storeys of most houses obliterated and the streets choked with rubble and bodies. About 600 infantry and 200 artillerymen had died in the explosion, along with 500 townsfolk. The governor had asked the townspeople to leave for the countryside shortly before the siege but around 1,000 had stayed.

The exact cause of the disaster was never established, with no living witnesses of the ignition. Artillery officer João de Sousa guessed that a French shell had ignited a powder trail from a leaking barrel as gunners took gunpowder from the magazine to the walls. Either that or a lucky shot had sent a howitzer shell through the castle doors directly into the magazine itself. However, Cox later claimed that the castle doors were always kept closed and were too thick for a shell to penetrate. Regardless of the truth of the matter, Cox realised that although the outer defences were largely untouched, with only thirty-nine barrels of powder remaining to him further defence was untenable.

Massena ordered a ceasefire and sent a party of officers to offer terms to Colonel Cox. Only Pelet and Captain Gama (a Portuguese officer in French service) were allowed to enter Almeida. Despite being blindfolded whilst being led to the governor, they saw enough to be shocked at the extent of the destruction within the town. The governor was well aware that the fortress was indefensible, but thought that he could hold out for a few days in the hope of a relief attempt by Wellington, who was only a day's march away. At a council of war with his officers Cox was dismayed at their eagerness to surrender with even his Lieutenant-Governor, Colonel Francisco da Costa, arguing for a rapid capitulation. The French offered reasonable terms, Massena's dispatch reading:

> The town of Almeida is burning. All of my siege artillery is in its batteries, and it is impossible for your allies to come to your aid. Render yourself to the generosity of the armies of His Majesty, the Emperor and King.[129]

To Pelet's surprise, Cox refused, but permitted some of his officers to go to the French camp to continue negotiations. Whilst talks were in progress d'Alorna, accompanied by General Manuel Pamplona and other Portuguese officers, rode along the glacis shouting greetings to the Portuguese soldiers on the walls. To the surprise of many, including d'Alorna and his staff, he received a rapturous welcome, many of the garrison cheering: 'Long live Marquis d'Alorna!'[130] and openly conversing with men their Government had denounced as traitors. Some officers even came down into the ditch to talk openly with the renegades.

Massena received Major Barreiros and Captain Mello behind the trench works and demanded the immediate surrender of the fortress. Initially playing for time as Cox had ordered, they requested that the garrison be permitted to march away under arms, but the marshal knew he had them at an enormous disadvantage and refused. However, though he realised that Cox was stalling, he did concede that the militia could return to their homes, but insisted that all regular troops would be taken prisoner. Mello returned to Almeida, but Barreiros signed the agreement and stayed in the French camp. Obstinate to the last, Cox refused to surrender and the bombardment began again. This time the cannonade inflicted more damage, with Barreiros treacherously directing French fire against his former comrades.

Early on the morning of 28 August, Cox accepted the inevitable and surrendered the town. Many within the French army believed his defence had been a gallant one, as Marbot conceded:

> That brave officer, not suffering himself to be intimidated by the horrible disaster which had just destroyed all his means of resistance, proposed to the garrison to continue their defence behind the ruins of the city. But the Portuguese troops, terrified and led away by their officers, especially by Bernado Costa... and José Barreiros... refused, and Colonel Cox, being unsupported, was compelled to capitulate.[131]

Almeida had fallen remarkably swiftly after eleven days of entrenchment and thirty hours of bombardment, but this was largely due to the Allies' incredibly bad luck. The French set about the repair of the town, but the outer defences had sustained little damage, most of the destruction being internal. Some 172 guns had been captured, along with numerous small arms but even more significant was the amount of food in the garrison's stores. Rations of 300,000 biscuit, 10,000lb of salted meat, twenty-four tons of wheat, 150 tons of straw and eighty tons of maize were amongst the spoils. This could have supplied the garrison for months and would be of enormous benefit to the French now that they were free to march into Portugal. Six colours had been taken from the Portuguese regiments and these flags were sent to Paris as trophies. Napoleon would be pleased at the victory as it meant the invasion was proceeding according to his timetable.

The French had sustained relatively few losses and had captured around 3,000 of the garrison, most of whom would be marching to Verdun as prisoners of war. However, to the disgust of Cox and the two other British officers with him, many of the Portuguese troops elected to serve with the French. They argued that the British had betrayed them and were heartened to see the return of d'Alorna, who promised to raise a regiment from these volunteers. Massena was reluctant to trust men who changed their allegiance so swiftly, but six officers and two hundred men, along with the entire 24th Regiment, were offering to swear an oath to the Emperor. When he authorised a unit of pioneers to be raised most of the 4th artillery and sixty of the 11th Cavalry also volunteered to serve under General Pamplona in Eblé's command. The militia were marched across the Côa and permitted to leave. Sadly for the French, Massena's suspicions were well founded and over the next few weeks they deserted in droves. Eventually so many absconded that Massena felt justified in disregarding the agreement and sent the remainder to France as prisoners. Men who had changed their allegiance once could never be trusted again and he cursed himself for squandering one of the fruits of his victory.

Wellington was dismayed at the fall of Almeida. He had hoped it would hold out for at least ninety days and once again he received severe criticism for not attempting to relieve the town. The Regency were unhappy about Wellington's strategy and Principal Sousa and the Patriarch argued that it would be better to oppose the enemy on the frontier rather than permit them to march into the hinterland and ravage central Portugal. They wished to replace many of Wellington's appointees with men of their own and concentrate a defence around Oporto, which they assumed would be the first French objective, as it had been during the last invasion. This situation was not helped by officers in the British Army, who sympathised with Portuguese misgivings and were worried by the French superiority in numbers. Wellington admitted: 'There is a system of croaking in the army, which is highly injurious to the public service, and which I must devise some means of putting an end to, or it will put an end to us.'[132] Charles Stuart, Wellington's political representative, argued continuously with Sousa over this matter and it was only resolved when Wellington threatened to resign and advise the British Government to withdraw from Portugal completely.

Colonel Cox was also blamed for an overly swift capitulation, even when the full facts were known. It was argued that he was negligent for not attempting sorties to delay the French progress against Almeida, but this was unfair considering that the bulk of his troops were untested militia and he could ill afford to lose men. A more justified criticism was his reliance on a single magazine for the bulk of the garrison's powder, though no one could have predicted that such a catastrophe would occur. Despite this Wellington eventually admitted: 'I have no fault to find with that unfortunate event excepting that they did not inform me as they might by telegraph of the exact nature and extent of the misfortune which had happened, and did not give me the option of saving the garrison...'[133] Furthermore, Cox had been betrayed by his officers and when Costa escaped from the French, Beresford had him imprisoned and later executed for cowardice on 22 August 1812.

Massena had won valuable time for his invasion plan but, infuriatingly, the invasion could not proceed straight away. He was unwilling to advance without amassing sufficient supplies of food and powder for the army and these took time to bring up from Salamanca. Several convoys were badly cut up by guerrilla ambushes and, in some cases, destroyed or carried off, which lengthened the process even further. It was not until 15 September that the three corps had concentrated and began to march into inner Portugal. Sufficient provisions for two weeks had been gathered in Almeida, the minimum that Massena considered necessary for success.

The army had lost nearly 2,000 men in the two sieges, along with 1,500 horses. As many as 6,000 men were sick and, though disease was always present in the army, the time spent in the trench works had increased their numbers. Marbot had only recently recovered from a severe fever and rejoined the staff at Fort Concepción. His growing dislike of Massena was strengthened by his failure to enquire after his health, and Marbot's scathing remarks about this stage of the campaign are no doubt coloured by this. French cavalry scouts brought back news that the Allies were falling back before them and Massena determined to march on Lisbon via the city of Coimbra in central Portugal. The British expected the French to take the more southerly route through the valley of the Mondego River, where the roads were adequate by Portuguese standards. However, Massena eventually chose a north-western route into the mountains of Viseu. Wellington was baffled, speculating over Massena's intent with French cavalry spreading out in several directions in order to conceal the army's destination for as long as possible. Indeed, initial scouting reports suggested that Massena might march in a totally different direction:

> Massena seems to be acting with extreme caution, leaving nothing to chance – Ciudad Rodrigo in his possession likewise Almeida, instead of making an immediate embarkation into Portugal he seems to meditate an attack on Badajoz the fall of which would give him the frontier from Galicia to the Guadiana...[134]

The fall of Badajoz would indeed improve the French position and make their rear more secure, and would allow the possibility of two simultaneous invasions from the north and the south that would be difficult to counter. This theory was given greater credence by the defeat of Spanish General Romana on 15 September, who lost 500 men and six cannons in an ill-advised foray in the south. He was only extricated by the fortuitous arrival of Madden's Portuguese cavalry and was forced to retire on Badajoz. The French did hope to move against the city, but Massena had reason to believe that Marshal Soult's army would besiege Badajoz in his stead and he had no wish to share the glory when Lisbon fell.

Only by 17 September did it become clear to a delighted Wellington that the French were pursuing the northern route, containing some of the worst roads in the country. Marbot commented caustically:

> One need only look at the map to see how unreasonable it was to go by Viseu on the way from Celorico to Coimbra; a mistake all the greater from the fact that Viseu is separated from the Sierra d'Alcoba by high hills, which the army might have avoided by marching down the valley of the Mondego. The neighbourhood of Viseu produces no corn or vegetables, and the troops found nothing there but lemons and grapes – not very sustaining food.[135]

However, Marbot was forced to concede that the maps in French possession were extremely poor and misleading. Furthermore the *Anfranceados* riding with them proved to be of less use than expected with their lack of local intelligence. Most of the exiles serving with Massena hailed from the Lisbon region and their geographical knowledge extended little beyond its peninsula. They covered their ignorance with bombast, Pelet recalling:

> The misfortune was that none of these self-styled strategists had gone over the ground they were describing, and they could not answer the only thing we asked them. 'Can a carriage go on this road? Is this river deep? Is this range of mountains impracticable?'[136]

In any case the Portuguese had never made much effort to map their country adequately and, with so little trade with Spain, central Portugal was rarely visited by those living in the coastal regions. French officers who had participated in the last two invasions were little help, not having campaigned within these provinces. Pelet also regretted the lack of topographical intelligence and did his best to ensure that extensive reconnaissance partially countered this dilemma. After the campaign he was furious to discover that far better maps were available in Paris that had not been provided for the expedition.[137] Consequently, Massena was forced to rely almost solely on his own efforts to scout the region.

Just why Massena opted for the northern route is debatable. Had he followed the Allied line of retreat he would have been obliged to fight on ground of their choosing should they decide to oppose his advance. Aware of the Allied plan to destroy Portuguese resources, he may have believed that the lands to the north would yield better supplies. Furthermore, the French army was renowned for its swift marching capability and, though the northerly route was at least ten miles longer than the road the Allies were taking, he may have hoped to overtake them. This could have enabled him to fall on the flank of any defensive position they had prepared, or even cut off their line of retreat from the capital. This would have been a masterstroke if it could have been achieved, but if this was indeed his plan he was confounded by the dreadful state of the roads in the area, most being little more than unpaved country tracks.

As the Allied army retreated it began to enforce the ruthless 'scorched earth' policy that Wellington had agreed with the Regency. British and Portuguese troops hurried the people on their way and if any refused it was not unusual for a few summary examples to be made, the French discovering men hanged or shot by the roadside. Observing the suffering of the peasantry, William Warre of Beresford's staff was sympathetic to their plight:

> It was most distressing to see them abandoning their habitations, and flying away from the miscreants, loaded with what little property they could carry away, crying and lamenting, followed by their helpless children, while the men drove away their cattle, and all uncertain where they might find a place of safety.[138]

All forms of shelter were burnt in the wake of the retreating army. Storehouses and granaries were emptied and cattle were driven off or killed. Although compliance with government orders was far from universal, Massena's army found little in the way of provisions and the countryside was largely deserted. They were marching into a man-made wasteland. If this were not bad enough, the *Ordenanza* were becoming bolder and more effective, especially under the leadership of regular officers such as Colonel Sir Nicolas Trant. The French artillery practically had to reconstruct large sections of roadway to allow the passage of their guns and, when Trant's force attacked the reserve artillery park strung out along the narrow lanes, they nearly met with disaster. Only the inexperience of his levies prevented him from tipping the guns down the hillside and destroying them when they fled at the approach of their escort.[139] Nevertheless, they inflicted some damage but the loss of this significant part of the artillery and a considerable portion of the army's baggage with the convoy could have forced Massena to fall back on Almeida. Progress was slow and Massena wrote to Berthier complaining how the terrible state of the roads slowed his march. The artillery suffered in particular. Colonel Jean-Nicolas Noël of VIII Corps recorded how difficult it was to drag guns over such terrain:

> The entire countryside was rocky and mountainous; there were no roads, merely narrow, dangerous and stony pathways where the artillery avoided accidents only with enormous difficulty... I had to send gunners, armed with pickaxes and mattocks, ahead of me to clear the way.[140]

The two sieges had proved a trial, but Massena's corps commanders were beginning to accept his authority now that success seemed to lie within their grasp. But the appearance of his mistress, still attired as a dragoon, provoked them once again. Sitting down to an informal lunch on the march under some lemon trees, Massena invited Ney, Reynier, Montbrun and Junot to join him. An awkward pause in their conversation occurred when Madam Leberton arrived to join them and it was taken as an affront. Ney found her presence particularly offensive. Amused at the generals' discomfort, Marbot later spoke to Junot, asking why he felt so aggrieved and hinting that their attitude was slightly hypocritical. He replied:

> Because an old hussar like me has his games sometimes, that is no reason for Massena to imitate them. Besides I must stand by my colleagues.' From that day forward the four generals were on the worst of terms with Massena, who, on his side, bore them no goodwill.[141]

It does seem remarkable that hardened campaigners, used to the occcasional squalor and immorality of army life, found the presence of a mistress quite so offensive, especially in an informal atmosphere. This slight affront was doubtless exaggerated by jealously and a wish to find fault.

Marbot even suggests that the six-day halt at the city of Viseu, which proved almost entirely deserted, was largely motivated by the need to find adequate quarters for the marshal's lady and his need to spend time in her company. This was probably malice on Marbot's part, but the charms of a young woman on a man twice her age certainly proved distracting. Previously she had travelled by coach, but owing to the poor roads had been obliged to ride and was consequently fatigued. Nevertheless, it is more likely that Massena halted the advance to enable the supply convoys and artillery to catch up with the army. This was the excuse that Massena later gave to Napoleon, and the fact that the guns and wagons were slowed by the appalling state of the roads gives it credibility.

Wellington had believed that Massena intended to take the road running south-west from Celorico to Coimbra, and had selected the ridge of Serra da Atalhada to fight a delaying action along that route. To this purpose he had constructed a line of earth redoubts along its crest and these were now useless. As the French struggled over the hills on poorly made tracks Wellington exulted over the fact that Massena had made such an error in marching to the north. He had surveyed the country extensively over the previous few months and found that much of the ground was suited to defence. He had made secondary plans for this eventuality. Accordingly he had selected a long ridge close to Coimbra as a highly defensible site. He felt confident that he could inflict losses on the French and significantly delay their march on Lisbon if he could concentrate enough troops to meet them there.

Chapter 6
Busaço Ridge

As the French advanced further into the hinterland *Ordenanza* and Portuguese guerrillas closed in behind them, killing stragglers, attacking foragers and cutting off their communications with Spain. Massena felt obliged to take everything with him on the march, including large numbers of wounded and sick who suffered appallingly in their ambulance carts as they scraped and bumped over the deeply rutted tracks. He was now committed to a march on Coimbra, partially because he hoped to find food supplies there. The two weeks' rations for the army, though husbanded carefully by the French commissariat, were dwindling rapidly. The countryside yielded little in the way of forage and parties sent out to gather it had to be given large escorts due to the hostility of the locals.

It was a frustrating war of ambush and murder that the French encountered in the hills and forests. Though better disciplined than their guerrilla counterparts, often fighting in regular fashion, the *Ordenanza* occasionally approached French troops masquerading as peasants, only to fall upon them treacherously. This, along with frequent acts of brigandage, shooting from cover or cutting the throats of sentries in the night, soon exhausted Massena's patience and he ordered all those taken in arms and out of uniform to be hanged or shot. Although the guerrillas were acting outside the rules of war, Wellington wrote to Massena imploring restraint in regard to the *Ordenanza*. He reminded the marshal that his own troops of 1792–1797 had been equipped in similar fashion and that such a policy would only perpetuate the bitter cycle of atrocity and reprisal. In reality Massena had little power to stop his troops shooting irregulars when they captured them and when the *Ordenanza* responded by torturing as well as killing those they captured, Wellington proved equally powerless to prevent such savagery.[142]

Wellington had decided to bar Massena's path at the Serra de Busaço about eight miles north east of Coimbra. Mindful of Portuguese opinions, he felt obliged to contest the enemy's advance and, having ridden over the area personally in the previous months, he knew the ridge was easily defended and that the French would have great difficulty dislodging a determined opponent stationed on the heights. It was a long, uninterrupted ridge extending about nine miles in length, dotted with rocky outcrops and sloping down steeply on its eastern side where the French were likely to approach. Several ravines ran down from the summit, which rose 1,800 feet above sea level in places. Though covered with heavy forestry today, the slopes were only partially wooded in 1810, along with patches of gorse and rocky outcrops in many places. The reverse slope was shallower in comparison and the summit quite broad and flat, in places extending to a width of between 300–400 yards.

Two roads crossed the ridge, the most important of which was the paved road between Mortagoa and Coimbra, which took advantage of a spur jutting out below the village of Sula on the slopes and surmounted the crest around the convent of Busaço. This consisted of a small chapel surrounded by a large ten-foot wall. Wellington took the convent as his headquarters and ordered the wall to be loop-holed for defence. Another country track climbed the ridge running from San Antonio de Cantaro to Palheiros along with two paths connecting small villages. Wellington suspected these four roads and pathways were the likely points for French assaults should they decide to attack him there.

By 25 September, Wellington had concentrated three divisions on the Serra de Busaço and hoped that two more would join him before the French arrived in strength. The Light Division were placed before the village of Sula on the lower slopes and Craufurd encountered the first elements of Reynier's II Corps when he marched them down on to the plain. Angry and humiliated after the affair on the Côa, Craufurd wished to restore his reputation by coming to grips with the enemy. Some skirmishing took place and Wellington was obliged to order Craufurd to retire to his initial position as the French began to deploy in force. It was only by rapid manoeuvre that a major engagement was avoided at this point, requiring considerable skill on Wellington's part.[143] Commissary August Schaumann recorded his impression of the great commander in the days leading up to the battle:

> *His orders were communicated in a loud voice, and were short and precise. In him there is nothing of the bombastic pomp of the Commander-in-Chief surrounded by his glittering staff. He wears no befeathered hat, no gold lace, no stars, no orders – simply a plain low hat, a white collar, a grey overcoat, and a light sword.*[144]

As the troops from both armies began to concentrate, Wellington deployed his men in an extensive line along the ridge, taking advantage of the reverse slope to shield them from enemy view. Though the Allies had around 50,000 men by 27 September, these were not enough to hold the entire ridge, although Wellington intended to make up for this deficiency by concentrating his defence on the tracks dissecting the hillside. He also ordered the construction of a military road along the crest line, knowing this would aid redeployment if he was outmatched at any point. He distributed his 60 guns in field batteries along the line and later received criticism for doing so on the basis that one or two large batteries would have been able to concentrate a heavier fire upon the French assaults. However, he was unsure at what points the enemy would attack and felt obliged to cover his entire frontage if possible, which was a wise course to adopt. After all, the military road would allow him to redeploy his guns should it prove necessary. Where the summit was flat enough, he even stationed two squadrons of dragoons. He knew that this was likely to be an infantry and artillery battle, but should the French carry the slopes he believed that a counter-attack by cavalry would be totally unexpected in such an area and might prove devastating.

Marshal Ney arrived on 25 September and ordered what appears to have been a rather haphazard reconnaissance of the Allied position. He determined that the area around the convent and the village of Sula was held in some strength and located the position of a battery of twelve cannon nearby, which most sources agree to have been Ross's battery. However, even from the highest point available to him he could only observe the position from 400 feet below the level of the summit, and therefore the bulk of Wellington's deployment would have been masked from view.[145] In addition, scores of light troops were stationed on the slopes, preventing close reconnaissance by his light cavalry. He believed that despite the steep gradient that would obviously hinder the infantry, the position was far less daunting than it appeared. By most accounts he was very confident of carrying the ridge and wrote to Reynier claiming: 'If I were in command I would attack without a moment's hesitation.'[146] However, this was on 25 September, when Ney assumed the force in front of him constituted little more than a rearguard. The next day, hearing that the Allies were bringing up more troops, he modified his view and became slightly more cautious.

Initially, Massena was delighted that Wellington had finally decided to offer battle. Many in the French army scorned the constant retreats that the Allies relied upon and shared their commander's wish that they would stand and decide the issue by force of arms instead of hiding behind fortifications. The chance of inflicting a serious defeat on the British could not be ignored and in any case the Allies lay between them and Coimbra and the need for supplies was becoming urgent. Yet many officers who trained their telescopes on the ridge quailed at the prospect of attacking such a position. In the valley they were exposed and the enemy could observe their moves and deployment. The only way to avoid their scrutiny was to assemble their formations at night, but an assault would have to wait until dawn. The difficulties of marching up the wooded, rock strewn hillside in darkness made a successful night attack unlikely and in daylight they would be exposed to artillery and musketry during a long climb up a precipitous slope.

Most of the senior commanders agreed with Ney's optimistic assessment and favoured a frontal attack on the ridge. With 65,000 men the French enjoyed good odds against the Allies, who possessed only 25,000 reliable British troops. Though aware of the presence of Portuguese forces, these were largely discounted as ineffective in ignorance of the extensive training that they had recently received. After all, the Portuguese had barely contested the occupation of their country under Junot, having so little faith in their army. Marbot was shocked when Massena accepted what he considered highly inadequate reconnaissance reports and, after announcing his intention to assail the ridge the next day, retired to Mortagoa without ordering further investigation. Having found and interrogated one of the local inhabitants, he claimed to know of the existence of a road between Mortagoa and Boialva, which might allow an outflanking move upon the Serra.

Marbot claimed that General Fririon and one of his fellow aides agreed that the prospects for a successful assault were poor and that something had to be done. Since only Pelet was permitted to submit suggestions directly to the marshal, they adopted the subterfuge of discussing his discovery within Massena's hearing. They spoke loudly and casually of their conversations with Ney's aides, bemoaning the fact that no attempt had been made to scout the area to the extreme left of the Allied position. Massena was intrigued and approached them to ask what they meant. What they told him gave him the notion of ordering another reconnaissance. However, Pelet refused to believe that Ney would submit such an inaccurate report and the plan was aborted despite Fririon's urgent entreaties. Infuriated by the constant bickering Massena allegedly snapped at him: 'You come from the old Army of the Rhine, you like manoeuvring; but it is the first time that Wellington seems ready to give battle, and I want to profit by the opportunity.'[147] In the early hours of the morning when the assault was about to begin, Massena murmured sadly to Fririon: 'Your suggestion of yesterday was worth considering.'[148]

Among the high command it is unclear exactly who supported and who opposed the battle plan and no doubt many who approved of the frontal assault remembered their objections only after the event was decided. However, some certainly voiced reservations and Pelet believed that it was one of Ney's outbursts that finally made up the commander-in-chief's mind:

> ...the interview between the Prince and the Marshal had been rather sharp. In front of everyone the Marshal loudly expressed his desire to attack and conquer all. He spoke in the same way to the Prince, who at first did not want to listen to him and was in rather a bad mood.[149]

Therefore it is quite possible that Massena felt obliged to attack in order to avoid losing face in front of his staff in the face of Ney's aggressive display of confidence. They were barely on speaking terms by this time and he did not wish to give Ney further reasons to question his competence or courage.

The essence of Massena's plan was to attack in two places using both Reynier's and Ney's corps whilst Junot's was held in reserve. Reynier was to attack up the San Antonio Pass, making use of the forest track leading up to the ridge's summit. This position had been incorrectly identified as the Allied right and Massena hoped that once the crest was carried this attack could turn to its right, attack along the summit and roll up the Allied flank towards the convent. In reality the centre of the Allied position lay at this point. When this attack was seen to be making headway, Ney was to send in his own columns up the paved roadway, assailing the village of Sula and fighting upwards towards the convent. He has been reproached for not timing his assault in concert

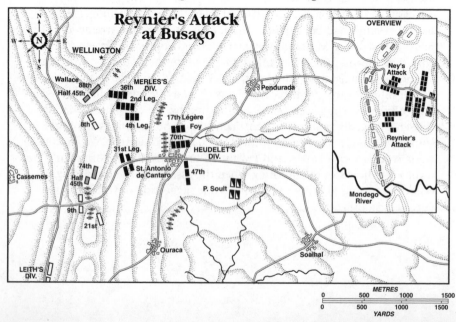

with II Corp's attack, but this would have been contrary to his orders, which still exist in the *Archives du Ministère de la Guerre* in Paris. Once Ney's forces had carried the ridge, they were to adapt their movements according to the progress of II Corps:

> *Marshal Ney will send his two columns of attack in the manner indicated when General Reynier is master of the heights, and when he marches on the convent of Bussaco. It will be for Marshal Ney to press the attack if he sees the enemy advance in a movement against General Reynier or a movement of retreat.*[150]

The attack began at 5.45am on 27 September in heavy mist. Two large columns of divisional strength began to toil up the slope, preceded by a large wave of tirailleurs and voltigeurs. These were under the leadership of generals Merle and Heudelet, and their advance was announced by a heavy French cannonade. Proceeding on either side of the forest track, their objective was the Pass of San Antonio, at the right of which Picton's Division was concentrated. The French gunners could fire on the slopes with relative ease but the summit, where the bulk of the Allied forces were deployed, was at the limit of their effective range and their bombardment did little damage. Colonel Noël recalled how his artillery could offer little support for the attacks:

> *The English occupied all the defensible points, and most importantly, a hamlet on the slopes. This was almost completely sheltered from our artillery... My division was sent to support the 2nd Corps... but in such an attack our artillery could not be of much help.*[151]

A bitter struggle ensued as the French light troops skirmished with Portuguese Caçadores and British redcoats on the lower slopes. Ensign

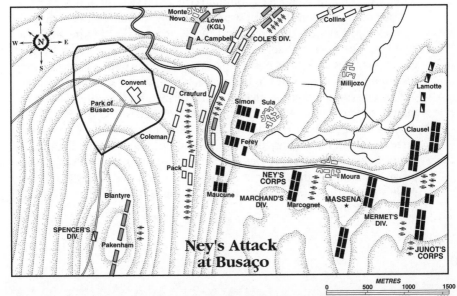

Ney's Attack at Busaço

William Grattan of the 88th Foot recalled that the British light troops were so hard pressed that men of the regiment began to be shot down where they stood in line as their own skirmishers backed towards them. The situation became serious enough for his Colonel to take a file of men from each company and send them to reinforce the light infantry. With drums beating, the French columns struggled upwards, their officers hurrying them forward shouting 'En Avant!' Allied artillery was sending round shot skittering down the slopes, but the early morning mist was hampering their aim. However, the effort of marching upward was tiring the troops and the French were losing formation as they neared the ridgeline.

As the mist started to clear, the right-hand column suffered greater losses as Arentschildt's KGL battery began to find the range. As the men of the 31st Léger heading the column advanced into the face of this punishment they were met by close-range musket fire from the British 74th and Portuguese 21st Regiments, who were placed either side of the artillery. Standing in a line two men deep they could bring every musket to bear on the advancing column which, with its narrower frontage, could not match their firepower unless they formed into line themselves. As they attempted this, the Allied infantry calmly reloaded and fired into them. Methodically the infantrymen rammed down cartridges with their ramrods, their exhaustive training making them some of the fastest firing soldiers in Europe. The British India pattern musket, known familiarly as the 'Brown Bess,' was slightly less accurate than its French Charleville counterpart, since musket balls rarely fitted snugly into its wide bore. However, this also made it quicker to load. At such close range there was little need for pinpoint accuracy and, with men falling by the dozen, confusion and disorder set in under the withering fire and Heudelet's column retreated down the hillside.

Four companies of the 45th were now firing at Merle's two columns as they approached the crest and Wallace brought up the 88th in support. The French had become confused in the mist, and by the numerous trees and rocks in their path, with a large body of skirmishers becoming detached from the main attack and taking station in a large outcrop of rocks along the incline. As he formed his line into column to march towards the 45th and the 8th Portuguese Regiment, these skirmishers began to fire upon them. Undeterred, Wallace detached three companies including his grenadiers to dislodge them and marched to meet the main attack. A vicious exchange of musketry volleys was in progress and, though a body of Portuguese militia fled, the 8th and the 45th steadfastly continued to fire until the 88th came up. Grattan recalled how:

> *Wallace, with a steady but cheerful countenance, turned to his men, and looking them full in the face, said, 'Now Connaught Rangers, mind what you are going to do; pay attention to what I have so often told you, and when I bring you face to face with those French rascals, drive them down the hill – don't give the false touch, but push home to the muzzle!'[152]*

After a brief exchange of fire, the 88th combined with the 45th to form a joint line and mounted a bayonet charge down the hillside. The French columns partly comprised men of the 36th and 70th Line Regiments, who resisted fiercely as a savage struggle ensued on the rock-strewn hillside. But their exertions in climbing the ridge had tired them and the men of the 'Fighting' Third Division soon gained the upper hand. The 36th were decimated in the fight and their colonel died fighting under the bayonets of the wild Irishmen of the Connaught Rangers as they swept down into his disordered ranks. The French broke and fled down the hill, pursued by a mixture of Portuguese and British regiments, who chased them to the edge of the hill, retiring only when French artillery began to fire upon them.

Wellington and his staff had observed the fight from close by and he rode up and congratulated Wallace on the performance of the 88th. It had been a valiant charge in the face of superior numbers and the outcome had been far from certain when they had rushed the French:

> *Marshal Beresford... expressed some uneasiness when he saw his regiment about to plunge into this unequal contest; but when they were mixed with Reynier's men and pushing them down the hill, Lord Wellington, tapping him on the shoulder, said, 'Well, Beresford, look at them now!'[153]*

With both his columns in full retreat, Reynier angrily ordered General Foy to make better time up the slope and restore the situation with his brigades. Offended by this tirade, having only been ordered to support the attack, Foy rode angrily to the head of the column, urging his men onwards. Cannon fire rained down upon them as they climbed but they reached the crest. Men of the Portuguese 8th and 9th Regiments opposed them, but were soon driven back by the sheer volume of their fire. Now that the location of this attack was known, General Leith had sent elements of his Division to support Picton, since there appeared to be nothing to his front. As the French were deploying into line on the plateau, the brown-coated Portuguese were retiring in considerable disorder, but two battalions of Leith's 9th and 38th Regiments appeared on the French flank and rear. Having believed that he was attacking the right flank of the Allied position, their arrival was an unpleasant surprise to Foy, just at the moment when victory seemed in sight:

> Meanwhile, my heroic column, weakened by the climb, reached the plateau; it was covered with enemy troops; those on our left made a movement and we were overwhelmed with battalion fire. Upon our front, the enemy, hidden behind rocks, assassinated us with impunity. The head of my column was thrown, in spite of me, to the right, and I was unable to deploy them and disorder ensued...[154]

Fired upon from their front, flank and rear the French could not stand and began to flee down the hillside. As Foy desperately tried to rally them, he received a bullet in the arm and was swept along with them as the retreat turned into a rout. Reynier's assault had failed.

Ney had waited patiently as the battle began and, in accordance with instructions, did not order his men forward until he saw Merle's column approaching the plateau through the slowly dissipating haze. Two of his divisions were to advance up slopes on either side of the Coimbra road over gentler slopes than Reynier's Corps were currently attempting. General Loison's division was to advance on the village of Sula and afterward assail Craufurd's positions where the ground rose steeply, whilst Marchand would take his column towards the convent. As the attack began Ney brought up a small battery of guns to just beyond Moura village. These fired on Craufurd's positions and provided the only truly effective French artillery support during the entire battle.

A steep ravine lay between the two huge French attack columns as they marched upward and, in the rocks and pinewoods of the lower slopes, their skirmishers met with a strong chain of riflemen and light infantry. This comprised men from the 95th Rifle Regiment and the 3rd and 4th Caçadores, who fell back slowly before them, contesting every inch of the rough ground. Ample cover was available to the riflemen and the tirailleurs could make little headway against them, forcing Loison to commit elements from his leading brigades to support them. By sheer aggression and weight of numbers the French light troops fought their way onwards, knowing they had to get close to negate the rifle's range advantage. Even so, the Allied skirmish line fell back slowly and inflicted great losses.

The village of Sula was taken but now Allied artillery began to concentrate their fire on the exits of the hamlet as the French advanced beyond it. Ross's battery, firmly ensconced within a natural rock

BUSAÇO RIDGE

embrasure near the convent, slammed round shot down the ridge into the advancing formations and Cleeve's German battery began to open up on Sula's approaches. Craufurd's main position was on a steep rocky knoll where the road curved around the hillside before ascending toward the summit. The French column aimed for the small windmill where he had his command post, struggling to surmount the sharply rising ground before it. Craufurd's two main line regiments lay in the hollow road behind him and as the French began to emerge over its lip he waved his hat crying: 'Now 52nd, avenge the death of Sir John Moore!'[155]

Breathless from their climb, the French were startled to see the red-coated ranks rise up suddenly before them from their concealed position. Already in some disorder, having struggled over uneven ground before climbing the incline, chaos set in as their officers frantically tried to get them into a firing line. Craufurd's two battalions delivered a shattering volley of musketry into their ranks from not much more than ten paces away, bringing dozens of men to the ground. Major Arbuthnot of the 52nd now wheeled three companies to fire into the column's right flank, while the 43rd did the same on the left. Caught in this semi-circle of fire, the French reeled under the fusilade and, after a brief exchange of musketry, turned and fled down the hillside, some losing their footing and tumbling down the slope. With their blood up the British infantry charged after them. Small groups of French infantry resisted as the fight degenerated into a brutal hand-to-hand struggle with swords and bayonets, but the French had no chance and were soon overcome. The fugitives were chased as far as Sula before their officers could restrain their men and General Simon was wounded and taken prisoner by a private of the 52nd during the running fight. Behind the Allied line, groups of wounded men collected, grimly waiting their turn to be taken to the surgeons. Yet their numbers were nothing compared to the steady stream of Frenchmen staggering or being carried down the hill and through the village. The hillside was strewn with dead men and wounded crying for aid.

Meanwhile Marchand's division worked their way up the ridge towards the convent. Portuguese light infantry contested their advance and it was only with difficulty that the French voltigeurs ousted them from the small pinewoods in the area. As the Caçadores fell back, the column came under the converging fire of three artillery batteries placed at the head of the ravine above them. Braving this fire they struggled upwards until opposed by four Portuguese battalions of Pack's Division before the convent. Deploying into line they exchanged volleys with the

103

Portuguese, the hillside becoming wreathed in smoke as they fired upwards. Yet the Portuguese stubbornly and firmly held their ground and General Maucune was wounded during attempts to storm the position. With one column routed and Marchand encountering serious opposition, Ney ordered him back. The convent area was clearly held in great strength and, scanning the ridge, Ney could see redcoats far to the left of Reynier's attack, revealing that he had been mistaken in judging the position of the enemy's right. He still held Mermet's division in reserve, but refused to commit more men against what appeared to be an insurmountable position. As the French trailed back down the ridge, the battle petered out into skirmishing along the slopes.

With the severe losses they had sustained, Massena agreed with Ney's assessment and never committed Junot's Corps to the battle. The French had lost nearly 5,000 men, with a remarkably high proportion of officers amongst them. In their valiant efforts to encourage the men General Graindorge had been killed and generals Foy, Merle, Maucune and Simon wounded. Fifty-two other officers had been wounded and II Corps had sustained slightly higher losses than VI Corps in the assault. In contrast, the Allied 'butcher's bill' was mercifully low. Wellington's Army had suffered 1,252 casualties, with about half being British and half Portuguese. Only two officers above the rank of major had been injured, Portuguese Brigadier Champlemond and Colonel Barclay of the 52nd, and none had been killed.[156]

The slopes were now littered with dead and wounded men, with scenes of carnage where the French columns had met the Allied lines. As he walked the battlefield that afternoon, Grattan observed that the dead had been rapidly stripped of anything remotely useful as both armies searched the slopes for their wounded. Going over the ground where his regiment had repelled the French:

> The rocks which had been forced by the three companies of the 88th presented a curious and melancholy sight; one side of their base strewed with our brave fellows, almost all of them shot through the head, while in many of the niches were to be seen dead Frenchmen, in the position they had fought; while on the other side, and on the projecting crags, lay numbers, who in an effort to escape the fury of our men, were dashed to pieces in their fall![157]

Commissary August Shaumann of the King's German Legion had been on the reverse slope of the ridge during the battle and afterwards came to observe the field. He recorded how, for the most part, the British and French fought without personal animosity and how unofficial truces were rapidly agreed:

> *With the help of my telescope I was almost able to distinguish each man. In the ravine there was a small stream, at which, with the most profound harmony, and as if nothing had happened, both French and English soldiers fetched water, and, as a sign of very special mutual esteem, exchanged their forage caps.*[158]

Massena had suffered a defeat but, despite a superlative Allied defence, had been repelled by the nature of the terrain as much as enemy action. Looking at the ridge today it is difficult to imagine contemplating an assault on such a strong position, but Massena was not entirely at fault. He had been let down by his subordinates with their poor reconnaissance and assessment of the Allied troops. Had the point of Reynier's attack truly been the Allied right flank, the outcome might have been different. As it was, even if this attack had been successfully established on the summit, they would have had at least 15,000 troops in their rear when they attempted to roll up the Allied line. Though it was true that the capability of the Portuguese Army was in doubt, Ney, Junot and Reynier had all faced the British before. With the benefit of their combined experience against British infantry, renowned for their defensive capability, they should have given better advice. Wellington was elated at the stubborn tenacity of his Portuguese troops but even he had been unsure of them in their first major trial.

The performance of the French troops had been incredible. They had reached the crest by a superhuman effort and only an incredibly tenacious defence had driven them back. Yet they had fought at a major disadvantage. The hillside progressed upwards in tiers, leading them to hope that each crest would be the last. Under the withering fire of skirmishers and cannon, their officers had understandably forced the pace and they had emerged tired and breathless at the summit to be met by the fresh Allied troops. Even so, they had achieved wonders against a nearly insurmountable position. Denied the use of his superiority in cavalry, Massena had also been handicapped by the inability to deploy artillery to successfully weaken the Allied line due to the length and height of the ridge. Wellington's choice of defensive ground had been faultless and Massena would not underestimate him again.

That evening, the gloomy French camp heard the sound of military bands playing on the ridge along with the Allied soldiers regaling Wellington with loud huzzahs as he rode along the line. Marbot believed that Massena should have mounted his horse and tried to inspire the troops with a rousing speech, as Napoleon would have done in his place, but he remained despondent. His subordinates, having previously urged him to attack, now magnified the scale of the reverse and advised him to retreat from Portugal altogether. This shook him out of his dark mood: 'Then old Massena recovering a little of the energy of Rivoli, Zurich, and Genoa, and many another memorable occasion, rejected their proposal as unworthy of the army and himself.'[159] He also spurned proposals to turn and march on Oporto. He had come to Portugal to take Lisbon at the Emperor's express command; not waste time on secondary objectives that would only prolong the war. The arrival of General Saint-Croix brought support for those counselling the possibility of turning Wellington's left. Accordingly, a new reconnaissance was mounted and the existence of a road between Mortagoa and Boialva was confirmed. The French set off that night:

> In order to conceal from the English the movement of such of our troops as were at the foot of the Alcoba, they did not march until night, and then in dead silence. But information was soon given by the despairing cries of the French wounded, whom we were under the sad necessity of abandoning… those who had lost their legs, or were otherwise severely wounded, were left lying on the dry heath, and as the poor fellows expected to have their throats cut by the peasants as soon as the armies were out of the way, their despair was terrible.[160]

These were the last troops to set out on the march and, despite French fears, Wellington was too cautious to mount an attempt on the rearguard once he perceived that the French were pulling out. General D'Urban recalled that the Allies were somewhat surprised that he failed to resume his attack:

> There was every reason to expect a general and persevering attack this morning, for it had not been the habit of Massena to give up his point. Towards daybreak appearances were suspicious for instead of becoming fainter the Enemy's fires became brighter. At 8 o'clock he was discovered in march and by 11 o'clock was evidently retiring.[161]

He went on to record that Wellington believed that the French had adopted one of three possible strategies. They could head north for Oporto to occupy the northern reaches of Portugal and see out the winter there, edge around the Serra de Busaço and head for Coimbra or turn south to cross the Mondego and march on Coimbra from that direction. Wellington had instructed the *Ordenanza* to destroy bridges in their path should they turn north, and the other two possibilities both entailed a march on Lisbon, which was already anticipated. Regardless of which course was taken D'Urban confidently predicted: '...we are again prepared for him and his wiles won't gain him a single march.'[162] Wellington had hoped that he might halt the French advance completely at Busaço and though he was well aware of the possibility of the French outflanking him, it was a disappointment nonetheless. He had little choice but to withdraw. However, he had achieved his objective of delaying the enemy and now resumed his withdrawal towards the capital, much to the annoyance of some officers who, emboldened by their victory, believed he should have attacked. The French encountered no resistance beyond a party of hussars at Boialva. The sight of more fertile land, suggesting the possibility of better supplies, heartened the dispirited troops and their officers made a great deal of the Allied withdrawal to inspire them.

As the 88th passed through Alcobaça the next day they found that the inhabitants were still there. They had not bothered to hide or destroy their food and possessions, in the hope that the armies would bypass them due to their location. Most of the villagers fled at their approach and the officers ordered the place stripped of anything useful to the enemy. Supply mules and carts were piled high with provisions and those who expressed qualms over such 'looting' were reassured that they were acting under Wellington's orders.[163] They wanted the French to encounter a desert, devoid of food and shelter. However, this event was not uncommon and trying to find the entire village supplies, hidden by the peasantry, in only a few hours would ensure that much was left behind for the French.

Commissary Schaumann was engaged in a constant struggle to move his supply wagons along the country tracks. Many of these contained wounded, whose sufferings were terrible as they were jolted along the rough highways. He witnessed harrowing scenes as long lines of civilians trailed alongside the army on the way to the capital. The roads were clogged with refugees, poorly clad and with few possessions, all hurrying to reach safety. 'Their flight was carried out partly in pursuance of orders, and partly from instinct; for they knew the French and their lust for murder and plunder, and were only too familiar with the ill treatment that awaited them.'[164] Schaumann saw old folk knocked down and trampled on the road, amongst other terrible sights. Many were angry, misunderstanding why the Allies retreated after a victory, and they doubted whether the British would stay to defend Lisbon.

Chapter 7
Que Diable!

Massena hoped that Wellington would make a stand in the region of Coimbra, but the Allies retreated before him, the Anglo-Portuguese Army crossing the Mondego and heading south towards the capital. Many French officers were mystified by Wellington's strategy, speaking contemptuously of his failure to support the border fortresses and unwillingness to meet them on equal terms. Though Busaço had been a disaster, the British had the enormous advantage of a strong defensive position, and yet they had refused to come down to fight them like men once the French onslaught was repulsed. They surmised that upon reaching Lisbon the enemy would have their backs to the sea and the matter would then be decided. The British would either stand and fight or take to the sea and flee to their island.

Sainte Croix's cavalry harried the rearguard, but failed to prevent the British crossing the Mondego at Coimbra and destroying the bridge behind them. Junot's Corps headed the advance and entered the town on 1 October. Most of its inhabitants had fled, yet some had tarried hoping that the French would be civilised conquerors. Pelet was approached by the town Governor who was:

> ...soon followed by a large number of inhabitants who had been outraged by the rigorous orders of the English and Portuguese generals, whose proclamations were still hanging on the walls, and frightened into hiding by the death penalty with which they had been threatened... In the streets we found a few bodies of people who were said to have been killed by military order before the departure of the troops. Most of the Portuguese complained bitterly about this loathsome tyranny and about having been chased from their homes.[165]

After constant warnings to destroy or carry their property away, the troops had followed their orders to the letter, and those that opposed them had suffered accordingly. It was a cruel policy, but already an effective one. However, many Portuguese were understandably reluctant to wreck their livelihoods and hid rather than destroyed supplies, to Wellington's annoyance. Massena's army contained many veteran campaigners, used to living off the land, who soon uncovered such hoards. In any case, there were considerable stocks of food in Coimbra's warehouses that the Allies had not had the time to carry off or burn. Yet Junot's men ravaged the town, looting anything of value, and those citizens who had remained regretted their decision as the soldiers tore through the streets. Massena was infuriated when he learnt of this, since the troops had carelessly fired food stocks and other supplies during the sacking of Coimbra. He gave Junot a severe reprimand and threatened to send him back to Paris if he could not maintain order in future.[166] In spite of this, Massena decided to present Marshal Ney with an expensive telescope, plundered from Coimbra's observatory, that had somehow come into his possession. Possibly he hoped this peace offering would help to resolve their differences, but it proved a poorly chosen gift. Ney returned it with a disdainful note saying that he was not in the habit of receiving stolen property.

Autumnal rains were now slowing the French advance. As they crossed the Mondego, militia and *Ordenanza* units closed in behind them, cutting off their communications with Spain. Almeida was already cut off by irregular troops under General Silveira who, though they lacked siege artillery to take the town, mounted an effective blockade. Militia units under officers such as Trant and John Wilson were ordered to harry foragers and intercept couriers as the French marched further into Portugal. In addition, Portuguese guerrillas, often little better than bandits, prowled the rural areas ambushing small parties of French soldiers and raiding their camps in the night.

Before leaving Coimbra, Massena had decided that only a small garrison was necessary for the town, knowing he would need nearly every man to capture Lisbon. He also left at least 3,500 sick and wounded troops under their protection. On 7 October Trant entered the town with 4,000 militia, easily overpowering their guards. Though the bulk of the wounded were carried on wagons to Oporto, considerable numbers were massacred by the militia, who slaughtered them as they lay helpless in the hospitals. The loss of Coimbra put an end to Massena's plan to use the town as a base to dominate central Portugal, but it was disastrous that the wounded had been left almost unprotected. When news reached the French ill feeling spread throughout the Army of Portugal at its commander's carelessness. These men could have fought again and it was foolish to have left them with so few soldiers to guard them in hostile territory. With national feeling running so high in Iberia, the savage end that many of them suffered was predictable and could have been avoided.

On 11 October Montbrun's cavalry found their way blocked by a

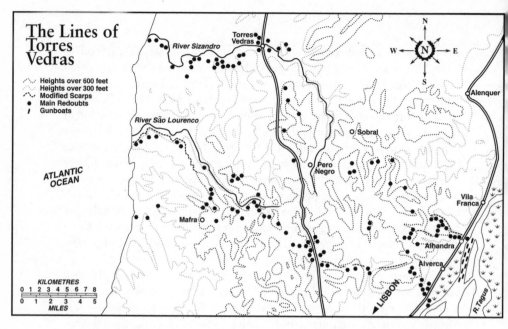

The Lines of Torres Vedras

Heights over 600 feet
Heights over 300 feet
Modified Scarps
• Main Redoubts
/ Gunboats

ATLANTIC OCEAN

River Sizandro
Torres Vedras
Alenquer
River São Lourenco
O Sobral
O Pero Negro
Vila Franca
Mafra O
Alhandra
Alverca
LISBON
R. Tagus

KILOMETRES
0 1 2 3 4 5 6 7 8
0 1 2 3 4 5
MILES

range of hills surmounted by a line of fortifications. Montbrun reconnoitred the position in detail and reported to Massena that this chain of forts extended many miles. On 14 October, Massena rode to the front to see for himself and was appalled at the strength of the works lying before him. Redoubts and forts, close enough to support each other with artillery fire, extended for miles amid the broken hill country. The enemy had excavated the hillsides, increasing the gradients of ridges and clearing dead ground of any cover where attackers could take refuge after failed assaults. Many streams and watercourses had been dammed, adding flooded areas to impede attackers and numerous support trenches and long lines of wooden stakes, barriers and impediments made the prospect of enduring the fire of the forts and marching past them bleak.

Despite spending the last six months in Iberia, Massena had heard very little about the vast construction operations that the Allies must have conducted to create these fortifications. Furthermore, although the lack of information from military sources was understandable with the communication and intelligence gathering problems in the Peninsula, not a word had been received from French spies operating in Lisbon.[167]

Rounding on his Portuguese officers, Massena demanded to know why he had not been informed of the nature of the ground north of Lisbon, since most of the exiles came from the region and should have been familiar with its geography. General Pamplona recorded how the renegades protested that these works were as much of a surprise to them as they were to Massena. Surely he could not have expected them to predict that Wellington would go to such trouble in creating these works they argued. Infuriated, Massena snarled: '*Que diable! Wellington didn't make these mountains!*'[168] He also held Junot accountable, since he had spent eight months in Lisbon and had marched over this ground during the Vimeiro campaign. Even without the fortifications surmounting them, the hills were a considerable obstacle and Massena should have received some warning of their presence.

Ordering an extensive reconnaissance, Massena personally inspected the lines, growing more and more despondent as he perceived their defensive capability. Resting his telescope on a farm wall he scanned one redoubt near Arruda for so long that the garrison fired a shot at the group of staff officers around him. The cannonball ploughed through the wall just as Massena was collapsing his scope and walking away, showering him with small fragments of stone. Turning, he raised his hat in acknowledgement of the gunner's fine shot and continued his ride along the lines. He had reached an impasse and would have to consider his next move very carefully. He must have asked himself how Wellington had managed to throw up so well planned a defence in such a short period of time. The answer lay in the events of the preceding year.

Following Soult's hurried retreat from Portugal, Wellington had put the breathing space the French had allowed him to good use. Knowing that the overwhelming number of enemy troops in Spain were almost insurmountable for a small army, he realised that the best chance for British success lay in outlasting the enemy. Spain was taking a long time to conquer and large French armies could only be assembled and maintained for a short period with the paucity of resources available there. Therefore, if he could fortify Portugal and provide himself with a secure base he had a good chance of surviving the third invasion and could continue to support his Spanish allies. Eventually he hoped to mount serious offensives into Spain. The problem lay in the fact that Portugal had one of the longest frontiers in Europe and could not be secured without massive expenditure. Such a project would also demand significant time; a luxury the French were unlikely to permit.

Wellington's eventual solution was to mount a three tier defence of Portugal – to establish popular resistance with a '*levée en masse*' raising militias and *Ordenanza*, to devastate the land before the French advance and to fortify the capital. Wellington had determined that the border fortresses could only delay the French and placed his main hopes on the defence of Lisbon. To this end he began the construction of a series of fortified lines that would totally cut off Lisbon's peninsula from the Atlantic to the Tagus estuary, denying the French the option of marching around them and forcing them to either attack or mount a siege. He eventually decided that two major lines of fortifications were necessary, with a far smaller third line designed to protect an emergency embarkation point.

Wellington had decided on this course as early as October 1809 and subsequently instructed his engineers to survey the areas in question. It was a mammoth undertaking and many doubted that it could be achieved in the time allowed. Their chances were not improved by the lack of trained engineer officers present in the army, a circumstance that was to hinder Allied operations throughout the war. Lieutenant-Colonel Sir Richard Fletcher of the Royal Engineers was given overall command of the operation, but he had only seventeen engineer officers to assist him in supervising the work, eleven being British, four Portuguese and two from the King's German Legion in British service. 10,000 Portuguese civilian workers were hired for the task of constructing the lines. They received only six vintems a day, which rose to ten when the work became full-time.

The lines were not designed as a continuous wall, but as a series of linked strong points of various sizes capable of mutual fire support. Many were small redoubts with only four guns, but larger fortresses were constructed at likely attack points such as the towns of Torres Vedras and Alhandra. These larger fortifications often possessed a glacis, ditch and embrasured gun ports. They were provided with bombproof shelters for their garrisons and strong parapets surmounted the walls, allowing infantry to fire over them. Wellington had decided to man the lines largely with militia and therefore provided inner defences such as internal ditches, primarily to bolster morale: '...these interior defences and retrenchments were intended to guard against a general panic amongst the garrison, which would necessarily be composed in part of indifferent troops, and also to prevent the loss of the work by the entry of assailants at any weak or ill-defended point.'[169] It was hoped that cannon fire alone would be sufficient to repel assaults but, in the case of enemy troops getting close enough to enter such works, the capability of the militia putting up stout resistance was uncertain.

Small windmills were commonplace in Portugal and were often adapted as inner fortifications, proving admirably suited to the task.

Arthur Wellesley, Duke of Wellington. Very much a man of his class and arguably the finest general that Britain ever produced.

Marshal André Massena. He rose from the rank of private in the French Army to eventually rival the Emperor himself as a general. *Maurier*

The Convent at Mafra where General Junot established his headquarters during the First Invasion of Portugal 1807–1808.

A typical view of the border region showing the mountainous and poorly tracked terrain that hindered the march of Napoleonic armies.

The western side of the Spanish fortress Ciudad Rodrigo with the cathedral in the background.

Another view of Ciudad Rodrigo's impressive defences.

A French storming party ascends the breach at Ciudad Rodrigo just as Governor Herrasti surrenders the town. *Philippoteaux*

The gorge of the River Côa beyond Craufurd's bridge. It was a difficult obstacle for troops without a crossing point, but virtually impassable for wagons and artillery.

The bridge over the River Côa where the end of Craufurd and Ney's controversial frontier action was fought out.

The devastation of the land before the French was enforced ruthlessly by the Allies when the peasantry resisted. *Raffet*

Below & opposite page: The people's fanatical resistance in Iberia led to a continuous cycle of atrocity and reprisal during the French occupation. *Goya's Disasters of War*

With small parties
always vulnerable to
guerilla ambush, the
French encountered
immense difficulties in
maintaining lines of
communication.
Philippoteaux

The gateway of São Francisco, the main entrance to the fortress town of Almeida.

Marshal Michel Ney. Although an excellent soldier, his constant clashes with Massena harmed French interests during the Third Invasion.
Meissonier

Craufurd's Rock, marking the point where the Light Division broke the back of Ney's main attack above Sula village.

Portugal's monument to the slain at Busaço, a highly significant battle in that nation's military history.

Massena's narrow escape while viewing the Lines of Torres Vedras, as a British round shot crashed through a wall beside him.
Delort and Laplante

A typical small redoubt in the Lines of Torres Vedras near Alhandra. Though crumbling and overgrown, two gun embrasures are still visible.

Fort St. Julien, the stronghold that protected Wellington's emergency embarkation point in the third defensive line.

The house where Wellington maintained his headquarters to monitor the Lines of Torres Vedras in the village of Pero Negro.

This Portuguese Hercules monument commemorates the lines that saved Lisbon on the site of a redoubt overlooking Alhandra. It is inscribed *Non Ultra*, meaning 'no further'.

Napoleon listened with increasing alarm and indignation as General Foy told him of Massena's difficulties.
Philippoteaux

A small footbridge over the Dos Casas at Fuentes de Oñoro. The picture is taken from the British side towards the French positions and the stream was totally dry in places.

The old village of Fuentes de Oñoro, viewed from the French side of the Dos Casas. It is still a warren of small lanes winding up the hillside towards Wellington's central positions.

The church of Fuentes de Oñoro, which marked the furthest extent of the French attacks and was the scene of brutal hand-to-hand fighting.

Massena's withdrawal from Portugal began a long series of retreats for the French, ending with their expulsion from the Peninsula.
Barbant and Delort

Although the right flank was driven in, repeated French cavalry charges failed to break the British squares as Craufurd and Houston conducted a masterful retreat across the plain.

The forward line ran a full twenty-nine miles from the Atlantic to the town of Alhandra and consisted of thirty-two redoubts mounting 158 guns. The majority of these strong points were small redoubts that made full use of the existing natural hill barrier. However, though many looked imposing when situated on the crests and summits of hills, this could restrict the forts' potential firepower, since their height would require such 'plunging fire' to reach certain areas that it would reduce the effect of musketry and cannon shot. Upon discovering this, redoubts were placed with greater care, but the existing high locations of many forts were felt to bolster the morale of their garrisons and they were retained.[170]

It was also considered unnecessary to follow the traditional star shape favoured by eighteenth-century designers due to the small size of most redoubts: '...this construction was latterly rejected, it being found to cut up the interior space, and to be almost fallacious with respect to flank defence, the breadth of the exterior slopes being in some cases equal to the whole length of the flanks to be obtained...'[171] With many forts situated on steep heights, this alone made them difficult for enemy gunners to obtain the necessary elevation to fire upon them directly. Furthermore, supporting ditches, flèches and abbatis[172] were considered sufficient protection against infantry attacks.

Yet even this was deemed insufficient and Wellington's engineers decided to improve upon the natural hillsides by steepening the slopes, blasting or digging away the hillsides with manual labour. These escarpments made the slopes extremely difficult for infantry to climb in places though:

> It never was presumed that scarps could be trusted to without defenders; but it was considered a great point gained to have rendered portions of ground of such difficult access as to be safely left to the guard of a small corps, or to unsteady troops, such as militia and ordinanza (sic)... [173]

As a further improvement, all cover was removed or cut away for several hundred yards in front of the lines, including forestry and olive groves. If a French assault failed, the troops would be denied a place to rally and re-form, and the artillery would have a clear line of fire to press their retreat.

Communication along the lines was essential and a military road was cut into the reverse slopes of the hillsides to allow troops to reinforce threatened sectors and provide easier access for the supply of food and ammunition. The Junta de Viveres had been established as a commissariat for the Portuguese forces who comprised the bulk of the line's garrisons. The British Government paid for about half of the supplies, but the junta proved inept in their task, often requisitioning rather than buying local corn and failing to ensure its proper transportation.[174] Wellington knew that one of the main risks of manning the lines was keeping the troops well provisioned and feared sickness and desertion as much as enemy assaults. It proved a constant struggle to maintain the flow of resources over such a large area and the military road was a sound investment. In addition a telegraph was installed along the line to give early warning of enemy attack. This was a variant of the semaphore system, comprising three masts with movable arms and flags. It relied on line of sight, but given clear weather conditions a message could be sent over the twenty-nine miles of the forward line in under seven minutes.

The second line blocked the four main routes into Lisbon via the valleys of Mafra, Montachique, Bucellas and Alhandra. A total of 447 guns were provided by the Lisbon garrison and considerable exertions were necessary to drag them up the hillsides:

> It was gratifying to observe... by what persevering and patient labour the peasantry, with their rude means of transport... succeeded in transporting 12-pounders into situations where wheels had never before rolled, and along the steep sides of mountains where horses would have been useless.[175]

Enormous effort was required to manhandle the guns into the redoubts, but the Portuguese proved equal to the task. Even the supply of food stocks and water proved difficult. The broken countryside was hard to travel over at the best of times, and the labourers, working in the heat, required large amounts of water that was heavy and awkward to carry in barrels.

The final line was based on the fort of St. Julien along the coast west of Lisbon. In addition to the fort itself, eleven redoubts mounting eighty-three guns protected the embarkation area for the British Army. Though confident of his preparations, Wellington was well aware that things could go wrong and, in the anticipation of a possible reverse, he made careful plans to evacuate his forces. As the Earl of Liverpool had written to him in November 1809:

> In the mean time you are aware that it must be our policy to remain in Portugal as long as we can remain there without risking our army. But we must secure the return of the army if a serious attack is made by the French upon the country. The delicate

question will be as to the time of the embarkation...[176]

Wellington had no wish to desert his Allies, but he knew that Britain would never forgive the loss of their small, professional army and hoped to avoid a repetition of the undignified scramble to the beaches that occurred during the retreat to Corunna. Considerable time and effort had been expended on finding a suitable evacuation point. Fletcher had surveyed several sites, including the small rocky outcrop of Peniche. This sea fortress situated on a narrow isthmus was perfect for defence and was considered a second Gibraltar. Unfortunately it lay forty miles north of Lisbon and outside the lines, so the beach behind Fort St. Julien was eventually chosen. On completion of the outer works, Fletcher wrote to Wellington, claiming:

> As long as this work could be held, its fire, aided by that of the fort would render it impracticable for an enemy to attack the troops assembled for embarkation, though they might suffer from the effects of a distant cannonade. The principal objection to this ground seems to be the confined space on which the army must remain while waiting to embark...[177]

The site was not perfect but it would serve. Though the locals considered the surf to be particularly rough at this point, Fletcher constructed three jetties to aid a potential naval operation. To the locals' surprise, they withstood the elements for many years. Hopefully, they would never have to be used.

The River Tagus proved a very wide barrier for the French to cross, but Wellington feared an amphibious attack, which could potentially outflank the lines. To counter this possibility he insisted on regular patrols by naval gunboats along the riverbanks and concentrated numerous vessels moored at various strategic points along the Tagus to oppose any river-borne raid. Should Marshal Soult overcome the fortress towns of Badajoz and Elvas to march upon Lisbon, a small chain of redoubts had been constructed on the far side of the Tagus immediately south of the city. However, British naval domination, along with the width of the Tagus, made this a doubtful French strategy. A long-range bombardment of Lisbon's docks could be mounted from the south, but it seemed that Soult's forces remained fairly inactive and Massena would have to cross the Tagus in force to try such a move.

In addition to huge logistical challenges, Wellington encountered considerable political opposition to his plans. The wealthy Sousa family and their political faction, which dominated the Portuguese

Government, resented having policies dictated to them and had not forgiven British refusals to even attempt to confine hostilities to the border region. In truth, the conflict would have wrought far less damage to the wealth and people of Portugal if such a course had been attempted and it took some effort to persuade them that Wellington's strategy was sound. Charles Stuart was foremost in representing British interests in Lisbon and considerable political tension arose when, as a foreigner, he was made a minister in the Government.

Luckily, Stuart was a diplomat of considerable skill, but he encountered serious problems, especially from José Antonio de Menezes e Sousa, who was very influential in the anti-French party within the Government. He was not alone in believing that the British withdrawal strategy had proved demoralising to the people and he lamented the huge cost and practicality of the fortifications. Though most of the redoubts were earthworks, they were eventually reinforced with stone to strengthen and preserve them against the elements. The eventual cost of the Lines of Torres Vedras was in the region of £200,000, a massive sum for the time. Though the British contributed to this, enormous manpower was used in their construction that was needed elsewhere. The age-old enmity between Portugal and Spain was also a factor, with the Government demanding the return of Olivenza, seized by the Spanish in 1801, a dispute that threatened the tenuous alliance. Luckily, memories of Junot's dictatorship and the fact that the Portuguese were relying on the British for national survival aided Stuart's cause.[178] Nevertheless, both he and Wellington were constantly badgered with enquiries and demands, adding to their already heavy workload.

Few efforts had been made to conceal the building of the lines, though Wellington had requested that no reports be made in the Portuguese newspapers. The sheer scale of the operation would have made his intentions obvious to anyone in the region of Lisbon, and the fact that their presence came as such a surprise to the French is an indication of their overconfidence and inefficiency. Furthermore, the depopulation of the lands the French were marching into made intelligence extremely hard to gather and francophobia in the capital rendered espionage difficult to conduct effectively. On the march back from Busaço, some Allied officers were surprised at the extent of the construction work, and many had been unaware of the project. Far from being built under a cloak of secrecy, they had been constructed in a low-key manner, which had done more to deceive observers than any cunning subterfuge.

In little over a year, Wellington had built a series of formidable barriers to protect Lisbon. However, many officers doubted their strength in the light of supposedly weak garrisons and previous French military achievements. Outwardly Wellington was very confident and had planned his defence in depth. Behind the lines he maintained his field army, initially in the region of Mafra, intending to utilise it as a mobile strike force that would march to counter any French breakthrough. However, he hoped an aggressive defence would prove unnecessary. He did not believe that Massena would risk heavy losses trying to overcome the lines and, writing to his brother William, he claimed: 'Massena is an old fox, and is as cautious as I am; he risks nothing... Although I may not win a battle immediately, I shall not lose one.'[179] His main weapon would be starvation and, should the French try to besiege the lines all he would have to do was wait.

Regardless of how effective the lines would prove, the cost of their construction and Wellington's three-tier strategy had been ruinous for the Portuguese people. Large tracts of land had been damaged or deliberately destroyed in the process of creating them. Farming was disrupted, with many vineyards, olive groves and forests destroyed. Though the Government promised compensation, relatively few received it and many farmers had their livelihoods ruined. The devastation of the land meant that this disruption spread far beyond the Lisbon region and the vast influx of refugees to the capital presented a huge problem. Even under normal conditions Lisbon had become a poor city and many British accounts testify to its squalid conditions. One officer recorded how it exacerbated the problems for the sick as far back as 1808:

> ...the pestilential vapours of Lisbon, where the atmosphere is impregnated with the exhalations from the filth and putrid carcasses of dead animals which are thrown promiscuously in to the streets during the night, which when evaporated by the... heat of the sun renders people in full health subject to serious indispositions; what effect must these have on the delicate lungs of a consumptive patient.[180]

Over the following two years Lisbon had become progressively more crowded, with the influx of British troops into the country and men such as Private Wheeler and Ensign Grattan recorded their shock at the state of the capital. In addition, the city was now filled with thousands of people who had fled before the French, due to the policy of depopulating the land before the enemy. The British Navy did their best to bring supplies into the city, but the bulk of these went to the army and the militia. Unsurprisingly, with such a large concentration of people in poor accommodation, sickness and disease spread like wildfire. Thousands succumbed to sickness and starvation with an estimated 40,000–50,000 people perishing during the period that Massena sat outside the lines. This constituted around two percent of the population.[181] Building the lines had been an unparalleled military achievement by the standards of the day, but the human cost of their construction had been terrible.

Wellington disliked the capital intensely and spent as little time there as possible. He maintained a house in the village of Pero Negro, from which he rode daily to inspect the lines and monitor enemy movements. He was well aware of what the people were suffering but did his best to maintain a façade of cold detachment, considering displays of emotion to be a sign of weakness. He cared about the dreadful plight of the Portuguese, but felt obliged to consider the larger picture. If the French overcame his efforts their suffering could be magnified considerably, with a vengeful army rampaging into Lisbon. He was unconcerned about his personal popularity and tried to present an impassive face publicly, concentrating on what he considered best for the nation. A firm opponent of republicanism, he believed that a French victory would spell disaster for Portugal and for Europe. In order to defeat French imperialism Portugal would have to endure.

Whilst Wellington toured the lines on a daily basis, malicious rumours abounded amongst the French that Massena was diverted by the charms of his mistress at his headquarters in Alemquer. However, he was acutely aware that morale in the Army of Portugal had plummeted upon reaching this forbidding chain of fortifications. With the benefit of hindsight, many believed that he should have tried to turn the British position at Busaço rather than suffer great losses in an ill-advised frontal attack. Some kind of demonstration was required to restore morale and improve the army's confidence in its leader. On 12 October Junot's corps began an operation to probe the Allied defences at the village of Sobral.

The French had determined that Sobral was a weak point in the lines, but it was in fact a false position established with the intent of inviting such an attack. The village itself was held by regular troops and barely fortified with minor barricades. Behind the village lay what the French believed were fairly weak, minor redoubts. However, beyond the reach of French reconnaissance lay a large fortress on Mount Agraço, strongly garrisoned by the Sobral *Ordenanza*, who were well aware of what the French were likely to do to their village. Initially the attack went well, with the British and King's German Legion troops yielding the village after a short exchange of musketry. However, as the French began to assault the hills behind Sobral they encountered strong resistance supported by fire from the redoubts.

Wellington had rapidly been informed of the move and ordered up the divisions of Cole, Picton, Spencer and Campbell once it became clear that the French intended to fight more than a skirmish. The next day almost 30,000 troops were concentrated behind this area of the lines. Junot continued to reinforce the attack and made some troop movements southwards, but soon realised that the defences had been strengthened in that direction. Advancing within sight of Mount Agraço, the French perceived the strength of the position and began to pull back. A private in the 71st recalled the intensity of the fighting. On the second day, after withdrawing from the village, the French rushed his battalion, which was stationed behind a mud wall:

> With dreadful shouts, they leaped over that wall... We were scarce able to withstand their fury. To retreat was impossible; all behind being ploughed land, rendered deep by the rain... It was a trial of strength in single combat; every man had his opponent, many had two. I got one up to the wall... I would have spared him, but he would not spare himself. He cursed and defied me, nor ceased to attack my life, until he fell, pierced by my bayonet. [182]

The 71st eventually got the better of their attackers in the brutal, close-quarter fight and pursued them over the wall for about a mile. The French retired to Sobral and halted the attack. Neither side suffered major casualties, and the affair was essentially a stalemate, but the French had confirmed the strength of the Allied defence. Massena had ridden up to view the lines for himself in the closing stages of the action and received the battle reports with dismay. The French had penetrated the line deeply enough to determine that a second line of defences lay beyond the first and the probe revealed that Wellington's army could respond quickly and efficiently to such moves.

Massena was at a loss and a subsequent council of war with his generals revealed deep divisions amongst them. Marshal Ney considered the lines too strong to attack without substantial reinforcements and Reynier was inclined to agree with him. The fact that even the impetuous Ney blanched at the sight of the constructions testifies to their incredible strength. However, Junot and Montbrun urged an all out assault, while the army's morale was still high. Marbot identified with their arguments: 'The English entrenchments formed an immense arc round Lisbon, at least twenty French leagues in length. Every officer of the least experience knows well that a position of this extent cannot present the same difficulties everywhere and must have its weak spots.'[183]

Marbot had reconnoitred along the lines in person and thought that many reports were exaggerated, believing that some observers imagined seeing a redoubt every time the earth had been disturbed along the line. Though it was true that diversionary attacks at various points, in conjunction with a strong assault, could have carried the forward line, the manoeuvre would certainly have been costly in terms of men, especially if opposed by the Allied field army if it arrived in time to counter the threat. Furthermore, an additional line of defences of indeterminate strength lay behind the first. Massena had underestimated Wellington before and was not about to do it again. This time there was no possibility of outflanking the long chain of forts, and he felt the need for caution after the losses suffered at Busaço.

After a fortnight of relative inactivity, Massena sent General Foy on a mission to the Emperor to request reinforcements and better assistance from Marshal Soult's forces in the south. He would have sent Saint-Croix on this urgent mission, but the famed cavalryman had been killed scouting the lines near Alhandra when his party had been fired upon by gunboats on the Tagus. Accompanied by a huge escort of 500 men, to ensure he got through, Foy reached Ciudad Rodrigo by 8 November and entered Paris on the 21st, where Napoleon questioned him for many hours. Prior to Foy's arrival, the Emperor had realised that Massena must be experiencing difficulties and had already ordered General d'Erlon to march with the 9th Corps to relieve Almeida.[184] He was angered by Foy's tales of the campaign, believing Massena had been reckless at Busaço and negligent in allowing the enemy to recapture Coimbra. However, beyond sending reinforcements, Napoleon had little practical advice to offer and clearly thought that Massena should be capable of overcoming the works protecting Lisbon.

Meanwhile, weather conditions were helping Massena come to a decision. His army was almost entirely under canvas before the lines and winter was setting in. The troops in the lines and the Allied Army fared little better, most having only tents or makeshift huts to protect them from the elements. As Ensign Grattan recorded: 'Although our situation was in every respect, better than that of the enemy, we were far from comfortable. Our huts, from want of any good materials to construct them, were but a weak defence against the heavy rains which fell at this time.'[185] As an officer, Grattan probably enjoyed better accommodation than most of the soldiers, meaning conditions would have been very hard within the lines.

As far as Massena was concerned his army was suffering for no good reason. It seemed vain to hope that Wellington would march out of the lines to attack him and blockading these hills served little purpose as the enemy was supplied by sea. Though the scorched earth policy had not been as rigidly enforced as Wellington had hoped, supplies were scarce and sickness was spreading through the army in the squalid conditions they were living under. Rather than besieging Lisbon, it seemed that the French were likely to starve long before the Allied forces, safe behind their fortifications. On 14 November Massena moved his army to see out the winter in Santarem on the Tagus, about fifty-five miles north of Lisbon.

When Wellington realised the French were pulling out he marched after them with his field army and established his headquarters at Cartaxo. Some attempts were made to press the French retreat, but it became apparent that they had established themselves effectively, as D'Urban recalled:

> Nov. 20. *This morning it is evident that the Enemy is in force in Santarem – he has completed an Abbatis along the whole face of the Upper Heights... and it is now clear that if the attack yesterday had not fortunately been prevented... we should have fallen into the Trap which had been set for us and sacrificed the two attacking Divisions...(sic)* [186]

Massena had fought a hard campaign, only to be thwarted almost within sight of his goal. His skills, however, had not deserted him. He constructed small-scale field works of his own, hoping that he would soon receive more troops to roust the British out of Lisbon. He was securely placed in Santarem and, while desultory skirmishing took place, Wellington realised that the French were far from beaten.

Chapter 8
The Retreat

The Army of Portugal remained at Santarem for months, enduring poor food and shelter, whilst the high command debated their next move. Massena had several options to consider, the first of which was to attack the lines in force. With the inadequate numbers at his disposal this seemed madness unless he received major reinforcement. Even with the necessary men it was likely to be extremely costly and casualties would probably exceed the slaughter at Busaço. The British had always been formidable in defence and a successful assault was likely to be a bloodbath even if it succeeded. In terms of the army's morale, this course should have been attempted as soon as they reached the lines rather than after weeks of inaction. The French had stayed relatively idle for months and the soldiers were naturally weakened by their poor diet and living conditions.

Alternatively, the army could return to the frontier region and could be resupplied around Salamanca. This would mean sacrificing everything gained during the past few months, but it would preserve the army and allow the possibility of another invasion. It was now clear that they had inadequate men for the task, and the Emperor might permit a greatly increased force for a fourth invasion. Marshal Ney favoured this course, but Massena viewed it as admitting defeat. If a fourth invasion took place it might well have a new commander-in-chief and he did not wish to end what was likely to be his final campaign in failure.

The third option was to march north and take Oporto, Portugal's second city. This would allow the campaign to continue within the region and allow the Army to be reprovisioned in an area relatively untouched by the recent conflict. Although it had proved unfortunate for Soult years before, Oporto was on the River Douro, which provided a good defensive line and a secure base for renewed attempts on the capital. Much of Portugal was devastated and Massena knew that the British were having difficulties convincing their Allies of the need to destroy large areas of the country in order to save it. For a long-term strategy this was a good move and raised the possibility of a political solution to the war without the need to take Lisbon.

Massena's final option was to cross the Tagus and invade southern

Portugal. The obvious drawback was the difficulty of crossing such a wide river knowing that the Allies would interfere with any such attempt. However, if the British riverboats were neutralised and a significant force crossed, the Allies would have difficulty sending sufficient numbers to oppose them and still man the lines. This being the case, the French would seize the heights of Almada opposite Lisbon with little difficulty. From this point they would be able to bombard the capital from long range and interfere with river traffic in the estuary. Relatively few troops would be behind them, their main concentration being at the border fortresses of Badajoz and Elvas. From this position it would be possible to aid Soult in reducing these fortresses and thereby gain his assistance for renewed efforts on Lisbon.

The fact that Massena was desperate to find a way out of his dilemma was amply illustrated by his eagerness to believe the tales of a British officer who had deserted and offered to provide the French with detailed plans of the lines. Several staff officers had reservations about the man's credibility but: 'You will hardly believe that Massena and Pelet, much as they despised the fellow, put faith in his tale, and wishing to profit by his advice, spent whole days over the maps with him, taking notes of what he said.'[187] When Junot met the deserter he claimed to recognise him as a spy who had tried a similar subterfuge before. This put Massena on his guard but the spy escaped that night, allegedly stealing some of his notes.

The French remained largely inactive during the winter, almost wholly preoccupied by the necessity of finding provisions. Nevertheless, Massena did make some attempt to prepare for crossing the Tagus, ordering General Eblé to mount a bridging operation. The centre of operations was at the small town of Punhete at the confluence of the Tagus and the Zezere (a tributary of the Tagus). Eblé managed to work wonders with tools he was largely obliged to improvise. Due to lack of transportation he was forced to take beams from houses in Punhete and Santarem to provide wood, but he produced a large number of boats and materials to construct a pontoon bridge. The work kept the men occupied and the possibility of spanning the Tagus was therefore an option. However, the British soon became aware of the move and Wellington ordered batteries set up opposite Punhete that began to harass French operations with long-range fire. It seemed a crossing would be unlikely to succeed without help from Marshal Soult's army. It was even more frustrating that the French could occasionally hear distant cannon fire from the direction of Badajoz, now under siege by Soult. Napoleon had ordered Soult to send 10,000 men to bolster

Massena's army, but he ignored the command. When Badajoz eventually fell the Emperor caustically remarked: 'He captured me a town, and lost me a kingdom.'[188] There would be no help from Soult.

Napoleon had mused over how to proceed but failed to produce any definite plan other than to send General D'Erlon with IX Corps to reinforce Massena. The trouble was that the conflict was so far away that his dispatches took weeks to reach the region, meaning circumstances could well have changed by the time of their arrival. However, the Emperor knew that every day that the Army of Portugal remained before Lisbon increased the likelihood of a political split between the Allies and weakened the resolve of the British Parliament. Pursuing the war was expensive and though the British troops were safely placed behind the Lines of Torres Vedras, defensive actions alone would not bring victory. However, they were pleased to hear that the French were suffering and were unlikely to sit before the lines much longer:

> The deserters who have arrived these last few days affirm, that the privations and miseries of the French are excessive; they are reduced to one-fourth part of a ration of bread, have no wine, brandy, or medicines of any kind; the greater part of the army is without shoes and without clothing; the cavalry have no forage and are again dying in great numbers...[189]

When D'Erlon's IX Corps arrived at Almeida on 14 December, Silveira's levies abandoned their blockade and retreated, being outnumbered and faced by regular troops. D'Erlon had a difficult mission to perform for the Emperor. He was obliged to reinforce Massena and at the same time maintain communications between Spain and the Army of Portugal. His attempts to fulfil both objectives were naturally doomed to failure. Generals Gardanne and Claparède were sent in pursuit of the various militia formations under Silveira, Wilson and Trant. The devastated state of the land made this no easy task:

> With all the Emperor's persipacity it was impossible for him at Paris to judge of the numerous difficulties which would hamper Gardanne in carrying out his orders. Napoleon could never believe that the flight of the Portuguese occupants at the approach of the French corps had been so universal that it was impossible to come across an inhabitant from whom one could receive the slightest information.[190]

These problems dogged the French campaigns in the Peninsula and, despite his brief sojourn into the war, Napoleon was far more used to the relatively genteel conditions prevailing in central Europe, where supplies were easily obtained along with intelligence. Nevertheless, the French drove the militia forces before them, winning a string of small victories and pushing them north and west. However, these triumphs had little strategic effect and the roads became no safer, couriers requiring large escorts in order to get through.

The news that IX Corps was marching to reinforce them cheered the Army of Portugal, but they were dismayed when D'Erlon arrived with a mere 6,000 men having left significant forces behind to bolster the garrison of Ciudad Rodrigo and fight the irregulars. Initially D'Erlon visited Ney at Thomar instead of travelling to Massena's headquarters at Torres Novas. This was not only against regulations, but was disrespectful of Massena's authority as commander-in-chief. When Marbot was sent to protest, he discovered that Ney, being convinced that no attempt on the lines would succeed, had suggested that D'Erlon march his men straight back to the border and that he was preparing to do so. Amazingly, D'Erlon had not been officially placed under Massena's command and considered himself subject only to the Emperor. Though the aide managed to convince him to report to Massena, the addition of 6,000 men was not going to make much difference.

The army had shown amazing tenacity but, even with the careful husbandry of resources, Massena knew that time was running out. Only a commander of his skill and experience could have stayed so long in such a hostile region and, as Wellington wrote:

> It is wonderful that they have been able to remain in the country so long, and it is scarcely possible that they can remain much longer. If they go, and when they go, their losses will be very great, and mine nothing. If they stay, they must continue to lose men daily, as they do now...[191]

The hardship and trials he endured during the siege of Genoa had provided Massena with valuable experience of operations of this kind, and he knew when to admit defeat. His army could only take so much without disintegrating or becoming totally ineffective. Hundreds had already succumbed through lack of food or disease and many were too sick to move unassisted. Soult was clearly not coming and attempts to bridge the Tagus and move southwards were too much of a risk in his absence. He decided to retreat northwards, but keep his options open regarding his eventual objective. The occupation of central Portugal was his preferred strategy but, should this prove impractical, a withdrawal to the frontier was still possible. His corps commanders had been of little assistance over the preceding months, constantly bickering and offering conflicting advice. Even the course of the retreat was questioned, and when Massena instructed D'Erlon to prepare his corps to move out he was answered with the lofty reply that he was only obliged to follow the Emperor's orders. This final disobedience was enough for Massena, who angrily retorted that he could take IX Corps his own way and damned him for his impertinence.[192]

The French retreat began on 5 March 1811. They withdrew slowly and quietly at first and efforts were made to mask their intentions, with straw-stuffed dummies set up in place of sentries along with the placement of false cannons in their earthworks. There was no room for surplus equipment and hundreds of ammunition caissons and baggage wagons were burnt, their horses being used to drag the guns. Retreating in three columns, the French were accompanied by hundreds of sick, who trudged dismally along or rode painfully in the wagons along the deeply rutted tracks. The troops had already tolerated months of hardship and a long siege, but their trials were only just beginning.

Though the move had been expected, the British were caught slightly off guard by the French subterfuge and the enemy managed to steal a day's march upon the Allies. Wellington immediately broke camp and followed the French. He had no intention of forcing a heavy engagement, but earnestly desired to prevent Massena from marching on Oporto. He had already sent word to the levies to prevent the enemy crossing the Mondego if possible and Trant's brigade had occupied Coimbra. The Army of Portugal was still a formidable force, but Wellington intended to snap at its heels and inflict some losses before they left the lands they had ravaged.

Embittered and angry, the French soldiers vented their frustrations on the towns through which they passed, looting and burning as they went. Those occupants who had remained were subjected to rape, torture and murder, whilst many French officers either participated or looked on apathetically. Private Wheeler recalled seeing numerous bodies in the streets of the towns and villages he passed through, the houses often being set alight to impede the Allied advance, as at Leiria:

The town had been on fire in several places, the houses were completely glutted (sic), doors, windows, shutters, and in many places the floors were ripped to pieces for fuel… the churches did not escape, the graves were opened, and the dead dragged out.[193]

The British saw many terrible sights marching in the wake of the French. Grattan recalled how beautiful towns such as Leiria and Pombal were wantonly destroyed and their inhabitants mistreated or murdered. The magnificent convent at Alcobaça was set afire in an orgy of destruction as the soldiers took a dreadful revenge on the people who had harried and ambushed them along the march. Grattan mused that: '...a century will be insufficient to repair the evils which a few months inflicted on this unfortunate country.'[194] Yet the sight of those villagers who had survived the French occupation was even more horrific. The French had starved over the preceding months, but those peasants who had remained were completely famished and suffering from exposure:

> *...we saw several women and children coming from their hiding places. Their appearance was frightful, scarcely able to crawl for the want of food, their deathlike countenances and their hollow sepulchral voices would excite pity from savages.*[195]

The Allies continued their pursuit, the path of their enemies being easily traced by the smoke on the horizon. Ney's VI Corps acted as the rearguard and conducted many skilful holding actions south of Pombal to delay their pursuers. Though an indifferent strategist, Ney was an accomplished tactician and made the Allies' task far harder than anticipated. He was fortunate in gaining such experience, as he would be forced to repeat this service for the Emperor on the famous retreat from Moscow the following year. Without orders, Ney decided to resist the Allied advance at Pombal on 11 March. British light troops drove the French back into the town and seized the bridge before the engineers could detonate their charges underneath it. Following this success they made an attempt on Pombal Castle, but were driven back by a counter-attack led by Ney in person with four battalions. As more British troops began to arrive, Ney relinquished the town and ordered parts of it fired to impede the enemy advance.

Meanwhile, Montbrun's cavalry were reconnoitring in the vanguard of the army and had reached the Mondego. They determined that militia were present in large numbers on the far bank and that the town of Coimbra was held by levies under Trant and Silveira. Montbrun conducted a poor reconnaissance, taking three days to find a suitable crossing point where a bridge could be thrown across three islets to allow a potential attack on Coimbra. In common with many officers he felt the campaign had foundered irretrievably and considered abandoning Portugal the best course. Therefore, his efforts during the execution of this task were somewhat lacking.[196]

The next Allied clash with Ney's rearguard occurred at Redhina on 12 March. The country was very hilly and covered with pine forests, making it ideal for rearguard actions, and Ney had chosen a strong position on a high plateau between the confluence of the Redhina and the Soure. He had his back to the bridge before the town, but had taken the precaution of covering the crossing with artillery in preparation for the inevitable withdrawal. The Light Division threw out a skirmish line and drove the French tirailleurs back after a sharp skirmish in the woods, but when they began to emerge onto the plateau they were met with a withering fire. Mermet's and Marchand's Divisions stood there to oppose them, supported by three cavalry regiments. The French infantry resisted stubbornly, supported by the fire of fourteen guns. Combined with a skilfully executed cavalry charge, the British advance was checked. As Pack's and Picton's Divisions arrived, Wellington decided to delay a serious attack until reinforced by the 4th Division due to the scale of resistance. However, Ney felt he had performed his task and, commanding his artillery to fire a sustained fusilade at the British, began to retire over the bridge. There was some confusion during the crossing, but Ney had achieved his objective, both sides losing just over 200 men. Wellington could have taken the opportunity to press the French retreat at this point, but considered it inadvisable to risk losing substantial numbers of men for little gain.

Arriving at Condeixa with the main body, Massena was forced to make a crucial decision. If he wished to force the Mondego and take Coimbra it must be now. If he were permitted thirty-six hours he could bridge the river and continue northwards. Asking Ney to hold his position at Condeixa as long as possible, he sent the wounded and baggage forward to Miranda de Corvo and reviewed his options. As the British vanguard approached they discovered Ney had thrown up abbatis to strengthen his position and was present in force. Wellington ordered the the 4th Division and the Light Division to occupy the French front, while the 6th and 3rd Divisions marched around both flanks to try to turn Ney's defence. After some resistance, Ney abandoned Condeixa, fearing that he would be outflanked, and withdrew to the east. In the distance Wellington could see elements of the main French body marching in the direction of Ponte de Murcella and realised that Massena had abandoned his designs on Coimbra.

After receiving further reconnaissance reports, Massena had been deceived into thinking Coimbra was held by between 20,000–25,000 men. In fact Trant had as few as 5,000, and was under orders to relinquish the city upon the first serious attack, Wellington deeming it unnecessary to sacrifice the Portuguese levies in the face of overwhelming numbers. However, as Ney withdrew he either forgot or deliberately failed to inform his commander-in-chief and British hussars came upon him and his staff. Both sides were surprised, but Massena's grenadiers stood firm and an aggressive display by his dragoon escort persuaded the cavalrymen to withdraw. Marbot recalled:

> The English, never dreaming that the French commander would be thus separated from his army, took our group for a rear-guard, which they did not venture to attack; but it is certain that if the hussars had made a resolute charge, they would have carried off Massena and all who were with him.[197]

Naturally this gave Massena even more reason to dislike Ney, whom Marbot felt had retreated long before he needed to at Condeixa. Indeed, Massena believed that the animosity between them had grown to such an extent that Ney might have wilfully placed him in danger. It seemed that everything was going wrong, and the burdens of command were added to by Massena's need to look after his mistress. Though a good rider, she had taken a series of hard falls riding over rough ground during the retreat and had to be carried along by two grenadiers. With the pursuit becoming more aggressive, she was likely to be taken by the enemy if they were hard pressed. Several times Marbot heard his commander exclaim: 'What a mistake I made in bringing a woman to the war!'[198]

The retreat was taking a severe toll on the Army of Portugal. After months of being cold and hungry, men were falling at the roadsides and with so few transport wagons many were simply left where they fell. The lucky ones were taken by the Allies as they advanced, but those discovered by guerrillas or the peasantry suffered severely:

> The Portuguese were not unrevenged (sic) of their destroyers, great numbers of whom had lain down, unable to proceed, from wounds or fatigue, and had either been killed by the peasantry, or died, unheard, amongst the devastation themselves or their fellows had made.[199]

Following the wanton destruction and the abuse of their people, many stragglers were tortured and mutilated before being put to death by the vengeful Portuguese. The invaders had despoiled their country and therefore paid a terrible price when they fell into the hands of those they had dispossessed.

As the French passed through Miranda de Corvo, constant and bitter skirmishing took place between the rearguard and British light troops as Ney did his best to ensure that small ambushes constantly waylaid the Allied advance. The cavalry in the vanguard were frequently attacked by dragoons firing carbines from the saddle, who then fled after causing disruption or engaged in brief, running fights with their pursuers. Marbot was caught up in a rearguard incident. Riding with a dispatch from Massena to Ney, he was fired upon several times by light infantry and, when returning, was challenged by a mounted infantry officer to single combat. At first refusing to acknowledge the challenge, he turned and rode at his adversary when accused of cowardice. As he did so, two hussars rode from the woods to ambush him:

> I was caught in a trap, and understood that only a most energetic defence could save me... So I flew upon the English officer; we met; he gave me a slash across the face, I ran my sword into his throat. His blood spurted all over me, and the wretch fell from his horse to the ground, which he bit in his rage. Meanwhile, the two hussars were hitting me all over...[200]

The aide managed to strike one of his assailants in the mouth, cutting his face open and forcing him to ride away. Seeing light troops from both sides approaching, and with musket balls hissing about them, the other hussar turned and followed, only to receive a thrust from Marbot in his shoulder as he did so. Though Massena praised his bravery, he admonished him gently for getting involved in outpost skirmishing, where an aide had no business to be. Marbot had been badly injured in the fight and, barely able to ride, was lucky to survive the retreat.

Firing Miranda de Corvo behind them, Ney's rearguard prepared to make another stand before the village of Foz de Arouce on the River Ceira. The bridge before the village was narrow and had been damaged by the peasantry but II and VIII Corps only crossed with difficulty. Massena ordered the rearguard across and to hold the line of the river, but unaccountably Ney left two infantry divisions in the meadows with the river at their backs, along with Lamotte's cavalry brigade. On 14 March, as the British approached, both Picton and Erskine assumed that Wellington would proceed with caution and attack the next day. However, despite the heavy fog that had come down, Wellington reconnoitred the French position and decided to attack at once, having observed the French seemingly dispersed and many troops cooking over their campfires.

As the British advanced, a confused action took place amid the mist. At first the French stood their ground in line, trading volley fire with the British infantry but soon at least two battalions broke and fled for the bridge. Seeing the crush of fugitives around the structure, many tried to ford the river instead and were swept away. The Ceira was in spate and the water was deeper than usual, with dozens of fugitives drowning. Ney led a bayonet charge with the 69th Line, partially restoring the situation. During the attacks made by both sides a curious incident took place, which apparently terminated the affair:

> We on the right bank then witnessed a sight unusual in war: two sides flying each from the other in complete disorder! Finally the panic on both sides was checked and English and French returned to the abandoned ground to pick up their muskets; but both sides were so much ashamed that, though they were quite close to each other, not a shot was fired nor any challenge exchanged, and they returned to their positions in silence.[201]

During the initial panic of the retreat, the French hamstrung 500 mules and horses for fear of them falling into enemy hands. The gruesome sight of these doomed animals foundering in the mud amidst a wash of blood sickened the redcoats as the French fell back before them, destroying the bridge as they did so. Grattan recorded that, in their wasted and starved condition, the animals would have been no good to anyone and that it was considered a bestial and savage act.[202]

On 16 March Wellington decided to halt his army's advance at Foz de Arouce. He was obliged to feed his troops by supply column from Lisbon and, though his improved commissariat was performing the task ably, the Portuguese were receiving next to nothing from their own supply masters. Obliged to feed both, the British commissariat could not cope and they would have to wait until sufficient stocks reached them. In any case, Wellington had achieved his main objective of denying the enemy a route into central Portugal and they now seemed bent on leaving the country. He had finally received reinforcements in Lisbon and the newly formed 7th Division was marching to join him. However, on 11 March Badajoz had capitulated and he had only just received the news. Though Soult's forces remained relatively immobile, he feared a move on the fortress town of Elvas and consequently dispatched troops to reinforce the south, leaving him with an army of roughly 30,000 to continue the pursuit.

The French had been allowed a breathing space and retreated along the line of the Mondego, reaching Colerico about twenty miles from Almeida. Trant's levies were shadowing them along the northern bank of the Mondego, but were unlikely to interfere seriously with French progress and Wellington was a couple of days behind. At this juncture Massena made a curious decision, motivated it seems by a stubborn refusal to admit defeat. He had also heard of Wellington's political difficulties, with doubts expressed in Parliament and by the Portuguese Regency about the ruinous cost of the war. He gave orders to march southwards on Guarda with the intent of crossing the Tagus out of reach of British interference and marching once more on Lisbon along the southern bank. The officers of his tired and ragged army received this news with shock and dismay. Ney angrily refused to obey his orders, knowing that the men needed rest, shelter and food before any offensive operations could even be contemplated. He wrote to his commander in the strongest terms, refusing to have anything to do with the plan and complaining: 'Since you always wait for the moment of greatest danger to make up your mind, I am obliged to prevent the total ruin of the army.'[203]

Massena was scandalised and wanted to dismiss Ney there and then. Pelet tried to calm him and emphasised what a triumph it was for the enemy that there should be such inner division within their army. The marshal relented but, after an exchange of angry recriminations, disregarded Pelet's advice and removed Ney from command, appointing General Loison over VI Corps in his stead. Ney was instructed to return to Spain and await the Emperor's pleasure whilst, to ensure his side of the story had the first hearing, Pelet was dispatched to Paris. Massena assured him: 'You do not need any instructions. You will see the Emperor and tell him everything that you judge proper.'[204] Throughout the campaign Ney had hindered him at every turn with insubordination, intransigence and abuse. Massena had finally had enough, though the army was shocked and bewildered by Ney's loss.

Once they reached Guarda, Massena ordered a three-day halt to rest his army and sent Junot and Reynier to conduct a wide-ranging reconnaissance of the region he intended to march into. D'Erlon had also refused to march on the expedition, and had taken IX Corps to Almeida, but the Army of Portugal still comprised around 40,000 men. At Guarda, Massena received several dispatches from Napoleon, nearly all of which were two months old, proving the folly of the Emperor trying to influence the campaign from such a distance. The reconnaissance revealed the area to the south to be largely barren and D'Erlon sent news that Almeida had only fifteen days' worth of provisions in its storehouses, with Ciudad Rodrigo in a similar state.[205] The army was short of ammunition, horses and transport. It was also underfed and nearly exhausted, despite the brief rest. Finally seeing sense, Massena abandoned his plans and decided to retire behind the Côa.

Wellington had resumed his advance and the leading elements of his army arrived at Guarda just as the French were leaving. Grattan of the 88th recalled that they came to within two gunshots of the town without meeting any cavalry vedettes. They could not take advantage of this negligence since the artillery and sufficient cavalry were taking some time to catch up with the advance guard and:

> ...we had the mortification to witness the French getting out of it (the town), bag and baggage, as quick as they could. The scene of confusion that the streets presented was great; infantry, artillery, and baggage, men, women, and children, all mixed pell-mell together, hurrying to the high road leading to Sabugal.[206]

The Army of Portugal was now headed for Almeida and Reynier's II Corps, comprising three divisions, was bringing up the rear. On 2 April Reynier had reached the town of Sabugal, situated on a bend in the River Côa. Knowing his position was isolated, Massena urged him to resume his march as soon as possible, but Reynier delayed, hoping to use darkness to cover his retreat. After a cautious pursuit, Wellington now decided that it was time to strike and hopefully inflict a grievous wound on the retiring French army. The dawn of 3 April was foggy with intermittent rain, but Wellington hoped it would assist his plans by masking the advance. The Light Division, with two attached brigades of cavalry, was to ford the Côa to the north, cutting off the French line of retreat and assailing their flank and rear. Simultaneously the 3rd, 5th and 7th Divisions would attack in force across the river against the town and hold the French in place. With luck Reynier's Corps would be severely damaged or even cut off and destroyed.

From the very beginning things started to go wrong with the Allied plan. General Erskine, commanding the Light Division, crossed far too high upriver with the cavalry and failed to engage in the action. The 1 Brigade of the Light Division under Colonel Beckwith also crossed at the wrong ford, with the fog limiting visibility to 100 yards. The ford was only four miles above Sabugal and far too close to the French positions. The green-jacketed 95th waded across the river up to their armpits in places, holding their rifles above the water. Luckily the French picket only fired a single volley at the struggling men before retiring. Meanwhile, the main attack was proceeding far too slowly, the mist adding to their confusion, leaving the Light Division dangerously exposed.

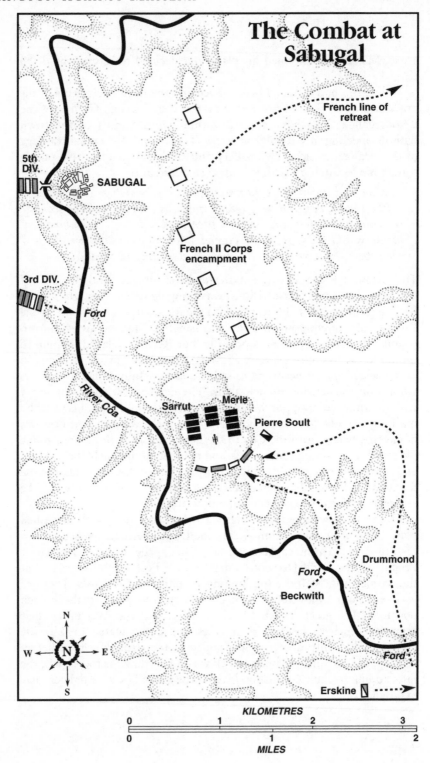

The Combat at Sabugal

French line of
retreat

5th
DIV.

SABUGAL

French II Corps
encampment

3rd DIV.

Ford

River Côa

Sarrut   Merle

Pierre Soult

Drummond

Ford

Beckwith

N

W ← → E

S

Ford

Erskine

KILOMETRES

0   1   2   3

0   1   2

MILES

Beckwith's Brigade comprised around 3,500 men of the 95th and 43rd Regiments and the 3rd Caçadores, considered some of the best troops in the army. He was lucky to have such elite and experienced troops as, after driving in the enemy skirmishers, he was soon confronted by Merle's Division. Though holding his own, Beckwith observed Heudelet's Division advancing in column, intent on outflanking him, and he retired to a small hill. With both sides eager for a fight, a fierce struggle now ensued. Three columns of French infantry advanced against the British line with the drums beating the *pas de charge* and their officers roaring encouragement at the head of their men. After pushing back the skirmishers, they were coolly received by the redcoats of the 43rd, who fired volley after volley into their columns. Vastly outnumbered, the riflemen and Caçadores also formed line shoulder to shoulder, firing their rifles like muskets into the oncoming masses. The French had brought up a couple of howitzers that lobbed their heavy shells high over the advancing troops to explode over the British position, but the broken ground limited their effect.

As the first attack was beaten off, one of the howitzers was left between the two sides and a struggle ensued for its possession. The French infantry advanced three times to contest the gun, only to be driven back. Reynier had recovered well from his initial surprise, but now the main attack could be discerned, with the fog beginning to clear, and it was time to withdraw. After a brief fight in the town, his infantry fell back in some disorder but were covered by the 31st Line and 47th Line who had not been engaged. The last act against the beleaguered 1 Brigade was a cavalry charge led by General Pierre Soult, who drove the British back from the howitzer to a dry stone wall. His dragoons bravely rode up to the wall to fire pistols and carbines at the re-forming infantry, but so many saddles were emptied by riflemen sheltered there that they were forced to turn about and flee.[207]

Wellington had failed to inflict decisive damage on Reynier's Corps, but the French had lost 760 casualties with eighty prisoners whilst the Allies suffered only 179 casualties. The Light Division bore the brunt of the British losses. For example, the 1st Battalion of the 43rd had suffered eighty casualties whilst 1 Brigade was engaging as many as ten French battalions, a stunning tribute to their fighting ability. The rain had diminished the use of musketry and the French should have possessed an advantage, with their preference for bayonet fighting over musketry, but the Light Division had repulsed them three times. Grattan had not taken part in the fighting, but walked the field afterwards and heard details of the fight. Whilst exchanging fire with the 43rd, the French had stuck the ramrods of the muskets into the ground before them to speed their rate of fire. The howitzer, now captured by the British, had been bitterly contested and all of its gun crew had perished in its defence. Grattan saw the body of a French artillery officer next to a gunner who sat with his back to the wheel of the gun as if resting:

> A round shot had taken off his thigh a few inches below the groin... The bare stump exhibiting a shocking sight – the muscles, arteries, and flesh, all hanging in frightful confusion, presented the eye with a horrid sample of the effects of those means made use of by man for his own destruction...[208]

Since the gunner had been killed by Allied artillery, this meant that he had died late in the engagement as Allied guns only arrived towards the end of the action. The French were nearing the end of their long, gruelling retreat, but they still had plenty of fight left in them and it was agreed that they had rarely fought better than at Sabugal. Though briefly pursued by cavalry, Reynier soon resumed an orderly withdrawal. The French had had a lucky escape, only the fog and the confusion saving them from a worse defeat.

After some skirmishing around Almeida, the Army of Portugal withdrew over the border to camps in the region of Salamanca. The retreat officially ended on 11 April. Massena's invasion had been defeated. Yet even now his authority was challenged. Though D'Erlon was now officially placed under him, Marshal Bessières questioned his requests for supplies, protesting that they belonged to the elements of the Young Guard that he commanded.[209] Once again, the Emperor had not made Massena's position clear to the army, a fact which protected his own authority but placed great strain on the marshal's ability to perform his role. After almost continuous fighting over eleven months, the Army of Portugal had earned a better reception.

Once Wellington had reached Almeida he halted, having reached the end of his resources. He swiftly blockaded the fortress and deliberated whether he should bring up a siege train to reduce it or move it south against Badajoz. On 10 April he issued a proclamation to the Portuguese people, announcing their deliverance from a cruel invader who had wrought terrible destruction on their country. They were free to return to their homes and professions, though the prospect of starting again in a man-made wilderness must have been daunting. The British were aware of the debt they owed to Portugal and several charitable relief committees were formed to help rebuild the country.[210]

London was well pleased with the outcome of the campaign and the Earl of Liverpool rushed to praise him:

> I congratulate you most sincerely upon the successful conclusion of all your operations, as far as relates to the defence of Portugal. The event has most fully confirmed all your predictions, and the eyes of the world are now completely open to the wisdom of the system upon which you have been acting.[211]

However, many bemoaned the enormous costs of protecting Lisbon which, though relatively cheap in terms of troops, had amounted to over nine million pounds. Even General Tarleton, a hero of the American Rebellion and sympathetic to the military, questioned what he believed to be unnecessary expenditure, claiming Wellington should never have retreated after Busaço and had squandered thousands of pounds feeding the refugees in Lisbon. This was the responsibility of the Regency, he insisted, adding: '…we were even obliged to supply the army in Portugal with red port, which was infinitely worse than sending coals to Newcastle.'[212] Wellington angrily refuted this, answering that such accusations were founded on propaganda published in the French newspapers. Ignoring the financial difficulties Perceval's Government was undergoing, he raged at the political 'betrayals' that dogged his achievements. In a letter to his brother he claimed:

> We aided the Portuguese government by our influence to purchase corn from the Barbary States and at Malta. But in point of fact the inhabitants of Lisbon were never in want, excepting what was occasioned by the speculations of those who monopolised the sale of grain.[213]

Regardless of how much expense Wellington had accrued, the occupants of Lisbon had suffered severe deprivation, with thousands dying from lack of food alone. With the loss of around two percent of their population during the third invasion, arguments over how much had been spent on the minimal provisions provided for Portuguese refugees were tasteless in the extreme. However, the money spent on the Lines of Torres Vedras had been justified. More than anything else they had stopped the French invasion in its tracks and prevented the sack of Lisbon and the loss of Britain's Continental base. If the lines had not been constructed and Lisbon had fallen, it is likely that the same critics would have damned Wellington for not taking such precautions. Wellington's ruthless defensive strategy had proved effective despite the cost in revenue and the despoilment of the countryside.

The failure of the third invasion of Portugal had grave implications for French efforts in the Peninsula. Massena had achieved next to nothing strategically and had lost between 20,000 and 25,000 men, along with vast amounts of equipment and supplies. It was not entirely his fault. Hampered from the outset by Napoleon's refusal to clearly establish his position as commander-in-chief, he had been beset on all sides by insubordination and outright refusals to obey his orders that would have crippled a lesser general. Though he managed largely to overcome these problems, he should not have been obliged to fight his own officers in addition to the enemy, a disadvantage caused by the Emperor's paranoia as much as his own actions.

A key error, mainly brought about by Napoleon's own orders, had been to spend so much time and effort taking the frontier fortresses. With the benefit of hindsight, Ney's advice to mask the strongholds and to march directly against Lisbon would have shortened the campaign and reduced the time Wellington had to prepare his famous defences. Enduring the long period before the lines (October 1810 to March 1811) had been a considerable achievement and even Massena's enemies acknowledged that only a man so well acquainted with the horrors of siege warfare could have tarried so long in the wilderness without his forces crumbling and dispersing through want of food and shelter.

Busaço had been a clear defeat, but Massena learned from his mistakes and, following this setback, he made relatively few serious errors of judgement. He manoeuvred his force skilfully and could not be blamed for Wellington's refusal to march out from his lines to meet him on equal terms. In Wellington's place he would have done exactly the same, as witnessed by his defensive strategy at Zurich. In terms of numbers the Army of Portugal was inadequate to force the Lines of Torres Vedras, but Massena had tried his best to circumvent them and Napoleon's failure to reinforce him sufficiently or compel Soult's support doomed them to failure. He subsequently attempted the next best strategy with his attempt on Oporto, which largely failed through his subordinates' unwillingness to comply.

Massena's one major error had been to pause and investigate the unrealistic possibility of following the southern bank of the Tagus to Lisbon, a reckless move that undoubtedly cost lives. Nevertheless, once he had discovered its impracticality he managed to extricate his army from a very difficult situation and bring it back to Spain. The mauling that II Corps suffered at Sabugal can be placed squarely on Reynier's shoulders and, largely due to Ney's accomplished handling of the rearguard, it was remarkable that the army did not suffer greater losses during a hazardous retreat. Few commanders would have fared so well in an undeveloped country with poor roads, constantly harried by guerrilla raids and obliged to forage for supplies in a virtual wasteland. With all the problems Massena encountered during the campaign it is a tribute to his abilities that he saved so many of his men. Thiebault summarised his difficulties succinctly:

> *...he was constantly disserved: first by the Emperor, who only gave him half the troops he required for success, and, to assist him, men who knew nothing of subordination... secondly, by those who had to guide him, and who, led by the Marquis of Alorna, led him all astray at Busaco... lastly by his generals, above all by Reynier, one of the most able men whom we had left, but who at Sabugal took no notice of his warning...[214]*

On the other side Wellington, already an experienced commander, emerged as a truly great general during this campaign. His handling of the army at Busaço was masterful and, despite being outflanked, his withdrawal to Lisbon was executed with great skill. Often accused of excessive caution, it should be remembered that his main concern was to preserve his small army and limit casualties – always the primary motivation of a decent general. The swift construction of an almost insurmountable barrier greatly assisted him in this. It has to be borne in mind that many generals would have balked at the scale of the task and not even considered such an operation. If he had merely tried to defend the city of Lisbon itself, the outcome of the campaign would have been less certain.

In contrast to Massena, Wellington's army had few generals experienced in the command of large numbers of troops, like Ney and Junot, and many were learning their trade at this level of operations. Indeed he was forced, often by political obligation, to endure lacklustre generals such as Erskine and Slade, whose efforts often hampered his operations whilst pursuing the French. In addition to Slade's poor leadership of the cavalry arm, Horse Guards had not permitted him sufficient cavalry, a deficiency keenly felt during the retreat. Furthermore, Wellington suffered political interference and meddling, which, while not as grave a handicap as Massena's problems, added to the burdens of his command. In the final analysis, the French had been rudely ejected from Portugal when authorities on all sides had predicted another victory for Napoleon's armies.

Chapter 9

A Last Chance

The only French presence remaining in Portugal was General Brenier's garrison in Almeida. The 6th Division and Pack's Portuguese Brigade were blockading the town but, until heavy guns were brought up from Lisbon, an effective siege was out of the question. The Army of Portugal, in a very bedraggled state, was now based around Salamanca and Wellington believed that it would be some time before the French would seriously contemplate offensive operations. After the fall of Badajoz, the situation in the south seemed to require his urgent attention and, leaving Sir Brent Spencer in command, he rode along the frontier to Elvas to assess the situation. Despite Beresford's capability, he felt obliged to see for himself.

Though he had ordered the Light Division to resume their role as border guardians to monitor French movements and harass the garrison of Ciudad Rodrigo, Erskine's suitability for this task was doubtful and he was no match for his predecessor. Though an experienced cavalry commander, he had gained a reputation for recklessness and was beginning to show signs of mental health problems that were slowly becoming apparent to his comrades. Shortly before his departure, Wellington had pulled the Light Division further back, and in his absence the situation deteriorated, with the garrison conducting aggressive probes and actions. Harry Smith summarised the state of affairs on the frontier: 'The Duke had gone into the Alemtejo, and Sir Brent Spencer commanded – a regular old woman, who allowed the French to commit all sorts of extravagances under our noses, when a rapid move on their rear from Espeja would have punished them.'[215]

In contrast, the garrison of Almeida appeared securely hemmed in. This was unsurprising, since Brenier had less than 1,500 men ranged against the 13,000 camped outside his walls. Following the disaster that had befallen the town in 1810, his time was largely consumed by the need to continue repairs and guard against an assault, even though the Allies lacked artillery. Indeed, the besiegers constantly interfered with his defence: 'The garrison had no means of providing for their cattle, but by turning them out to graze upon the glacis; and we sent a few of our rifles to practice against them, which very soon reduced them to salt provisions.'[216] Wellington believed that Almeida was poorly provisioned and that a blockade alone might force their capitulation. He was mistaken in this as the garrison possessed adequate food stocks, but their position was a precarious one nonetheless.

Meanwhile Massena was encountering great difficulties in Salamanca. The reverses his forces had suffered in Portugal infuriated the Emperor and he gave Pelet a stormy reception when he arrived in Paris. Napoleon kept repeating that a mere 30,000 men under Wellington had repelled the Army of Portugal, comprised of over 60,000. Pelet replied that Massena had never possessed that many troops, citing only 40,000 at best (a gross underestimate) and reminding him that the British were supported by at least 15,000 Portuguese regulars, not to mention the *Ordenanza* and other irregulars. Yet Napoleon refused to countenance this and during a long interview confronted him with the information brought by Foy from Santarém. He spoke derisively of Massena's performance during the campaign, remarking: 'What would have become of you if, on the day following the battle of Busaço when you were making your movement right, Wellington had fallen upon you with a victorious army?'[217] Pelet loyally defended his commander, but it seemed clear that Napoleon was firmly set against him. Furthermore, though he listened politely to Pelet's account of Ney's actions, he never issued more than a slight reprimand to the marshal and soon gave him another appointment.

General Thiebault, one of Massena's former aides, was military governor of Salamanca and the arrival of the Army of Portugal presented him with many difficulties. The ragged force required accommodation, food and clothing in enormous amounts and Massena expected Thiebault and Marshal Bessières, Duke of Istria, to provide it. Napoleon, sick of the rivalry and inefficiency of his governors, had created the Army of the North under Bessières in January 1811 to unite the northern provinces. This was an enormous task for 70,000 men, including elements of the Imperial Young Guard, demanding the suppression of revolts in mountainous territory ideally suited to guerrilla activity, guarding the coastline against raids from the British Navy and containing upwards of 16,000 regular Spanish troops in the north-west. Now he was expected to assist Massena's forces, its commander insisting:

> The Army of Portugal is not a territorial army. Its business is to face the English army, and fight it wherever met with. It has retreated to Salamanca in order to save Rodrigo, and if possible Almeida, and to cover the Army of Northern Spain itself; and

therefore it ought to be fed by the Army of the North, since Spanish Estremadura is part of that army's territory.[218]

Massena had a right to demand this, but French resources were already stretched without the presence of over 40,000 half-starved soldiers to add to their problems. Yet Thiebault venerated his former commander and was overjoyed to see him, providing a warm welcome in Salamanca. However, the presence of his mistress distressed him:

I had heard of this folly and regretted it, since it had the worst possible effect in the army; besides, the marshal was really old enough to dispense with this kind of camp furniture. My interest in him and his reputation made this person's presence painful to me, and it was awkwardly enough that I allowed myself to be presented to the fair dame, who was in truth nothing much to look at.[219]

Nevertheless, Thiebault endeavoured to be a good host and entertained the couple at a formal dinner. Yet, having tactfully accepted the presence of Massena's concubine, he was appalled when, without warning, his guest's sordid reputation for embezzlement suddenly arose, with Massena requesting:

'My dear general, here is a statement of 80,000 francs arrears of pay due to me. Kindly have them paid to me out of the fund that you have just received. On this occasion I reckon upon your old friendship.' The perspiration stood on my forehead. 'Prince,' I replied, 'this fund is destined for a special purpose; it belongs to the subsistence of your army.'[220]

Despite Thiebault's protests the marshal was implacable and browbeat him into a promise to yield the funds at the first opportunity. The Governor was mortified and distressed that a man he respected would make such a demand, writing: '...never did my conscience exact a more painful sacrifice.'[221] Massena may have been owed the money, but with the sufferings of his army this appeared unpatriotic and selfish to say the least and, considering the reverence his former aide clearly held him in, the tale is almost certainly true. Yet the Emperor was clearly displeased with him and he probably suspected his replacement was imminent unless he rapidly restored the military situation. He probably doubted that Napoleon would honour the debt if he were removed from command due to the uncertain relationship between them. However, in the light of Napoleon's usual generosity towards his marshals, this seems unfair.

Letters from Berthier, conveying the Emperors's wishes, were constantly arriving in Salamanca berating Massena and demanding action. The Emperor wanted the army to relieve Almeida and to slight the fortress, rendering it useless. This would remove a formidable obstacle for another invasion, but what Napoleon really wanted was the defeat of the Allied field army, and he hoped such an attempt would draw it out. The letters were full of criticism, claiming, amongst other things, that Massena should have occupied Coimbra before withdrawing from Santarem. However, Berthier also wrote:

> The Emperor hopes that you will soon find an opportunity to take a striking revenge. The Emperor has not forgotten your fifteen years of success and he has complete confidence in you... We appreciate all the difficulties of your position, and hope that you will find the Duke of Ragusa easier to handle than Marshal Ney.[222]

Marmont, Duke of Ragusa, was travelling to take command of VI Corps, and this letter implied that Massena had a last chance to restore himself to favour. Just as there was no excuse for failure in military thinking; a major battlefield success would pardon all former sins. Fortunately, many conscripts and invalids were present in Valladolid and Salamanca to bolster his force and he had been able to replace most of the 6,500 horses he had lost in Portugal. Massena also asked Bessières to provide 8,000 infantry and replacement artillery.

However, Marbot, still recuperating from his wounds, recorded that when the reinforcements were observed approaching on 2 May, the troops mistook them for an advance guard. Only 1,500 cavalry, six guns and thirty gun teams accompanied Marshal Bessières, who received a frosty reception from Massena. Seeing his fellow marshal's dismay, Bessières protested that recent revolts made it impossible to reduce his army any further, but this failed to placate him. Massena was so angry that, careless of who overheard him, he told his staff: 'He would have done much better to have sent me a few more thousand men with ammunition and provisions, and to have remained at the centre of his province than to come examining and criticising what I am to do.'[223] He believed Bessières had come in person in order to undermine his authority and he had no need of another commander to confuse the army hierarchy even further.

Thiebault was equally scathing and believed that Bessières' failure to bring adequate reinforcements endangered the enterprise, the marshal having initially promised to provide at least 10,000 men. The Army of the North had its own battles to fight, but a conversation with the marshal implied that Massena's suspicions were well founded:

> '...I am come, like a French cavalier at the head of a handful of heroes.' At these words I looked at him; it did not need his accent to remind me of his origin, and I feared to detect some second thought concealed behind his chivalrous gasconade. Next moment he betrayed it by saying that to collect the infantry division of which Massena had spoken would have taken too much time.[224]

Nevertheless, Massena had between 47,000 and 48,000 infantry, thirty-eight guns and around 4,500 cavalry. He was going to honour his obligation to Almeida's stranded garrison, but his true intent was to force the Allied army back over the Côa and inflict a decisive defeat upon it if possible. In a rousing address to his troops on 2 May he appealed to them:

> '...the enemies of Napoleon the Great have the audacity to blockade a fortress which they durst not previously attempt to defend. Soldiers, if your valour then intimidated their columns, will not your valour now punish them for their temerity; will you not bring to their recollection that you are still the same brave fellows... who drove them to their trenches at Lisbon?'[225]

In the south, Wellington had examined Elvas's fortifications and conferred at length with Beresford. The southern fortresses were far greater in size and armament than their northern counterparts and the task of regaining Badajoz seemed daunting when he reconnoitred the place on 22 April. However, his reconnaissance revealed how edgy the garrison was, when the garrison sent out three battalions to cover the withdrawal of a 200-man working party after spotting Wellington and his small escort.[226] Wellington intended Beresford to move against Badajoz shortly and entertained hopes of retaking the city. Useful as this visit had been, Wellington was alarmed to hear news of ominous movements around Ciudad Rodrigo and cut short his stay. Many in the Anglo-Portuguese Army were pleased when Wellington rejoined them after a long and hurried ride:

> As a general action seemed now to be inevitable, we anxiously longed for the return of Lord Wellington... as we would rather see his long nose in the fight than a reinforcement of ten thousand men any day... I'll venture to say that there was not a heart in that army that did not beat more lightly, when we heard the joyful news of his arrival...[227]

French activity had escalated, with large amounts of supplies being carried into Ciudad Rodrigo and Marshal Massena preparing his headquarters in the town. The actions of the Spanish guerrillas had not been up to their usual standard, with several supply convoys reaching there with little difficulty. This may have been due in part to the reduced assistance from the Light Division.

Wellington guessed that Massena's objective was Almeida, but believed that he could hold the town. Though he could withdraw and hope that the dearth of supplies would drive the French back once more, he was not prepared to allow the French to remain in Portugal. The main problem with Almeida from the perspective of defending Portugal was that it lay on the eastern bank of the Côa. If Wellington withdrew over the river the French were likely to increase its garrison and a few months might see them strong enough to base their army in the region and, protected by the Côa's gorge, it would become a staging area for another invasion. The Portuguese had been invaded three times in three years, but with their lands ravaged and the people sick of war, Wellington must have doubted their resolve to continue resistance. He wished to take the conflict over the border into Spain, not repeat the dark days of 1810, and was determined to block Massena's march and give battle. The Allies had between 30,000 and 37,000 men, but the Portuguese regiments were malnourished and suffering from sickness and desertion due to the Regency's supply mismanagement. He outgunned Massena's force with forty-eight cannon to the French thirty-eight, but was inferior in cavalry having only 1,800 against 4,500 French horse. Notwithstanding, he was confident of success, writing to Lord Liverpool on 1 May:

> The enemy may be stronger than they were when they were obliged to evacuate Portugal, and they may have been reinforced by detachments of troops under the command of Marshal Bessières; but I still feel confident that they have it not in their power to defeat the allied army in a general action.[228]

One reason for confidence was that he was able to choose his own ground for this battle. Knowing the route the French would be obliged to take for Almeida, he selected a ridge on the edge of the plains of Leon as a defensive position. The ridge lay between the two rivulets, the Dos Casas and the Turones, and grew progressively steeper towards the north. The Dos Casas widened to the north and was a difficult obstacle, having steeper banks and being strewn with rocks further upstream. Wellington placed the 5th and 6th Divisions along this line, anchoring his left on the ruined fortress of La Concepcion.

The village of Fuentes de Oñoro lay on his right. Comprising rugged granite-built cottages, it was low lying and rose up the hillside in tiers, the church being the largest and highest building in the hamlet. The Dos Casas was narrow and shallow at this point and did not present much of an obstacle, but the confused warren of small houses and walled gardens was certainly defensible if exposed to artillery fire. Here Wellington stationed twenty-eight light companies drawn from the 1 and 3 Divisions including British, Portuguese and King's German Legion troops, their combined strength amounting to around 1,800 men. These were under the command of Colonel Williams, who also had a full battalion of the 83rd in support.

Behind and to the left of the village were the 1st, 3rd and 7th Divisions. The Light Division lay in reserve along with the 1 and 2 Cavalry Brigades under Major-General Slade and Lieutenant-Colonel Von Arentschildt (KGL). South of Fuentes de Oñoro, the land was considerably flatter and more open, though broken with woods and marshland in places. Wellington predicted that the village would become the focal point of the battle, but nevertheless posted Julian Sanchez's irregulars, both infantry and cavalry, to the south in the village of Nave de Haver and a small British detachment in the village of Poço Velho. He did not expect a serious attack on this flank, but felt it prudent to take precautions. The Allied line was roughly eight miles long.

Five miles in the Allied rear lay the chasm of the River Côa, if anything deeper at this point than to the north, where Craufurd had fought his rearguard action the previous year. In the event of being forced to withdraw, various fords and the bridge at Castello Bom were the only viable crossing points unless the force retreated north-west to the bridge at Almeida. Although the fortresses' guns did not cover the bridge, the move would involve a considerable detour over difficult ground, with the grave possibility of interference from the garrison as the forces masking it would also be forced to retire. Massena was aware of this and, though he acknowledged the strength of the Allied position, recorded: 'Yet this position of the enemy was not without danger to them, since they had behind their front the rocky bed of the Coa, and but a single carriage communication, sufficiently difficult, by Castel Bom.'[229] It was a risk to have such a serious obstacle in the army's rear, but Wellington thought his position sufficiently strong to make retreat unlikely.

The French moved west from Ciudad Rodrigo on 2 May on two

parallel roads. Allied cavalry scouts soon detected their manoeuvring and several small clashes occurred as they fell back towards Wellington's position. Massena began to scout the enemy position on the afternoon of the 2nd. This time he intended to proceed cautiously after his previous underestimation of Wellington's ability and the strength of Busaço Ridge the year before. He determined that the village was the key to the Allied position and later wrote: 'This village is hidden by the nature of the ground, and placed in part on the foot of the little hill which the enemy possessed. I hoped to carry it, and keep it...'[230] To the north he deemed the land too rugged and difficult for a successful attack, but if he could occupy the enemy there, a large attack on Fuentes de Oñoro might break the Allied line and an advance along the ridge. He deployed Reynier's II Corps to the north, aiming to engage the British 5th Division with: '...orders to favour, by petty attacks, the grand movement of the army, and to manoeuvre in such a manner as to unite with it in proportion as it gained ground upon the enemy.'[231] Simultaneously, Ferey's Division from Loison's VI Corps would assault the village. He concentrated the bulk of his forces before Fuentes de Oñoro, including IX Corps under D'Erlon, and held his cavalry under Montbrun and Fournier in reserve. Junot's VIII Corps was also placed before the village, but further to the right, where they were close enough to march in support of Reynier should it become necessary.

The French army was in good spirits. Charles Parquin, a second Lieutenant in the 20th Chasseurs, recalled: '...everyone was eager to come to grips with the English.'[232] Parquin was a relative newcomer, having recently ridden to join Montbrun's Cavalry Division. However, Massena's popularity had waned after the horrors of the retreat, Parquin revealing one source of discontent: 'Unfortunately for the army Marshal Ney, le Brave des braves, was no longer there... a difference with the Prince of Essling had deprived the army of his talents and his sword.'[233] They were eager to avenge their humiliations at the hands of the British, but Parquin was not the only one to remark that the great cavalry leader's absence weakened their army.

The battle began on 3 May as Reynier began to probe the extreme left of the Allied position. Wellington suspected that this attack might be only a feint, but was sufficiently concerned to order his reserves to march in support of the 5 Division. The Light Division arrived to find some large-scale skirmishing in progress across the Dos Casas, but found their support unnecessary. Meanwhile, Ferey sent ten battalions across the stream to storm the village. Though the streams were at a high-water mark during this season, the Dos Casas was rarely more than a couple of feet deep before the village and the infantry splashed across it with ease though under heavy fire. Light infantrymen fired from the houses and over walls at the oncoming French and lined up across the narrow village lanes to block their progress. Yet firepower alone was insufficient to stop the onslaught as they struggled up the slope through the tangle of walls and gardens and the action turned into a brutal hand-to-hand struggle.

The light companies fought hard in the narrow streets, but the numbers sent against them were overwhelming and the French determinedly pushed them back up the hillside towards the village church. Here Colonel Williams mounted a counter-attack with his reserves that drove them back almost to the Dos Casas. Ferey then committed his second brigade, attacking at two separate points. Williams was severely wounded and the light infantry were again driven back through the village. Richard Brunton was among the hard-pressed troops. Since the action on the Côa he had been promoted and transferred into the 6th Caçadores under Colonel Pinto. His company: '...were hotly engaged disputing its possession from 12 o'clock until it became nearly dark, when the 71st and 79th came up to our support and very opportunely, for we were completely exhausted and the enemy constantly reinforced...'[234]

At one point the red-coated Hanoverian Legion, in French service, advanced upwards through the village and were mistaken by their garb for a British unit. It was only when they formed a firing line and fired a volley into the British before them that the error was discovered. However, as the fight began to go against them they were fired upon by the French 66th Line and also by their own artillery as they fell back through the streets, these blunders possibly costing the French the action.[235]

Observing that the fight was going badly and that the Allies were about to be forced out of the village, Wellington committed two Highland regiments to reinforce Williams and they mounted a determined bayonet charge down the hillside and into the village. One soldier of the 71st remembered Colonel Cadogan addressing the men as they prepared to move down the hillside:

'My lads, you have had no provision these two days; there is plenty in the hollow in front, let us go down and divide it.' We advanced as quick as we could run and met the light companies retreating as fast as they could... they called to us, 'Seventy-first, you will come back quicker than you advance.' We soon came full

in front of the enemy. The Colonel cries, 'Here is food, my lads, cut away.'[236]

It was rare for Wellington to order fighting in built up areas and unusual that bayonet clashes were contested so long. In the tortuous lanes of the village the two sides came upon each other at short range and, after a brief exchange of fire, had no time to reload before they were upon one another with sword and bayonet. Usually such affairs would be short lived, and often the psychological threat of the bayonet alone was enough to make one side break and run, but here both sides stood and fought with steel and musket butts. Harry Smith witnessed the charge from outside the village and remarked on the number of French officers he saw struck down, leading a column up the hill along with scores of men on both sides. Despite Smith's extensive military experience, it was: '...the only real bayonet conflict I ever witnessed.'[237]

Along the lanes and in the houses, groups of men lunged at each other and fired at point-blank range as the Scots forced the French back through the hamlet. One anonymous soldier's account conveys something of the savagery of the fray:

> *In this affair my life was most wonderfully preserved... a bayonet went through between my side and clothes, to my knapsack, which stopped its progress. The Frenchman to whom the bayonet belonged fell, pierced by a musket ball from my rear-rank man. Whilst freeing myself from the bayonet, a ball took off my right shoulder wing and killed my rear-rank man, who fell upon me. Narrow as this escape was, I felt no uneasiness; I was become so inured to danger and fatigue.*[238]

The streets had become choked with bodies and the wounded grasped at him as he stood over them and fired at the enemy, begging for assistance. Unable to help them, he recalled trampling over the dead and wounded as the 71st and 79th pursued the French over the Dos Casas. They chased them further, but French cavalry checked their advance and they were forced to retire in some haste.[239] Four more battalions from Marchand's Division were now sent against Fuentes de Oñoro, but the Scots resisted fiercely and held the line of the stream. According to Allied sources, the French were only able to recapture a few houses on the eastern bank, but Massena's account differs. He claims that after desperate attempts to oust his men: '...the greater part of the village remained in our hands during the night.'[240] Had this been true, the French would almost certainly have attacked in force the next

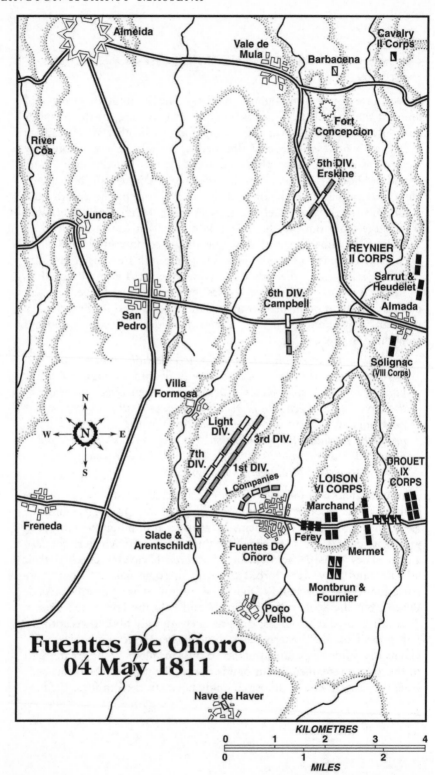

Almeida

Vale de
Mula

Barbacena

Cavalry
II Corps

Fort
Concepcion

River
Côa.

5th DIV.
Erskine

Junca

REYNIER
II CORPS

Sarrut &
Heudelet

6th DIV.
Campbell

Almada

San
Pedro

Solignac
(VIII Corps)

Villa
Formosa

Light
DIV.

3rd DIV.

N

7th
DIV.

1st DIV.

W   E

L.Companies

LOISON
VI CORPS

DROUET
IX
CORPS

S

Marchand

Freneda

Slade &
Arentschildt

Ferey

Fuentes De
Oñoro

Mermet

Poço
Velho

Montbrun &
Fournier

Fuentes De Oñoro
04 May 1811

Nave de Haver

KILOMETRES

| 0 | 1 | 2 | 3 | 4 |

| 0 | 1 | 2 |

MILES

morning to try to break the Allied line above Fuentes. Nevertheless, desultory firing continued into the night, but the fight for the village was over for the present.

On the following day some skirmishing took place across the Dos Casas in the early morning, but the fighting soon died away as a truce was agreed at 10 o'clock to retrieve the wounded in the village. VI Corps had suffered at least 650 casualties the previous day and both sides entered the village to clear the streets of the dead and wounded lying heaped in the alleys and gardens.

Massena realised that he had underestimated the strength of the village and that another frontal attack, unless combined with and supported by another manoeuvre, stood little chance of success. Sending out his cavalry, he spent the rest of the day scouting and searching for weaknesses in the Allied defences. If Napoleon had been in command, it is unlikely that he would have acted in such a patient and methodical manner. Ever impatient, he would never have given an enemy a day to prepare for his next assault unless presented with no choice but to do so. His tactical doctrine relied on speed and surprise, with a willingness to gamble against the odds if necessary. In contrast, Massena was cautious and prudent and, knowing the calibre of his opponent, refused to take risks. At Zurich he had waited an entire month for an opportune moment to strike. He believed the key to defeating Wellington was to outwait him, and the delay of a single day was insignificant if it might lead to victory.

Montbrun's cavalry reconnaissance swiftly determined that the Allied right was held by relatively few troops and that the bulk of those present were irregulars who were unlikely to put up serious resistance in a major engagement. Furthermore, the ground there was open and favourable for cavalry action, conveying little advantage to a defender. Massena had discovered Wellington's weakness; his right was thinly held and could be turned. He later wrote: 'I reconnoitred carefully the flank of the enemy... I found an accessible ground between Nave D'Aver and Posobello, and I resolved to direct the army thither. The orders were sent off in the evening, and the movements were executed during the night.'[241] Reynier would make a similar demonstration on the Allied left, as before with the intention of drawing the enemy reserves to that sector. Ferey's Division would remain poised before the village with IX Corps drawn up in its rear in two widely-spaced lines. This was intended to mask the fact that the rest of VI Corps were no longer positioned behind them.

The bulk of the French cavalry, upwards of 3,500 men, was to attack on the British right at the village of Nave de Haver and continue their attack toward Poço Velho. This attack was to be supported by three infantry divisions from VI Corps and VIII Corps, comprising about 17,000 men. The rest of the French army was deployed in front of the village as before, where a second assault would be mounted in conjunction with this flanking attack on Wellington's right. If the Allied flank could be successfully turned it would place their line of retreat to the fords and bridge at Castello Bom in severe jeopardy. If they were cut off, the Anglo-Portuguese Army would have grave difficulty in crossing the gorge of the Côa and the single bridge near Almeida would not be enough for the entire force to cross in a hurry. Furthermore, a successful attack on the village, with the divisions behind it weakened through supporting the Allied flanks, stood a chance of breaking the enemy centre. If Massena's plan succeeded, Wellington would be forced into a difficult retreat towards Almeida that might end in disaster for the Allies and a conclusive French victory.

Although the French moves had been conducted in darkness to conceal their intentions, Wellington had spent the day riding from one vantage point to another observing enemy movements. In addition, his cavalry had been actively probing and monitoring the enemy positions and he had noticed patrols to the south which led him to suspect that Massena intended some sort of move there. During the day he had withdrawn most of the exhausted light companies from Fuentes de Oñoro and replaced them with battalions from the 71st, 79th and 24th. Another attack on the village was anticipated and Grattan recalled:

> On our side we were not inactive: the avenues leading to Pozobello and Fuentes were barricaded in the best manner the movement would allow; temporary defences were constructed at the heads of the different streets, and trenches dug here and there as a protection against the impetuous attacks expected from the cavalry of General Montbrun.[242]

Indeed, Wellington appears to have been more concerned about renewed attempts on Fuentes de Oñoro attempting to split his army in two than any attempt on his flanks. Craufurd now returned to considerable acclaim from his troops:

> ...General Craufurd made his reappearance amongst us from England (4 May), and was welcomed with much enthusiasm by the division; although a strict disciplinarian, the men knew his value in the field too well not to testify their satisfaction at his return. The Caçadores, particularly, caused much laughter among

us by shouting out in Portuguese... 'Long live General Craufurd, who takes care of our bellies!'[243]

Although still held in poor esteem by many of his officers, it was acknowledged that Craufurd's handling of his Division was far more capable than that of Erskine, who now returned to command the 5th Division. Once again, the Light Division was held in reserve behind the Allied centre.

Yet Wellington had some concern about his right wing and sent two squadrons of cavalry to Nave de Haver and placed the 7th Division in and behind the village of Poço Velho. He later wrote that he:

...imagined that the enemy would endeavour to obtain possession of Fuentes de Oñoro and of the ground occupied by the troops behind the village, by crossing the Dos Casas at Poco Velho (about two miles to the south of Fuentes); and in the evening I moved the 7th Division, under Major-General Houston, to the right, in order, if possible, to protect that passage.[244]

However, the 7th were new arrivals in the Peninsula and therefore the least experienced division in the army. It appears that Wellington thought the French were only planning a minor manoeuvre to threaten communications and induce him to weaken his centre. He believed that the main attack was likely to be concentrated against the village. The ridge running west of Fuentes de Oñoro was eminently defensible and it would have made more sense to withdraw his right flank to this position entirely instead of inadequately reinforcing it with a weak division. The troops along his eight-mile frontage were thinly stretched already, but perhaps Wellington feared a successful move cutting off his retreat, although if the enemy could not break his line, there was little to worry about in that direction. Since the defensive position he had adopted was intended to cover Almeida from possible relief, combined with the fact that the French possessed insufficient strength to bypass his position and enter into Portugal, it was unnecessary to extend his right. Even historian Michael Glover, a keen Wellington partisan, called this decision: '...one of the most questionable moves which Wellington ever made.'[245] Yet Wellington was not completely autonomous and many of his staff approved of the redeployment, Sir Brent Spencer in particular earnestly supporting it. The morning would tell whether his line could survive the French onslaught.

Chapter 10
The Most Dangerous Hour of the War

Redeploying quietly under cover of darkness had been difficult and the French troops on Massena's left flank had only a few hours to rest. Few slept, knowing what awaited them on the morrow. The attack would begin shortly after first light and, though a low early morning mist hung over the fields, the day promised to be bright and very hot. Parquin greeted one of his superiors as they tightened the girths on their saddles and made last minute preparations for the advance:

> I noticed that Major de Vérigny had had his beard trimmed. His gauntlets and his shirt were clean, his boots highly polished and his spurs gleaming. He was riding his best horse, a fine Turkish mare... His colpack was crowned with its plume and its bag fluttered in the wind. His moustache had been waxed and turned up. In short, he was immaculately turned out. I complimented him on his appearance. 'My dear Parquin, this is how one should look when one is meeting the enemy,' he said. 'One is never too well dressed when the cannon roars.'[246]

The Allies were also settling in to their new positions. Houston had placed the 85th Regiment and the 2nd Caçadores in the village of Poço Velho and deployed the rest of the 7th Division behind the hamlet and slightly inclined towards Nave de Haver. In that village two squadrons of the 14th Light Dragoons had ridden up in the night to reinforce Sanchez's irregulars. Speaking with the famous guerrilla leader, Captain Thomas Brotherton inquired about the precautions he had made to defend the village and was assured that they were extensive. In the darkness it was difficult to confirm this, but he recalled: 'It was a strong post, on an eminence, surrounded by stone wall enclosures, similar to those in Ireland, and no cavalry alone ought to have carried it.'[247]

As the morning mist began to dissipate, Brotherton spied a large body of men just before the tree line of the woods to their front. Sanchez confidently told him they were his own pickets, but, to his horror, Brotherton suddenly realised that they were a squadron of

French cavalry just as they mounted their horses and began to advance. As the alarm was sounded, it became clear that a huge force of cavalry was headed for the village. Observing the odds, Sanchez made no attempt to defend Nave de Haver: '...but the *brave* Don Julian, as the Spaniards called him, took himself off immediately with his whole force to the mountains, and left me with my two squadrons to shift for myself.'[248] Brotherton clearly believed that with the irregular infantry they could have at least held the French advance for a while, but Sanchez was not prepared to risk his men against a large body of regulars. The two squadrons of dragoons skirmished with the advanced French units but were forced to retreat, being massively outnumbered. Those guerrillas on foot dispersed and fled but the French sabred many of them, the horsemen eagerly riding them down, wishing to avenge scores of ambushes and raids they had suffered at their hands. Isolated groups turned to fire on their pursuers or made brief stands amongst the houses, but were rapidly surrounded and mercilessly slaughtered by the vengeful cavalry.

The British cavalrymen were bloodied but had not suffered serious casualties as they thundered up to the village of Poço Velho, glad of the sight of the red-coated infantry drawn up there. Yet Brotherton was puzzled at their nonchalant attitude:

> ...but as they did not commence firing on the French cavalry that were closely pursuing me, I rode up to the first officer I could approach, and asked him why he did not fire and stop the progress of the enemy. He replied with astonishment, 'Are those French?'[249]

This was a battalion of the 85th Regiment who had never seen action before. Brotherton swiftly confirmed the identity of his pursuers and the infantry began to open a brisk fire on the horsemen. Numerous horses and men fell in the leading ranks, but the cavalry only retired a brief distance and more squadrons rode up to their support, reforming and obviously preparing for a major attack.

Private Wheeler of the 51st Foot also recalled that his battalion, drawn up on the plain to the right of the village, was casually cooking rice for breakfast when round shot began to fall amongst them from horse artillery that had unlimbered to their front. An immense body of cavalry was observed spreading out in squadrons on the plain before them. These were the brigades of generals Fournier and Lepic, and to their rear the leading elements of Marchand's infantry could be seen marching in a column of double companies from Nave de Haver.

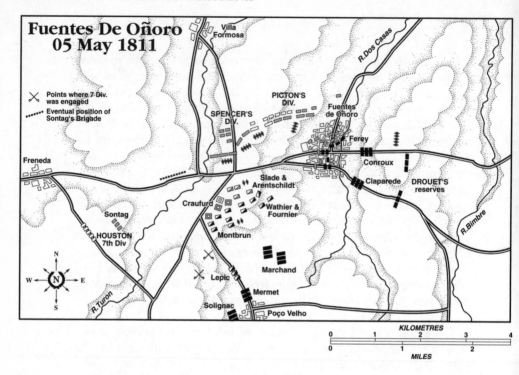

From his vantage point above Fuentes de Oñoro Wellington could now see the danger. Once again Reynier was attacking on his left, but without much conviction, and it was likely to be a mere distraction attack. He judged that Erskine and Campbell's Divisions could hold their own there and in any case his main concern was the right flank and they would have to fend for themselves. The 7th Division could not possibly stand against the huge attack that was being concentrated against them and he decided to commit the Light Division to their support. He ordered Craufurd to march to the threatened flank, attempt to extricate Houston's Division and cover their withdrawal.

Around Poço Velho matters were becoming serious for the Allies. The skirmishers had been pushed back into the village and French infantry were beginning to form for an assault. On the plain, Wheeler recalled that they only had two Portuguese cannon supporting them to the right and that one of them was rapidly dismounted and put out of action by French artillery fire.[250] The gun teams then swiftly retired with their other piece and the French gunners began to fire upon the infantry standing in line. Their exposed position made them an easy target and as they were softened up, the cavalry began to make repeated charges against them: 'The C.B. Regt now opened a fire, as did the Portugueses over our heads. It was a dangerous but necessary expedient, for our fire was not sufficient to stop the cavalry, so we were obliged to lay down and load.'[251]

The French infantry assault soon drove the 85th and the 2nd Caçadores out of the small village with some loss and they retreated in disorder. The 7th Division was forced to adopt square formations as the cavalry menaced them, reducing their firepower and slowing their rearward movement. The compact mass of bayonet-tipped muskets presented an near insurmountable anti-cavalry defence, but was also an inviting target for enemy artillery and the infantry who were approaching. Once weakened by their fire, the horsemen would charge in and destroy the squares. Luckily for the Allies, the leading elements of the Light Division were now approaching and Rifleman Costello recalled how he entered woods to the left of the village to help cover the withdrawal:

...where the 85th regiment were very roughly handled by the enemy. This was the first time since their arrival in the country that they had been engaged. Opposed, with their conspicuous red dresses, to the old trained French tirailleurs, it is no wonder that the gallant 85th should have suffered so severely. When we came up, however, our practiced fellows, in their dark clothing, from the murderous nature of their arms, soon turned back the advancing French...[252]

Craufurd conveyed orders to Houston that he was to withdraw to the higher ground between Fuentes de Oñoro and the village of Freneda. He would cover the 7th Division as they retired across the plain, but it was a fearsome prospect since the rocky slope lay three miles to their rear. Seeing the scale of the French manoeuvre, Wellington had decided to pull in his right flank and yield the road to Castello Bom. Once this had been accomplished there was no prospect of using the fords and the bridge behind them if he had to retreat. The single bridge near Almeida was a dubious escape route for the entire army and Wellington now placed his hopes on holding the line to avoid such an eventuality.

Both divisions began to retreat across the plain as large numbers of French cavalry milled about them at the edge of musket and rifle range. Craufurd had brought up some horse artillery and the batteries of Bull and Ramsay fired upon the French cavalry, hoping to arrest their progress. With practised skill, Craufurd formed the men into close columns of companies moving in pairs – one formation remaining in square while the other withdrew. Riflemen were sent into the scrub and outcrops of rock around them to snipe at the cavalry and check the advance of French infantry, whose skirmishers were beginning to approach and fire upon them. A slow and painful shuffle across the plain began as French artillery fire ripped into the squares, often knocking down many men with one shot as the projectiles bounced over the plain wreaking havoc.

Despite the remarkable orderliness of the withdrawal, the French cavalry had a rare chance to attack infantry who were barely supported by other arms. Their officers knew it, and as the 20th Chasseurs formed up for a charge they tried to urge their men on to greater feats. Major de Vérigny tried to inspire Parquin's squadron:

> 'Parquin,' he said, pointing to a chasseur who was under fire for the first time and whose pale face betrayed the apprehension he felt, 'Parquin, I can see by this fellow's face that he is going to make good use of his sabre when we charge.' The chasseur, who immediately recovered his determination at these words, brandished his sabre and declared: 'You may count on that, sir.'[253]

The trooper kept his word and in the charge that followed rode right into the British ranks, hacking down wildly at the men around him with his sword, but he was swiftly shot down and killed. Parquin was also struck in the face by a bullet fired up at him at point-blank range and was forced to leave the field.

Every charge on the squares was fiercely resisted. The first rank knelt, holding their muskets at the slope, presenting a hedge of bayonets to the horsemen as their fellows levelled their firelocks and fired over them at the approaching cavalry. Wheeler recalled: 'One of our men shot a horse, the dragoon made an attack on him with his sword, but Maxwell, for that is his name, ran him through the body with such force that he could not extricate his bayonet without placing his foot on the fellow's ribs.'[254] The rush of the horsemen was intimidating but without more artillery support or infantry to weaken the formations, they stood little chance of breaking their formation.

Meanwhile, the vastly outnumbered British cavalry charged continually against their French counterparts. Some Frenchmen were said to be drunk and wheeled about haphazardly,[255] yet they outnumbered the dragoons and their brave attempts to hold them back from the infantry were near suicidal:

> ...a squadron of the 1st Royal and of the 14th Light Dragoons gallantly dashed in amongst the enemy and performed wonders, but they were soon obliged to fall back – for the enemy

outnumbered them twenty to one or more; we now sorely felt the want of artillery and cavalry.[256]

Brotherton was involved in the brief and violent cavalry clashes as the horsemen whirled back and forth across the plain. Each time they retired to reform their ranks, French artillery would target them, knocking down horses and riders in a flurry of blood and dust. It was brutal, close-range fighting with sword and pistol: 'I had my charger shot under me, and got on a troop horse which was also shot under me, through the head, by the pistol of a French officer, so closely that my own face was singed.'[257]

With combined arms the French should have been able to decimate the stricken Divisions, but Mermet's infantry had paused inexplicably around Poço Velho and the Allies were beginning to lengthen the distance between them. A trail of casualties lay stretched over the plain, but they would have been even greater if the men had not kept their order. The cavalry persistently harried the retreat and tried to dislodge the riflemen operating in the scrubland. Costello was forced to run to the cover of the 51st's square on several occasions.[258] Wheeler recalls his somewhat eccentric Colonel's outbursts during the retreat:

> *'That fellow is out of step, keep step and they cannot hurt us.' Another time he would observe such a one, calling him by name, 'cannot march, mark him for drill, Serjeant Major. I tell you again they cannot hurt us if you are steady, if you get out of time, you will be knocked down.' He was leading his horse and a shot passed under the horses belley (sic) which made him rear up. 'You are a coward' he said 'I will stop your corn three days.'*[259]

Yet the situation was desperate for the Allies and as Napier wrote in his account of the war: '...there was not during the whole war a more perilous hour.'[260] If Montbrun's cavalry could delay the retreat until their infantry came up the entire Allied right wing might collapse. The situation was grave indeed, and at one point during the retreat Colonel Mainwaring of the 51st apparently took the drastic step of burning his regimental colours, fearing that they would fall into enemy hands. These were symbols of the Regiment's pride, which they were supposed to defend to the last, and this virtually unprecedented act reveals how desperate the situation had become. Mainwaring would later suffer for this 'defeatism' when Wellington heard of it.[261]

It seemed that the French were on the verge of victory, as Thiebault later recorded:

...having by a magnificent movement turned the enemy's right flank, it became master of the fairly accessible ground lying between Nave de Aver and Pozo Velho, and was in a position to take Wellington in flank and rear, and throw him back into the cul-de-sac formed by the Coa, the Agueda and the Douro. In this situation, among the crags with which the banks of those torrents bristle, the English army would have been certainly lost...[262]

The troops placed before Fuentes de Oñoro had remained inactive until mid-morning. Observing that his flank attack was succeeding, Massena ordered an assault on the village. Once again Ferey's Brigade splashed through the Dos Casas and Claparède's Brigade from IX Corps attacked the village to his left. French artillery began to pound the village in a heavy bombardment to cover the attack, bringing walls and roofs down upon the defenders as dust and smoke rose above Fuentes. Commissary Schaumann, posted in the rear at the bridge of Castello Bom, had ridden to observe the action from the ridge and observed the fearsome struggle below:

The French attack, particularly their gun fire (they usually fired salvos of six), was terrible, and the carnage in the streets was, if anything, worse than on the day before. The whole place rang with the clash of bayonets, the cheers of the men, and the chatter of muskets. Death flew forth from the churchyard wall and from the village church, which had been crenelated like a fortress by our men, and pierced with embrasures.[263]

The French pressed upwards through the narrow streets, rousting the defenders out of the houses and heading up towards the church. The 71st and 79th fell back before them, fighting house-to-house but gradually being overrun. Wellington ordered the 24th Regiment and the 6th Caçadores to support them, but General Drouet now committed ten more battalions to the attack, including grenadiers of the Imperial Guard. He hoped these elite shock troops would force the Allies out of the village and smash through Wellington's centre. The attack was even supported by some dragoons on the right of the village, and some of them clattered their way into the winding streets where a series of savage fights was in progress:

A French dragoon, who was dealing death around, forced his way up to near where I stood. Every moment I expected to be cut down. My piece was empty; there was not a moment to lose. I got a stab at him, beneath the ribs, upwards; he gave a back stroke, before he fell, and cut the stock of my musket in two.[264]

Brunton also encountered cavalry on the edge of the village. His Caçadore battalion was to the right of Fuentes de Oñoro, defending series of walls and broken ground. The dragoons charged a weak point in their position where the ground was flatter and marshy, riding down many of the Portuguese as they tried to flee. Brunton's company was cut off from the rest of the battalion when the horsemen got in between them and: 'We lost many men and the other wing was partly dispersed, but I maintained my ground and after dark rejoined the Brigade with what remained to their surprise, as they had imagined we were all taken.'[265]

Being forced out of the lower part of the village, the Highlanders were pushed back into its upper reaches. A fierce fight took place around the churchyard as the Highlanders fought among the tombstones with the French, but the enemy soon had possession of the church and its environs. The village was theirs and they began to re-form into line around the churchyard. One last effort would see them crown the ridge and if they could carry it and were reinforced with enough men, the Anglo-Portuguese Army would be cut in two.

Meanwhile, Houston and Craufurd's Divisions had nearly reached their new position. They had performed the incredible feat of retreating nearly three miles, harried all the while by the enemy. It justified Wellington's faith in Craufurd, since without careful handling and rigid discipline the troops would have broken and routed during such a long retreat. It was a crucial point in the battle and Massena recalled:

> *The enemy had his right routed, and the corps that composed it fled dispersed towards the centre, where they could unite behind the English regiments that were coming in great haste from the left... from the summit descend two ravines, very rocky and difficult... Lord Wellington filled these ravines with tiralleurs, stationed on the back part a good deal of artillery... Before our infantry could arrive, the enemy had had time to cover the summit... with several lines of English infantry...*[266]

Despite their inexperience, the 7th Division had performed well under fire and endured a hazardous retreat that would have broken most troops. Their escape had seemed impossible, yet the French infantry lingered around the villages instead of quickly following up their cavalry's success. Loison was advancing slowly, but Mermet's Division spent far too long around Poço Velho, exchanging fire with skirmishers instead of ignoring their fire and advancing swiftly to take advantage of the situation.

Massena realised he had a chance here to cut off the Allied line of communications through Castello Bom and possibly destroy Wellington's right flank. He sent word for Lepic's Brigade of Imperial Horse Grenadiers to exploit his success, but was mortified when Lieutenant Oudinot brought Lepic's insolent reply: 'Where is the guard Cavalry?' shouted Massena. 'General Lepic will not move, Prince,' replied the aide, 'he says he can only take orders from the Duke of Istria.'[267] There was some delay while Marshal Bessières was found and Massena was infuriated at the waste of time, every minute seeing the beleaguered Divisions slipping further away.

Lieutenant Freer recorded how the artillery of Bull and Ramsay's batteries continually played upon the enemy, covering the withdrawal. Ramsay's horse artillery had fallen back steadily over the plain, pausing at various stages to fire into the enemy masses before hitching up the guns and riding to another firing point. However, he lingered too long and his battery was surrounded as the cavalry swept by them. Undeterred, Captain Ramsay calmly ordered the gunners to limber up the cannon to their teams and: 'The guns when passed by, by the enemy, succeeded in escaping by charging through them and joining the (British) cavalry.'[268] The French cut at the gun teams as they rode by and the gunners fought their way through, though unaccustomed to using their swords in such a mêlée, as their guns skidded and jolted behind them. British cavalry rode to their assistance, holding back the enemy horsemen as the gunners careered past the infantry starting to form on the rocky slope. They were met with rousing cheers, this narrow escape becoming one of the most famous incidents of the battle.

The two Divisions now took up position along the slope between the villages as the French began to deploy before them. William Stuart of the 30th Regiment recalled how the Allied position had changed: '...our right towards the heights of Villa Formosa – our line was now formed into two sides of a triangle: from Fort Conception to Fuentes D'Onoro...'[269] The right flank had essentially swung back like a door, forming the southern half with the village of Fuentes jutting out at the point of this triangle. Wellington must have been mortified at the reverse on his right but, due to the skill and discipline of his troops, the Allies had retrieved the situation, performing this incredibly dangerous manoeuvre successfully.

The 85th had suffered a mauling, losing about a quarter of their number in Poço Velho and during the retreat, as had the 2nd

Caçadores, but the rest of 7th Division suffered only ninety-two casualties during the hazardous withdrawal with the Light Division losing only sixty-seven. However, the cavalry had lost heavily, with 140 casualties of all ranks and 100 horses. Their heroism had saved the infantry from worse, but their losses should have been far higher considering the numbers matched against them. Montbrun was finally reinforced by the infantry but did not feel strong enough to force the new Allied position. Kincaid recorded the first French attempt:

> The enemy followed our movement with a heavy column of infantry; but when they came near enough to exchange shots, they did not seem to like our looks, as we occupied a low ridge of broken rocks, against which even a rat could scarcely have hoped to advance alive; and they again fell back and opened a tremendous fire of artillery...[270]

The French attack had stalled and, seeing their inaction, Wellington felt confident enough to withdraw the Light Division to their former place behind and to the right of the village. However, as 7th Division adjusted their positions on the new defensive line, the Guards of Stopford's Brigade became overconfident and sent out skirmishers. Observing this, the French cavalry charged the men strung out in open order and around a hundred men were killed or taken prisoner, Colonel Hill being among the captives. Grattan of the 88th had a clear view of the action and recorded his frustration at the sight:

> Our division was posted on the high ground just above the plain; a small rugged ravine separated us from our comrades; but although the distance between us was short, we were, in effect as far from them as if we were placed on the Rock of Lisbon. We felt much for their situation, but could not afford them the least assistance, and we saw them rode down and cut to pieces without being able to... even discharge a musket in their defence.[271]

The battle had now reached its crucial point. Things were going well for the French in the village but the action on the right was coming to a halt, with Montbrun demanding reinforcements and limiting his attacks to the cannonade against the ridgeline. The British responded in kind, gradually getting the better of the artillery duel with their advantage in guns. Both sides mounted unsuccessful cavalry charges on their opponent's batteries to little effect. Captain Knipe of the 14th was mortally wounded charging French guns in front as the gunners switched loads and flayed the approaching dragoons with grapeshot.

163

Above the village, Wellington observed that the attack on his right was bogged down and the skirmishing on his left was no cause for alarm. Had Montbrun continued to press home his assaults, in conjunction with a renewed French attack on his centre being prepared in Fuentes, the situation would have been very serious, but now he only had one threat to counter. The 88th and the 74th were positioned above Fuentes de Oñoro as Pakenham rode up to Colonel Wallace and commented on the fugitives pouring out of the village and the French forming up there:

> ...when Sir Edward Pakenham galloped up to him, and said, 'Do you see that, Wallace?' – 'I do,' replied the Colonel, 'and I would rather drive the French out of the town than cover a retreat across the Coa.' – 'Perhaps,' said Sir Edward, 'his Lordship don't think it tenable...' 'I shall take it with my regiment, and keep it too.' – 'Will you?... I'll go tell Lord Wellington so; see, here he comes.'[272]

Pakenham soon returned, along with General Mackinnon, who would lead the attack. The 88th and 74th advanced silently at first, well aware that they were in full view of the French and most of the Allied army and that much depended on this assault. As they crested the ridge they were met by sporadic musketry fire from the houses and observed men of the French 9th Line forming line with bayonet-tipped muskets outstretched, preparing to receive them. Grattan led the advance company and:

> ...I turned round to look at the men of my company; they gave me a cheer that a lapse of many years has not made me forget, and I thought that that moment was the proudest of my life. The soldiers did not look as men usually do going into close fight – pale; the trot down the road had heightened their complexions, and they were the picture of everything that a chosen body of troops ought to be.[273]

Weary after fighting uphill through the village, yard by bloody yard, the French proved no match for the wild Irishmen of the 88th, who were fresh and eager for a fight. After a brief but vicious contest around the church, the 9th Regiment began to give ground. Grenadiers of the Young Imperial Guard opposed the redcoats' onslaught but were gradually pushed back through the streets. During the chaotic fracas one group of about a hundred guards fled into a cul-de-sac by mistake, becoming trapped. Grattan recorded: '...the result is easily imagined;

troops advancing to assault a town, uncertain of success, or flushed with victory, have no great time to deliberate... every man was put to death...'[274] The two battalions harried the French back through the streets unmercifully, even pursuing them over the Dos Casas until French artillery began to fire upon them, halting their advance.

Massena was now approaching the end of his resources. Most regiments were down to five cartridges a man and he sent back to Ciudad Rodrigo for more ammunition. Riding up and down the line, he despaired of his attack on the Allied flank. It had gone so well initially, but now his brigade commanders were hesitating and some were even refusing to obey orders. Riding northwards he found that Reynier had attempted very little there, achieving nothing except tying down the two divisions opposed to him. Both of these were fresh and an attack by II Corps stood little chance of success with the difficult ground in front of them. In the centre he had lost at least 1,400 men during the day's fighting, but the divisions of Ferey, Claparède and Conroux were exhausted and to mount another attack was folly. Wellington was still far from being defeated and Almeida was certainly beyond his reach for now.

Once again the French artillery resumed its bombardment of Fuentes de Oñoro. Its defenders took cover in houses and behind walls as round shot crashed and ricocheted around them. Pakenham rode along the streets shouting encouragement to the soldiers, but every time he paused, the ground about him would be torn up by cannon fire as the gunners tried to target him. Colonel Cameron of the 79th was killed at this time and Wallace was knocked down and covered with stones and dust as a wall he was sheltering behind was blown in. Though several of his companions were killed, he emerged unhurt. The streets were strewn with dead and wounded and:

> ...this proceeding was attended with little loss to us, and was fatal to many of their wounded, who lay in a helpless state in the different streets, and could not be moved from their situation without great peril to our men – and they were torn to pieces by the shot of their own army.[275]

Crouching in the streets and houses, the town's new defenders endured the cannonade in the heat and dust until dusk, but the Allied line had held and the battle was over.

In the evening a truce was agreed and men of both armies entered Fuentes de Oñoro to begin the sad task of removing the dead and wounded. They lay piled in the streets or within the houses, where many wounded had crawled to escape the cannon fire raining down on them. The Highlanders of the 79th had suffered in particular, yet the men of many regiments lay sprawled in the dusty, rubble strewn lanes, the manner of their fall clearly evident:

> *Among the dead that covered the streets of Fuentes, it was quite a common thing to see an English and a French solider with their bayonets still in each others' bodies, and their fists convulsively grasping the butt ends of their muskets, lying on top of each other. At one spot in the village I saw seven, and at another, five, French officers killed by bayonet wounds.* [276]

In the savage street fighting the French officers had led by example and suffered accordingly. The loss of officers from the Army of Portugal was almost triple that of their enemies, with twenty-eight killed and 158 wounded compared to nine killed and fifty-seven wounded on the Allied side.[277]

On both sides the field hospitals were filled to overflowing. Many had suffered horrific injuries in the close-quarter fighting in Fuentes and the vicious cavalry clashes on the plain. Wounds from splintered stone were commonplace after the long artillery bombardments on the village and many had lost limbs from the passage of round shot. Parquin had been shot in the mouth, but was relatively lucky compared to some of the wounded, recording with a cavalryman's nonchalance:

> *When the major learned that I had been wounded he was kind enough to send a message enquiring how I was. I took a pencil and wrote a note for him saying that my wound would not be serious, but to take six of my teeth seemed excessive on the part of the English.* [278]

Field hospitals had been established in many of the surrounding villages and Grattan visited one at Villa Formosa, where many of the 88th's casualties had been taken, where he witnessed terrible sights. Peering through a grating in the wall of the *quinta* (yard) of a large house he observed more than 200 men waiting to have limbs amputated, whilst more were constantly carried in:

> *...their limbs were swollen to an enormous size. Some were sitting upright against a wall, under the shade of a number of chestnut trees... The streams of gore, which had trickled down their cheeks, were quite hardened with the sun, and gave their faces a glazed and copper coloured hue; their eyes were sunk and*

fixed... they resembled more a group of bronze figures than anything human – there they sat, silent and statue-like, waiting for their turn...[279]

Watching and in one case assisting the surgeons conducting the dreadful work of sawing off shattered and infected arms and legs, Grattan saw the horrific human cost of the battle. Outside the hospital he found an enormous pit being filled with corpses, twelve to fifteen at a time, who were earthed over before more were flung in. Vultures were already beginning to hover, turning the pretty village of Villa Formosa into a ghastly charnel house.

Prisoners from both sides were marching disconsolately into captivity, Schaumann seeing many being led past him at his post near the bridge of Castello Bom. A French Chasseur Colonel complained to him that he had not been fed by his guards:

'Sacré dieu,' he cried, 'our men have as much meat, bread and wine as they can possibly carry in their haversacks; but you beggars have nothing.' I pointed out to him somewhat resentfully that, unlike the French army, we English did not live on spoil and plunder, and that an English soldier could not therefore be expected with his ration to entertain a chasseur colonel to a meal. 'March!' I added... In a great rage he drew his bearskin down over his eyes and walking angrily across the bridge, muttered... 'Bien, en avant donc!'[280]

Wellington had withdrawn the fatigued troops from the town and committed the Light Division to its defence. He half expected an attack the next day as the French had not moved, but this was not to be. Massena still felt obliged to carry out his Emperor's instructions if he could. He felt that another attempt to push Wellington off his ridge was likely to be futile, but the presence of the army might aid the withdrawal of Almeida's garrison. He offered 6,000 francs to any man brave enough to try to get through the Allied lines to the beleaguered town. Three men volunteered and under instructions to masquerade as deserters if caught, they were given tiny dispatches about two inches by one inch and told to swallow them in the event of capture. Two were taken but André Tillet of the 6th Light Infantry got through to General Brenier.[281]

Brenier's orders were to slight his defences and to attempt a retreat by way of Barba de Puerco. To confirm that he had received the message he was to fire four salvos from his heaviest guns at ten o'clock the following evening. This being done, Brenier spiked his guns and placed charges under some of the fortress defences with timed fuses. Massena's army remained before Fuentes for five days but on the 10th they withdrew and that evening they heard the muffled report of heavy explosions from the north-west. The Allies carried out a tentative, half-hearted pursuit, the vast superiority the French enjoyed in cavalry making them too strong a quarry for the Allies as they withdrew across the plains. Almeida's garrison had crept out in the night and, to the amazement of both armies, managed to evade the blockading troops and cross the border into Spain, a key bridge having been left unguarded. Wellington was livid:

> I was then quite sure of having Almeida; but I begin to be of the opinion... that there is nothing on earth so stupid as a gallant officer. They had about 13,000 men to watch 1,400; and in the night of the 10th, to the infinite surprise of the enemy, they allowed the garrison to slip through their fingers and to escape, after blowing up some of the works of the place! There they were all sleeping in their spurs even...[282]

Many, such as Grattan and Wheeler, believed that the troops blockading Almeida had been negligent and they were subjected to some ridicule in the Anglo-Portuguese Army. However, Wellington was so incensed that he ordered official inquiries to be made and Lieutenant Colonel Charles Bevan, whom he held accountable for the debacle, eventually committed suicide over his disgrace.

Though the battle had been a stalemate rather than a decisive Allied victory, the French had been thwarted in their aims, neither relieving the garrison nor defeating Wellington's army. Furthermore, during the three-day battle the French had lost an estimated 2,844 casualties compared to 1,800 sustained by the Allies. Both sides claimed the battle as a victory but Massena had lost his last chance of restoring his reputation. He gained some satisfaction from the fact that Almeida had been partially slighted, with the garrison escaping, and used these factors to claim a success, though his euphoria was short lived.

The performance of both Wellington and Massena at Fuentes de Oñoro remains contentious. Parquin believed that his commander-in-chief barely emerged from his command tent during the battle, despite the initial successes his army gained, citing the cavalry actions on 5 May in particular. In the eyes of many, Massena was a tired old man, well past his prime and living on his former glories. Parquin did not mourn his departure, commenting: '...the Duc de Raguse arrived to take over as the marshal commanding the army; everyone was glad of his arrival.'[283]

In contrast Thiebault believed that his former mentor had been beset by innumerable problems, especially amongst his own high command, and that it was remarkable that he had achieved as much as he did. Had it not been for the inertia on the French left during the outflanking manoeuvre, he could and should have beaten Wellington. He placed the blame squarely on the commander's subordinates:

> But it has to be said, painful and humiliating as the remembrance may be, that when victory was secure... when the men, elated in the highest degree... asked for nothing more than to come to close quarters... French generals refused to fight. As a result of that incredible disobedience, which Massena had no longer the energy required to punish by blowing out the brains of one of the generals who were defying his authority... our troops stood still with success before them and recoiled from victory...[284]

Thiebault also complained that Wellington had benefited from great good fortune which, considering his right wing was obliged to retire a full three miles, is a well founded observation. As for the poor performance of Massena's commanders, many historians agree with Thiebault's assessment. Fortescue claims that the French suspected that Wellington may have brought Beresford's army back along the frontier and that more troops lay concealed behind the crest than was actually the case. This could have been one reason for their hesitancy to assail the slope to the south of Fuentes and Fortescue believed that they should have pushed their advantage on the flank. The British cavalry should have been entirely destroyed in that sector considering how badly outnumbered they were and they were lucky not to have taken greater losses.[285] Napier agrees that Massena's initial success on 5 May should have brought greater benefits and that gross insubordination lay at the root of his failure. Junot had been inactive as his second-in-command, Reynier had dithered ineffectually in the north and several generals had refused to commit their troops to the fight. In summary he commented that for Massena: '...the machinery of battle would not work.'[286]

From the British point of view they had successfully blocked the French path to Almeida, stood firm during three days of fighting and obliged the enemy to retire into Spain. The escape of the garrison was an annoying factor but strategically irrelevant to the campaign. However, the battle had been very close and Ensign Mills wrote:

I have learnt one thing since I came to this country, and that is to know how easily England is duped; how completely ignorant she is of the truth of what is going on here... At Fuentes the French completely turned our right; Lord Wellington in his dispatch slightly notices it, and would lead you to think that the troops on the right were withdrawn rather than, as was the case, driven in; and then they give him what he himself never dreamt of claiming, a victory.[287]

Publicly, Wellington had indeed announced that Fuentes was an Allied victory, but could hardly have done otherwise during wartime. However, his private view differed and in later years he admitted that: '...he committed a fault by extending his right too much at Poco Velha; and that, if the French had taken advantage of it, there might have been bad consequences, but that they permitted him to recover himself and change his front before their face.'[288] Clearly he considered himself fortunate that the attack there had not been pressed home with more conviction, though it must be said that, when he became aware of his error, he retrieved the situation admirably.

If Wellington's right wing had disintegrated during its long retreat, the consequences for the army could have been catastrophic. In Thiebault's opinion, the Allies could then have been trapped with near impassable rivers on each side and the entire army captured or destroyed. This is backed by Wallace's comment before mounting a bayonet charge in Fuentes as being the lesser of two evils. Generally, Wellington's handling of his army at Fuentes de Oñoro had been masterful, but this one key error nearly cost him the battle. During his momentous career he rarely misjudged a situation, but this must stand as one of his worst mistakes. He owed his deliverance to his own self-confidence, well-trained officers, disciplined troops and the French failure to exploit their advantage.

Wellington never sent a victory dispatch to London, which traditionally entailed a promotion for the aide de camp chosen to bear it. He did not count the battle among his victories, though it could hardly be said that he lost the action. Four years later he would comment on how close a victory Waterloo had been, but in comparison his monumental struggle against Napoleon never witnessed the near collapse of his army's flank. He was honest enough to concede how near he had come to defeat, writing two weeks after the battle:

Lord Liverpool was quite right not to move thanks for the battle of Fuentes, though it was the most difficult one I was ever concerned in, and against the greatest odds... If Boney had been there, we should have been beaten.[289]

Chapter 11

The End of the Old Fox

On 10 May in Ciudad Rodrigo, General Foy delivered two letters to Massena from Marshal Berthier conveying the Emperor's displeasure. The first contained a tirade of criticism for his conduct during the campaign. Considering the old enmity that existed between them, writing these reprimands on the Emperor's behalf must have been satisfying for the resentful Berthier. A great deal of the dispatch was unfair and took no account of the incredible difficulties Massena had faced. For example:

> Old soldiers are grieved to see such a fine army fleeing from 25,000 British, and manoeuvring to evacuate the country without the honour of a battle. Prince, the Emperor charges me to inform you that he expected more from your energy, and from the opinion he had formed of you as the result of the glorious episodes in which you have so frequently taken part.[290]

Of course, Massena had brought the Allies to battle while this dispatch was in transit, but it would not be enough to save him from disgrace. Just as he had claimed with Pelet, Napoleon refused to consider the Portuguese soldiers and irregulars in his calculations, in complete ignorance of how effective they had become. The second letter informed Massena of his dismissal and replacement with Marshal Marmont, Duke of Ragusa. It was a blunt and unnecessary rebuke and, to add insult to injury, he was ordered to hand over the majority of his staff to his successor and return to Paris immediately.

Massena did not linger in Ciudad Rodrigo but, after a stormy encounter with Foy, whom he accused of turning the Emperor against him, left for France the next day. Napoleon was furious over the failures in Portugal and the ambiguous results of Fuentes de Oñoro failed to placate him. After his arrival in Paris, Massena was kept waiting for weeks before an audience with the Emperor was granted, only to be greeted with the taunt: *'Eh bien! Prince d'Essling, vous n'êtes donc plus Massena!'*[291] He was then subjected to one of Napoleon's tantrums, which included a string of accusations and taunts about missed opportunities in the Peninsula. Under similar circumstances, many French officers had been reduced to tears when confronted by the engraged Corsican after letting him down, but Massena dispassionately stood his ground in near silence. Occasionally he would challenge the wild charges made against him, but Napoleon rarely paused for breath on such occasions and he would take no excuse. In the final analysis Massena had failed.

Massena's involvement in the Peninsular War had led to shame and disgrace; in contrast Wellington's fortunes would go on from strength to strength during the conflict. However, in the immediate aftermath of Fuentes he received bad news from the south. Marshal Soult had attempted to relieve Badajoz and Beresford had, according to instructions, opposed his march towards the city. The resulting battle at Albuera on 16 May had been extremely bloody with Beresford coming close to seeing his right flank destroyed in an error that bore an eerie similarity to Wellington's mistake at Fuentes. Beresford was on the verge of ordering a retreat, but was saved by his subordinates when, without orders, generals Lowry Cole and Sir Henry Hardinge brought up 4,000 men of the 4th Division to support the threatened flank. The battle had been a slaughterhouse, with 6,000 Allied casualties compared to 8,000 French. Only Soult's decision to retire gave the British the opportunity to claim a victory in this controversial action.

Reading Beresford's honest and gloomy report on Albuera, Wellington snapped to the staff officer who brought it: 'This won't do. Write me down a victory.'[292] News of a near defeat would make dismal reading in London and, since the Government was struggling to ensure that Parliament persevered with the long and unpopular war, its effect could be devastating. Though Wellington did not doctor the dispatch as much as his French counterparts would have done, he nevertheless played down Allied losses and how close Beresford had come to defeat. It may have been unethical, but the fate of the Peninsula and Europe still lay in the balance and he justified his actions by saying: 'they would have written a whining report upon it, which would have driven the people in England mad. However, I prevented that.'[293] Harking back over that year's events, *The Annual Register* gave a fairer summary:

> *That the action of Albuera was really a victory on the part of the allies, the result rendered undeniable, for the French general was completely foiled in his attempt, and was obliged to quit the purpose he had in view. It was, however, so dearly purchased, that in a sober estimate the day will perhaps be reckoned (more)*

among the disastrous than the triumphant ones, for the loss
incurred seems to have exerted a serious influence on subsequent
transactions.[294]

While 1811 also saw the British fail to take Badajoz and retire across
the border, it proved a watershed for the entire conflict. Never again
would Wellington be compelled to retreat as far as Lisbon, and
Massena's invasion was the last major French offensive to come so close
to success. Early the following year Wellington took Ciudad Rodrigo
and, turning south, invested and captured Badajoz by April. The fall of
the Spanish frontier fortresses secured Portugal and on 22 July
Wellington won a remarkable victory at Salamanca. Prior to this the
French had formed the inaccurate view that Wellington was dangerous
only as a defensive general and his attack and the conclusive defeat of
Marmont's army came as an unpleasant surprise. Both the Marshal and
his second in command General Bonet were seriously wounded in a
battle that saw the French lose 14,000 casualties. Only a staunch
rearguard action by General Foy allowed the French to retreat without
suffering greater losses and the defeat broke their hold over northern
and central Spain.

On 13 August 1813 Wellington entered Madrid for the first time, but
was forced to relinquish the city when the French renewed the
offensive. However, the tide had irretrievably turned in the Peninsula;
Napoleon's disastrous invasion of Russia crippled the French Army and
reduced the chance of sufficient reinforcements being made available
for Spain. On 12 June 1813 Wellington inflicted a crushing defeat on
the French at Vitoria, where King Joseph was nearly taken in the rout
that followed and a vast amount of loot, acquired from all quarters of
the Peninsula, was captured in the French baggage. French military
power was broken in the region after Vitoria and the fall of San
Sebastian on 27 June was the last major obstacle to ousting the French
from Spain.

From 25 July to 2 August Marshal Soult mounted a desperate
offensive over the Pyrenees to try to restore the situation, but this was
swiftly forced back. France itself was now under threat and, having
driven the invaders from the Peninsula, Wellington invaded France in
1813 as the combined might of Europe converged on Napoleon's
capital. His offensive culminated in the Battle of Toulouse on 10 April,
when the French capitulated after Napoleon's first abdication.

During this time Massena had languished in semi-retirement as
Napoleon mounted one of the greatest invasions the world had yet seen

against Russia. Portugal's resistance to his Continental System was insignificant compared to the increasing reluctance of Tsar Alexander to conform to demands that were so damaging to the Russian economy. Determined to bring the Russians to a decisive battle, Napoleon pursued them further and further into the hinterland in a campaign that surpassed even the Peninsula for its horrific conditions and the ferocious manner in which it was fought.

Massena was deliberately overlooked when the high command was picked for the Russian venture. Beset by ill health and premature old age, he was likely to have turned down any command offered. The years had given him ample reason to dislike Bonaparte and, remembering his revolutionary ideals, he loathed his increasingly autocratic style. When walking with a friend in the grounds of his house he pointed out that the stream running over his land flowed down towards Malmaison, one of Napoleon's favourite retreats. 'I piss on him when I want to,'[295] he casually remarked. Yet, with Wellington's increasing success in Spain, France required his services and he was offered command of the Army of Portugal once again by the Regency Council governing in Napoleon's absence. However, during the journey southwards he fell ill at Bayonne on 26 August. Massena had never fully recovered his health after years of hard campaigning and, with a chronic stomach inflammation, was forced to relinquish the command.[296]

Napoleon had lost thousands of men in his disastrous invasion of Russia. Even the incredible slaughter at the Battle of Borodino and the fall of Moscow failed to force the Tsar to negotiate and the retreat that followed witnessed the virtual destruction of Napoleon's *Grande Armée*. Though his political and military positions were desperate, the Emperor still denied Massena a corps command but appointed him Military Governor of the 8th Military District at Toulon. This was an important position, as Toulon was crucial to France as the main naval base for the Mediterranean. Massena was responsible for the protection of a long stretch of coastline and commanded the *Garde Nationale*.

The years 1813–1814 proved to be the swansong of the French Empire. Massive armies were concentrated against the French and, one by one, Napoleon's allies began to desert him. For years he had led France to victory, humbling some of the greatest powers in Europe, but now everyone urged him to make peace. His marshals, with an average age of forty-nine, were tired of war and wished to enjoy the estates and privileges that Napoleon had bestowed upon them rather than risk them in further conflict. The Allies were offering generous terms, allowing Napoleon to retain power if he conceded that France would return to its former borders, but the Emperor was intractable. Despite the odds, he set out in pursuit of a great victory that he hoped would restore France's position as the greatest power in Europe. He had humbled the Continental armies before and believed he could do so again.

While Napoleon fought for the survival of the Empire, Massena quietly pursued the demands of his governorship. Toulon was a great port but the English still dominated the oceans and with news of the loss of French ships in the region, Massena wrote to the Emperor, fearful of an attempt on the city.[297] Napoleon replied that a British landing was more likely at Genoa but in fact the Allies saw little need to open another front in the war since the French were being forced out of the German states and Wellington was manoeuvring to cross the Pyrenees.

The Battle of Leipzig shattered Napoleon's attempt to confine the fighting to Germany. Renowned as 'The Battle of the Nations,' it was the largest battle of the era. Between 177,000 and 195,000 French troops and their allies were ranged against as many as 365,000 Allied troops by the end of the confrontation. Bernadotte, a one time Marshal of the Empire and now Crown Prince of Sweden, changed sides, bringing Swedish forces against Napoleon to combine with the might of Russia and Prussia. Hemmed in, the French lost 73,000 casualties during a three-day battle while the Allies lost 54,000. Though coming close to victory, Napoleon was eventually forced to retreat over the River Elster. He lost 20,000 men in the city of Leipzig when a bridge was destroyed prematurely and the rearguard was stranded. Prince Poniatowski, a recently appointed Marshal, was drowned trying to swim the river and Generals Lauriston and Reynier were captured along with many others.

As the Allies invaded France, Napoleon still refused to negotiate and, though he conducted a brilliant campaign, winning a string of minor victories, defeat became inevitable. Many troops had been left in Germany garrisoning fortresses and cities now under siege, which he sorely needed, and he could no longer rely on his marshals. Following the battle of Laon on 9 March, Marmont opened independent negotiations with the Allies that eventually led to the surrender of Paris, in which Joseph Bonaparte played a part. Marshal Murat tried and failed to make a secret deal to retain his kingdom of Naples in return for deserting the Emperor. On 4 April the marshals rebelled en masse. Further slaughter was futile, they argued, and on 6 April 1814

Napoleon was persuaded to yield to the inevitable at Fontainebleau.

The Emperor abdicated in favour of his infant son, but a secret agreement had been reached between Tsar Alexander and Talleyrand for the restoration of the Bourbon monarchy. On 26 April the Comte de Provence landed at Calais and was proclaimed Louis XVIII. Napoleon travelled into exile on the Isle of Elba in the Mediterranean. Massena reluctantly gave his allegiance to the king. As a republican he hated the idea of a return to the monarchy, although he had always entertained misgivings regarding Napoleon's autocratic form of government. He was not alone in this – nearly all of the marshals followed suit. Their political views varied enormously but in the end the wish to retain money, status and power overcame any reservations they entertained. Louis was glad to receive Massena's fealty and awarded him the Grand Cross of the Order of Saint Louis. He also wished to make him a peer, but now the borders of France had been redrawn once more he was unable to do so, for Massena had lost his French citizenship. His native Piedmont had been returned to the Kingdom of Sardinia. The problem was resolved by an Act of Naturalisation on 20 January 1815, which saw Massena become a Peer of France.[298]

Massena retained his position as a Military Governor under the Bourbons as the country adjusted to a short period of peace after over twenty years of almost continuous war. Wellington had been recalled to London after the fall of Toulouse and received the congratulations of the Regent and the Government. In the House of Lords he was granted the unique privilege of having five plaudits of nobility read out for him in a single day, conferring the titles between Baron and Duke. He was then sent to Paris as the British Ambassador to the Court of the Tuileries. Following the political maelstrom in the wake of the Napoleonic wars, the Congress of Vienna was to be convened with the intention of planning Europe's future and he was to play a role. There he encountered an old adversary:

> I knew Massena afterwards well in Paris; and met him first at a dinner at Marshal Soult's, who was then Minister of War... Massena was much excited at first seeing me, made a great noise, and greeted me very cordially. 'Ah, Monsieur le Maréchal, que vous m'avez fait passer des mauvais moments!' And he declared to me that I had not left him one black hair on his body; he had turned grey, he said, all over. I answered that I thought we had been pretty even – things nearly balanced between us. 'No,' he said, 'how near you were taking me two or three times!' – which I was.[299]

It is interesting that the two former opponents should have got on so well, particularly as many of Napoleon's marshals shunned Wellington when they met him through resentment of his victories over them. Perhaps it testifies to the pair's devotion to their craft and mutual professional respect, whereas many of the marshals saw soldiering as a means to an end. Massena lacked the vanity of his fellows and, clearly delighted to meet a man whose talents had finally surpassed his own, seemed to bear no grudges. Rarely generous with praise, Wellington respected Massena enormously and complimented him in turn when they discussed the Lines of Torres Vedras: 'My Lord, you owe me a dinner – for you made me positively starve.' Wellington laughed. 'You should give it to me, Marshal, for you prevented me from sleeping.'[300] It was the first of several conversations between them in which they discussed each other's strategies and mused over the fortunes of war during the time when they had been adversaries. Criticised, perhaps unfairly, for his supercilious attitude towards the ranks and the 'lower orders', here was Wellington happily discussing high concept strategy with a former sergeant who had risen through the ranks. The fact that both had fought and overcome similar trials appeared to break the social and national barriers between them. It resembled a meeting between old comrades rather than a confrontation between former enemies.

France was unhappy under the Bourbon restoration and even as a convinced Royalist, Wellington looked disdainfully upon the inept and overindulgent Louis XVIII. By anyone's reckoning, he was a poor substitute for the man who had dominated the Continent. As the national representatives in Vienna debated their plans to restore the balance of European power, a bombshell disrupted their plans. Napoleon Bonaparte escaped from exile on Elba and landed between Antibes and Caen on 1 March 1815. After only a year of Bourbon misrule he received an ecstatic welcome from the French population as he marched with a tiny force inland. The coastline where he landed was under Massena's jurisdiction but, considering their recent past, he headed northwards rather than entering Marseilles or Toulon and risk trusting him. He later recalled:

> I heard later that the latter wept with joy on hearing of my return, but he told my emissary that the attitude of Marseilles was so hostile that he would have to arrest him to save him from the fury of the mob... although Massena was attached to his old colours, under which he had fought for more than twenty-five years, he would not act rashly.[301]

Napoleon was a shrewd judge of men. Whilst contemptuous of the Bourbons, Massena regarded the return of his former master with some trepidation following their differences and, although he had implemented many Republican policies, an Emperor was still a dictator. Massena went through the motions of sending men against the new threat and publicly denounced him to his troops, though without great enthusiasm. Napoleon's supporters rallied about him and by the time he entered Paris Louis XVIII had fled and he was restored to power on a wave of public support.

Massena felt that he had honoured his new oath to the monarchy but, now that the Bourbons had abandoned France, he was no longer bound by any obligation. When edicts arrived from the Emperor he obeyed them without hesitation, endeavouring to win over support in the Midi region despite its reputation as Royalist country. Nevertheless, the Emperor, worried about the Var frontier region in his district, decided that he needed a more reliable guardian and appointed Marshal Brune in Massena's stead. Massena was recalled to Paris, where Napoleon teased him about his conflict of loyalties:

'Well, Massena, so you were going to serve against me…'

'Sire,' replied Massena, 'You know quite well that my flag has always been that of my country. If I was mistaken, it was against my wish.'

'Against your wish! Come, come! You would have thrown me back into the sea if I had given you time to collect your troops.'

'Certainly, Sire, so long as I believed that you were not recalled to France by the majority of Frenchmen.'[302]

Napoleon had given Massena little cause for personal loyalty over the years and must have realised that his return had placed him in a difficult position. Whilst many of his former marshals gave evasive replies to similar questioning, Massena's honest response must have been refreshing to a ruler well versed in cynical, self-serving politics. He was not vindictive and indeed offered him an active command in his forthcoming campaign with Europe forming a new coalition against him. However, pleading ill health, Massena refused to accept the appointment and once again the Emperor marched without him. During the campaign of the Hundred Days, which culminated in the Battle of Waterloo, he was also offered the Governorship of Metz, which included the 3rd and 4th Military Districts, but again felt unable to assume the position with his failing constitution.

After Napoleon's final defeat, a provisional government was formed and, with the enemy advancing on the capital, Massena was appointed commander-in-chief of the National Guard in Paris. As the Allies approached, he was present at the council of war that debated whether to resist or treat with the enemy. For once, Massena urged peace during the stormy session that followed. The line of the River Seine was defensible but Paris would be subject to a ruinous bombardment, he argued. In any case, following the Emperor's second abdication, Frenchmen had little cause to fight. The anti-war faction gained the ascendancy and the French Army withdrew over the Loire to allow the Allies to enter the city as negotiations took place. As governor of Paris, Massena performed the difficult task of calming the excited population in a city flooded with Bonapartists, deserters and malcontents. When Louis XVIII entered the capital accompanied by Allied forces there were no major incidents, testifying to Massena's efficiency in the task.

In contrast to the Emperor, the Bourbons wished to punish those who had been disloyal and immediately set about hunting them down, despite Allied pleas for restraint. Hundreds were arrested, imprisoned or executed. One of the most notorious cases was that of Marshal Ney who, though sent to capture the 'Corsican Tyrant,' had immediately switched allegiance and fought for Napoleon at Waterloo. Charged with treachery in the presence of the enemy, Massena was asked to sit on the courts martial that would try him along with Augereau, Mortier and Moncey. As president of the courts martial, Moncey refused to sit in judgement on his former comrade-in-arms and was replaced by Marshal Jourdan. Massena also wrote to the Minister for War twice asking to be excluded, citing both ill health and bias towards the accused.[303] Nevertheless, he was overruled.

However, Ney solved Massena's dilemma by insisting on a trial by his fellow lords in the Chamber of Peers and the army gladly passed on the responsibility. This was a bad move on Ney's part since the army was likely to have absolved him on the grounds that the Allies had issued an amnesty for those who had fought under Napoleon. The Chamber condemned Ney to death and he was executed on 7 December in the Luxembourg Gardens. He had given Massena ample cause for animosity during their frequent and acrimonious disagreements in the Peninsula, but he spurned a chance for revenge and was not among his jurors. After all, no one was more aware of the crisis of allegiance that the Emperor's return had caused and to hide behind the façade of a show trial was not the soldier's way to settle a difference.

Shortly afterwards, Massena resumed his post as Governor of the 8th

Military District but his past came back to haunt him. Louis XVIII was determined to avert any repetition of 1815 and wished to remove all those from office whose loyalty was suspect. Many of those who had rallied to Napoleon were exiled or punished, especially amongst the army. On 1 January 1816 Massena fell victim to this purge when he received an accusatory message on behalf of the king:

> The various letters written by Your Excellency on 3 March to the Minister of War and on 13 April to the Prince of Eckmuhl have furnished proof of the negligence with which Your Excellency received the first reports of Bonaparte's landing, and the activity which you subsequently displayed in placing under his orders the Military District, the government of which the King had confided to you.[304]

The letter ended with his dismissal from his command and the removal of all privileges, including pensions and annuities. This was grossly unfair, as he had been unaware that the Emperor himself had landed for two days and Paris was nearly five hundred miles from Marseilles, making the delivery of a swift warning unlikely. Although he had acted with some duplicity, he had stayed loyal to the monarchy until Louis himself had left the country, which left him no choice. It was a spiteful act by a regime that was not destined to last.

Yet Massena was not sent into exile and could finally return to his estates and enjoy his retirement. After years of soldiering in the French army he was hardly penniless and still possessed a considerable fortune amounting to around forty million francs, the origins of which were somewhat obscure. However, the rigours of his hard life were catching up with him and he died on 4 April 1817, only one month short of his fifty-ninth birthday. Despite his philandering, his wife Rosalie had remained loyal and was present at Père Lachaise Cemetery, where Massena was buried with full military honours, ten marshals of France attending the funeral. The headstone read simply MASSENA, with the words Rivoli, Zürich, Génes and Essling underneath.

Many in France mourned his passing, and the English press recorded the death of their former enemy in a host of obituaries. The *Gentleman's Magazine* recalled his sobriquet 'the favourite child of victory' and in a list of his achievements expounded on what was perhaps his greatest victory: '...that memorable campaign of Switzerland, which the battle of Zurich rendered so decisive and so glorious: 70,000 prisoners were the fruits of this campaign, where he had to contend against two great captains, Prince Charles and Marshal

Suwarroff.'[305] His wife, two sons and a daughter survived him. Even though his final campaign was fought against Britain's foremost general, the journal conceded that in the Peninsula he: '...displayed anew the firmness of his character in the midst of difficulties of all kinds with which he was surrounded and which he had to surmount.' [306] This was a generous tribute coming from his former enemies.

Whilst mourned by his contemporaries, he remained a mysterious and enigmatic figure to many. Having come to know the marshal well in Spain, Madame Junot believed that most people only knew him by his reputation as a skilled strategist and tactician, along with his reputed vices for womanising and embezzlement:

Massena had as much regard for me as I believe he could have for anyone who could be of no service to him. He used often to come and chat with me in the morning, and these visits were very agreeable to me, as they afforded me some insight into the character of a man who seems to have been but imperfectly known to many of his biographers.[307]

The trouble with assessing Massena's character is that, being no lover of the written word, he left no memoirs and the majority of his family papers are of a functional nature. This was the case with many military men, though some of his contemporaries left reams of paperwork, and historians are fortunate in the memoirs of two of his aides, Marbot and Thiebault, both of whom were accomplished diarists.

Most historians, while acknowledging his undoubted military talent, bemoaned his vices and to some extent exaggerated them. Oman was among them, remarking: 'Massena was hard, suspicious, and revengeful; an intriguer to the finger-tips, he was always prone to suppose that others were intriguing against himself.' [308] This assessment seems unjust. In addition to Massena's single, disastrous foray into politics, he was far from diplomatic in military circles either. Whilst capable of great cunning on the battlefield, his dealings with subordinates in the Peninsula imply that he underestimated the effects of provoking them and he failed to placate them or outmanoeuvre them, being forced to endure their obstinacy and insubordination. Far from being vengeful, he went to great lengths to disassociate himself from Ney's trial when many would have leapt at the opportunity to avenge the harm that his old rival had done to him.

Massena had laboured long in the service of France and, though he had a weakness for money and women, had triumphed on many battlefields. During his final exile on the island of Saint Helena in the Atlantic, the former Emperor mused over his misfortunes and reminisced over his former glories to an enthralled audience. The cult of Napoleon was far from diminished and, dictating to his entourage, he embellished his legend, belittling his own failings and blaming others for his downfall. Whilst not bitter about Massena's role in his saga, he rarely mentioned his old rival and when he did so was rarely inclined to be generous:

> Asked by Dr O'Meara to say who was the ablest of his generals, Napoleon replied: 'That is difficult to say, but it seems to me it may have been Suchet; once it was Massena, but eventually one had to consider him as virtually dead; Suchet, Clausel and Gérard were the best French generals in my opinion.'[309]

Massena had fought dozens of successful actions in Italy, notably at Lodi and Arcola, and was second only to Bonaparte as a commander at this time. Later, with the Austrians and Russians driving all before them, he saved the Republic at Zurich and resisted long enough at Genoa to allow Napoleon to win his victory at Marengo. Not only did Napoleon display little gratitude for either feat, but he was also inclined to downplay their relevance, especially in the case of Genoa. On the Danube Massena's stubborn defence of Aspern village enabled the Emperor to claw his way back from the brink of defeat and his actions at Wagram had contributed to Napoleon's last decisive victory. Though it was true that his performance in Portugal had not been of this calibre, he was beset by a host of problems and received little help from the over mighty subordinates foisted upon him by his master. At Fuentes he had broken and driven in the Allied flank, a reverse far greater than anything Wellington suffered at Waterloo. Ironically, during a conversation with Croker, his old enemy gave a fairer assessment:

> 'You thought Massena their meilleure tête militaire?'

> 'Yes I did. While he was opposed to me I never could make an attempt on his line but I was sure to find him in force opposite to me. I should say, as far as my own experience goes, that he was their best.'[310]

Wellington and Napoleon were the greatest generals of their time, yet they never bestowed praise lightly. For Napoleon, Massena was only as good as his last success and his remarks seem churlish and ungrateful. However, his rival's honest tribute was a fitting epitaph for the man who had nearly beaten Wellington.

Chapter 12
Touring the Peninsula

Visiting the Iberian Peninsula is fundamental for anyone wishing to gain an insight into the nature of the Peninsular War. It is particularly useful since the conflict was dominated by the constraints of geography and climate, which can only be appreciated in the region itself. Though road atlases and battlefield maps are available, Ordnance Survey maps are very hard to obtain due to lack of demand and security regulations for both countries, so it is wise to plan a trip bearing this in mind. A vehicle is necessary for a tour of this kind and it is advisable to buy plentiful drinking water due to the risk of dehydration in such a hot climate. Sensible headgear and skin protection is also important. The trip recounted below traced a circuitous route of around 500 miles starting from Lisbon, travelling south-west into Spain, following the border to Ciudad Rodrigo and returning to Lisbon tracing the approximate path of Massena's invasion. It took a week and, though it covers the main sites of interest, there are many more locations that would have been desirable to visit. For example, the battlefields of Sabugal and Vimeiro had to be left out because of time limits. A close watch on the time should be maintained if you wish to make your hotel before nightfall and allow enough time to locate and examine the sites.

LISBON – PORTUGAL
Lisbon is a large city so it is essential to have a street guide, especially with its occasionally confusing one-way system. In contrast to many of the locations on this tour, the traffic is always intense and it is advisable to start early to avoid congestion. Finding a hotel that provides parking is recommended, as most streets are constantly double-parked. Consequently, vans and lorries frequently stop to unload in the middle of the road and drivers should proceed carefully, as minor accidents are commonplace. Most of the buildings are modern, though neglected and derelict structures are common. This, along with the rubbish often piled on the pavements, recalls the experiences of Private Wheeler and others in this city during the nineteenth century. However, people are usually friendly and helpful. A visit to the castle is highly recommended, with its Napoleonic exhibits along with the Porto (fortified wine), which is usually excellent.

ELVAS – PORTUGAL. BADAJOZ AND ALBUERA – SPAIN

It is best to drive straight down to the coast and follow the River Tejo (referred to as the Tagus in nineteenth-century accounts) to Lisbon's large suspension road bridge. The road across the bridge immediately runs into the A2-IP7 motorway, which leads straight to Elvas. Although a string of redoubts was built from Almada to the Costa da Caparica to guard the southern approaches, nothing remains of them as the area is almost entirely built over. The estuary narrows at this point, but it would still have been too wide an obstacle for the French to cross without serious naval support, though they could have mounted a long-range bombardment of Lisbon's docks from this location.

The motorway continues past Setúbal and Évora and changes name several times as it progresses. By the time it reaches the fortress town of Elvas it has become the A6-IP7 E90. Choose any of junctions 9 to 12 to leave the motorway and drive down to Elvas. Elvas is largely unspoilt and its bastions and gatehouse are built on an impressive scale. Some of the surrounding hills show signs of supporting fortifications, with straight lines and levelled areas at their summits, though most have a few modern houses built upon them. The town is extremely photogenic, although, from a historian's point of view, it is disappointing that no major incidents occurred here during the Peninsular War, as it was never besieged.

Rejoining the motorway, the drive into Spain towards Badajoz, constructed to counter Elvas, is easier now there are no longer customs controls to contend with. Badajoz is the ideal place for booking the second hotel on this trip, but if you wish to visit the battlefield of Albuera it is advisable to drive straight through and leave sightseeing until your return if you plan to do it in a day.

The town of La Albuera is south-east of Badajoz and simple to find by following the N432 out of the city. There are few identifying features for this battlefield and it is intriguing to speculate about why Beresford chose to fight in this area. There is a small monument to the slain that is worth a visit. The area itself is fairly open, with sloping ground rather than clearly defined hills and ridges, and it is easy to see why the French superiority in cavalry was such an advantage during this controversial action. There are two nearly identical monuments in the village of La Albuera at either end of the main street. Both have colour depictions of Spanish, Portuguese, British and French soldiers and they are worth stopping for. Interestingly, they both include a quotation from Lord Byron's poem about Albuera in each relevant language.

Retracing the route back to Badajoz it is possible to undertake a brief inspection of its defences, though you have to be economical with the time in Elvas and Albuera in order to do so in just one day. Entering the old city, the best course is to walk the entire circumference of the defences, starting at the castle. Badajoz was built on a vast scale, but the fortifications are neither as complete nor as photogenic as its rival across the border. The city is expanding and many structures have been demolished for improved road access, though all of the main bastions remain. The castle walls are largely intact and efforts are being made to reconstruct various areas on the town side of the structure. The walls Picton's men attempted to scale with ladders in the siege of 1812 are still intact and well preserved. Badajoz was besieged several times during the war and its possession was considered vital strategically. Sadly it is the least photogenic of the border fortresses due to modern development.

FUENTES DE OÑORO AND
CIUDAD RODRIGO – SPAIN

As a general rule, Spain is far better for road signs than Portugal, although you have to keep your wits about you as you may get only a single warning for some exits. Follow the EX100 out of Badajoz and, changing to the N630, skirt around Cáceres heading north. There are several medieval castles on the route to Ciudad Rodrigo, but it is inadvisable to stop unless you have planned for this in your itinerary. It is important to be highly selective with so many interesting sites separated by considerable distances. Just after the River Tajo and the major lake it flows into, turn on to the EX109 going past Coria and Moraleja. Heading towards Ciudad Rodrigo, the road changes into the CL526 and the town should be found with no difficulty. Depending on time constraints it may be wise to visit Fuentes de Oñoro before Ciudad Rodrigo. Again the fortress town is ideally placed for booking a hotel.

Be warned that there are two places called Fuentes de Oñoro, the old village being the one of historical interest. They are separated by about half a mile. Driving along the N620 E80 you will see the old village on your left before entering into the new village which is right on the Portuguese border. There is a turning into the old village on a bend, which will save enormous time but is not signposted and is consequently easy to miss. It may be difficult to turn into considering the speed and level of traffic here. If you fail to see this turning, the new village centre is easy to find, being on the main road and surrounded by a cluster of souvenir shops. It is just before the old border station, which is now inactive. It is possible to turn left and then proceed parallel with the route you came along and find the village by instinct using country lanes. Alternatively, you can retrace your route and search for the turning again.

The streets of old Fuentes are very narrow and winding, making it easy to see how French units strayed and found themselves trapped in dead ends during the bitter street fighting. Depending on the season, the stream of Dos Casas may well be completely dry, except for the odd stagnant pool here and there. The streambed makes a useful reference point and it can be followed to the old footbridge, which marks the centre and the point of many of the French attacks. The road here winds uphill towards the church, which approximately marks the centre of the British line that the French came so near to breaking. The churchyard no longer exists and there is a newer graveyard on the east bank of the Dos Casas, where the French would have deployed. A small memorial stands near the church and just above this location is the vantage point that Wellington used as a command post for much of the battle.

Retracing the route back to Ciudad Rodrigo, the city is impressive from a distance. Ciudad is smaller than Badajoz, but saw many sieges, its possession being vital for the French invasion of Portugal and the later British incursion into Spain. The glacis and the double lines of ditches still exist virtually unchanged and it is possible to walk the entire circuit of the walls in an hour or two. The bastions are in better condition than those at Badajoz and are constructed using better quality stone. The cathedral tower is a dominant feature and still bears the marks of cannon fire. Though the breaches that the British pounded into the defences in 1812 were repaired by Wellington, a plaque marks the approximate spot where General Craufurd was killed in the storming and can be found on the reverse side of the fortress wall near the cathedral. The bridge across the River Agueda still exists and the city is very beautiful, making it easy to see why Ciudad Rodrigo attracts so many tourists. The Hotel Paradores in the castle itself is recommended both for its facilities and the marvellous view over the river and city. Of all the frontier fortresses, Ciudad Rodrigo is the most impressive visually and is very photogenic. Try to spend a second day here if possible.

OUTLYING VILLAGES FOR FUENTES – SPAIN AND PORTUGAL, ALMEIDA – PORTUGAL

Driving back through Fuentes de Oñoro you can visit the villages of Poço Velho and Nave de Haver on the British right flank. Follow the N332 south along the border and though Nave de Haver appears in road atlases, Poço Velho is too small for most maps. Luckily both are well signposted and easy to find. The battle was very much a border incident and this area of the field is mostly in Portugal. The small church in Poço Velho is worth a photograph, along with the general lie of the land around both villages, but the houses are fairly modern and little exists from the time of the battle. It is easy to see how the French superiority in cavalry proved so decisive on this flank due to the open nature of the landscape here. A visit to Freneda, which marks the furthest extent of the British withdrawal, is worthwhile since an old house next to the church is where Wellington reputedly stayed before the battle. There is a plaque on the wall proclaiming this fact. The land also changes along the route of the British retreat. There are plenty of rocky outcrops where riflemen stationed themselves during the fighting withdrawal and the land becomes progressively more rugged, beginning to slope upwards. The French cavalry would still have been able to press the retreat, but their use would not have been quite so effective here and you can easily understand why they kept pausing to wait for infantry support.

Turning back, head north along the N332 and drive directly to the old fortress town of Almeida. Finding the town should be no problem, but although the town is built on a slight eminence, it is set far lower down than the other fortresses. This was by design, since its lower silhouette presented a harder target to besieging artillery. The defences are virtually complete and their appearance benefits from the red and yellow lichen on the dressed stonework. The gateways are impressive and the main entrance contains the local tourist office, which provides good maps of the fortress. It is the smallest of the frontier strongholds and walking the entire circumference of the structure should not take much more than an hour. The ruins of the castle near where the disaster occurred in 1810 are easily found and testify to the power of the monstrous explosion.

Take the N340 out of Almeida towards the Côa, where Craufurd fought his controversial action against Ney's vanguard. A modern road bridge now spans the gorge, but fortunately the Portuguese road builders decided to retain the old bridge underneath the structure.

However, the positioning of the new bridge means that from most angles the old bridge cannot be seen from the road. It is possible to park on the road above and walk down to the river. Examining the Côa at this point you realise how difficult an obstacle it presented to an army, making possession of this bridge particularly vital. The old bridge has a very pleasant aspect, quite out of keeping with the terrible slaughter that took place around it. A stone monument and a cross stand in the centre of the bridge and on the western bank. Its three-point span would have handicapped a direct charge across it and it is easy to imagine British and Portuguese sharpshooters firing down from the steep banks of the gorge above it.

Continuing on into central Portugal, the journey to Coimbra is relatively easy along the N324 and then the A25-IP5. Joining the E80, which skirts around Guarda, be aware that you may only get one warning for motorway exits and that you are suddenly offered a choice between a northern and southern route. The northern route is the one required for Busaço and Coimbra. Depending on how much time you have spent touring the sites it is probably best to leave an examination of the battlefield until the next day.

BUSAÇO – PORTUGAL

If approaching the battlefield from Coimbra, take the IC2 and then the N1 northwards. You need to drive through the park and the grounds of the Busaço Palace Hotel in order to get to the battlefield, and the museum here is excellent. The Portuguese Army runs this museum and many of the exhibits were picked up from the battlefield itself. A small but useful map of Busaço Ridge is provided on their leaflets. The long ridge, though layered, is incredibly steep and this cannot be truly appreciated until you actually stand on the ground itself. Unfortunately, the area is now heavily wooded, which was not the case in 1810, and this obscures much of the field. Nevertheless, it is impossible not to marvel at the courage and determination of the Frenchmen who toiled up the slopes to face a prepared enemy. Likewise, it is difficult to understand why Massena failed to try a flanking move as soon as he saw this formidable natural obstacle in his path.

The commemorative obelisk is easy to find, signposts directing you straight from the museum. It is an impressive monument to the fallen and the posts of the encircling fence are in fact small cannon barrels sunk into the ground. Behind the obelisk the convent wall that was incorporated into the Allied defence still exists, though you may encounter some trouble finding Wellington's command post without the museum leaflet. This lies at the end of a very narrow forest track only just wide enough for a vehicle. It is worth the effort for the stone plaque, but forestry almost completely conceals the view Wellington would have had from this point.

Heading downhill from the obelisk, Craufurd's command post near the village of Sula can be viewed from the road by the old windmill marking the spot. The cluster of rocks that Craufurd stationed himself behind is marked with a plaque and is slightly more photogenic than Wellington's command post, since this place is not so heavily wooded. Sadly the road that led to the point of Reynier's attack no longer exists and extensive woods and lack of footpaths suggest that it would be difficult to pinpoint accurately and not worth the effort to seek out. However, it is worth driving into the valley to observe the ridge from the road where Ney deployed his VI Corps. The area where VI Corps attacked is obvious, but determining the point of Reynier's assault is more of a challenge.

Returning to Coimbra, the next destination is the battlefield of Roliça, one of Wellington's earliest battles in the Peninsula. Travelling along the A1-IP1 motorway, it is advisable to change to the IC2 at junction 10 near Pombal in order to avoid driving through Leira, where several road changes would be required. You then join the A8-IC1 and head towards Nazaré on the Portuguese coast. Driving past Caldas da Rainha and the impressive medieval castle at Obidos, be prepared to leave the motorway at junction 13.

Roliça is impressive, with a high observation platform marked with a cross on top of an extremely steep hillside. From the point of view of the British it is easy to see how an assault would have been difficult, even when using the gullies to the left of the gorge you are likely to drive through. The gorge is very obvious, being flanked by two large jutting hills, and you drive onward to the small village of Columbeira, which is unlikely to appear on many maps. Go past the old church and uphill along the farm tracks, where brown signs direct you to the viewpoints of this popular beauty spot. The area is studded with windmills and planted with numerous vineyards and orchards. Once you have located the viewing point with the cross, work your way along the tracks to its right and you should come across the iron-fenced gravestone of Colonel Lake. Lake had pressed forward up the gully at the head of the 29th Regiment, encountering overwhelming numbers and taking fire from both flanks. You understand how this occurred when you see the nature of the ground; the strength of Delaborde's skilfully chosen position becoming immediately apparent. He had left himself an easy line of retreat and you can imagine Wellington being dismayed afterwards following Delaborde's masterful performance. Luckily for the British, not all his French opponents would fight so well.

The battlefield of Vimiero is also close by and after rejoining the motorway can be found by leaving at exit 10 and heading towards the village of Campelos. However, bearing in mind the length of this journey it may be preferable to drive straight back to Lisbon via the A8 and attempt it on another day if you want enough light for decent photographs. Throughout this kind of journey it is wise to be ruthless about your priorities and, if in doubt, leave sites for another time. Remember that these routes involve considerable distances and that drivers are likely to have had enough by the end of the afternoon.

THE LINES OF TORRES VEDRAS – PORTUGAL

If staying in Lisbon itself, set out as early as possible to avoid the heavy traffic and follow the coastal road westwards past the enormous city road-bridge. The road is signposted for the town of Cascais and if you keep the ocean in sight on your left it is unlikely that you will stray from the route. There are several old military bases and fort-like structures along the coast, but the fort in question is the São Julião, which will appear on your left just as you reach Oeiras. The fort was protected by a string of small batteries and redoubts, though little evidence of them remains. This was intended as the embarkation point for the British Army if they were forced to abandon Lisbon, and several jetties used to extend from the beach under cover of the fort's guns. The fort itself is worth photographing, but bear in mind that it is still an active army base and if you approach it too closely the military police may take exception.

Just before Cascais, turn north towards Sintra and on to the town of Mafra. Mafra contains an impressive convent built on a palatial scale, which is truly magnificent and difficult to miss in the centre. During the first invasion of 1807, General Junot used this appealing building as his headquarters and it is easy to see why. Next to the convent stands a modern war memorial depicting three Portuguese soldiers from medieval, Napoleonic and twentieth-century wars. There are plaques naming a variety of campaigns and battles, along with some of the regiments involved. It is unusual and worth closer scrutiny.

Leaving the N116 after Sintra, travel by minor roads through the villages of Murgeira and Gradil. This area is part of the second line of defences in the lines of Torres Vedras. Scanning the surrounding hillsides and peaks, you see levelled areas and altered hill scarps, but few fortifications are obvious here. The Royal Park of Tapada contains the remains of four redoubts and the large wall skirting the park was used as part of the defences. Continuing along minor roads heading for Sobral, the route should take you under the motorway and on to join the N374 and subsequently the N115 into the town. The Great Redoubt stood on Monte Agraço to the east of Sobral, which is sign-posted 'Forte de Alqueidão'. Its remains are impressive but it is difficult to find. The Portuguese have made great efforts to preserve this structure, its walls and ditch being well maintained.

The small village of Pero Negro, where Wellington kept his headquarters during the siege period, is easier to find, being posted and marked on most maps, unlike the Great Redoubt. If you turn left just before the railway station and the small level crossing, you should discover Wellington's house, which is marked with a plaque and currently used as a schoolhouse. Every morning Wellington would ride from the property to survey the lines and receive reports on enemy movements.

Take the N248 north-west from Sobral to find the old town of Torres Vedras. The town is dominated by the old Moorish castle, included in the lines as fort number twenty-seven. It is worth navigating the tiny streets uphill to the castle, which provides a good view of the surrounding area. A relatively short way out of town is fort São Vicente, which has been restored to something approaching its former glory. It contains earth traverses, some of which were later faced with stone, revetted banquettes for infantry and strategically placed gun embrasures.

If possible, pause here and complete the rest of the tour the following day, but you may have enough daylight to visit the southern defences along the Tejo if you have made good time. Travelling south along the lines you may spot occasional signs of small redoubts and forts, but bear in mind that detours will almost always take longer than expected and should only be attempted if time permits. The southern end of the line started at Alhandra on the Tejo, which is the first destination. Travelling east along the N9, join the N10 just above Vila Franca. Driving through Vila Franca you may see the famous Hercules statue standing on a tall column on the hillside. The statue is white and stands out against the hillside, but binoculars or a telescope may be necessary and the buildings along the route only allow the occasional fleeting glimpse. The exit is just after the town of Alhandra when travelling

towards Lisbon, but can be very difficult to find. The turning is marked
with two signs for Solbanhino and Palacio. Road atlases are likely to be
inadequate for the small lanes now encountered and the best course is
to drive up the hillside watching closely for a small yellow sign reading
'*Linhas de Torres des Monumentos*'. It is unfortunate that the
Portuguese fail to provide the numerous signs that most countries place
to mark sites of historical interest, especially with the wealth of
interesting locations. This one is easy to miss and instinct and
perseverance may have to be relied upon. The area is heavily wooded
and contains a large quarry with industrial buildings, meaning some
areas are restricted. Most of this applies to limiting access to various
roads, some of which are blocked with large boulders. The Portuguese
are generally very easy going, but quarry workers around here may
challenge you if you stray off the paths.

The Hercules statue is imposing and has two plaques
commemorating Lieutenant-Colonel Richard Fletcher, considered the
main designer and creator of the Lines of Torres Vedras, along with the
general British and Portuguese input into Wellington's vast and
farsighted project. The column base is inscribed '*NON ULTRA*',
meaning 'No Further' in Latin. The statue stands on the site of a
redoubt, but all traces of this have been removed. It is a very good
position for a fort with extensive views out over the Tejo and the
estuary. British gunboats would have ranged even further east than this
point, adding to the formidable nature of the defence.

The more adventurous could follow the rough tracks to view the
remains of smaller fortifications north of this point. Retracing your
route to the fork in the road before the statue, travel uphill along the
narrow and rough track. Following the crest of the ridge you will see
the well-preserved remains of a redoubt to your right. Walking into the
structure you will find that it is wedge-shaped, terminating in a
triangular point facing eastwards. There are four stone-faced
embrasures and a small powder store still exists in the centre. However,
this small redoubt is heavily overgrown on the inside, limiting
photographic possibilities. The sides of the redoubt have been faced
with stone to preserve them and, if you are determined to get good
photographs, it is possible to clamber down the steep, overgrown
hillside and shoot up at the structure. Be extremely careful here and
wear long trousers, since gorse and thorn bushes cover the area. The
redoubt is very well positioned with good views down the precipitous
slopes. Observing it from five hundred yards further on it was hardly
visible on the hillside despite its good state of preservation. This would

have presented a formidable obstacle to the French considering it was one amongst many mutually supporting structures.

Driving further you will encounter a small battery site, which is again stone-faced on both the wall and the gun embrasures. Sadly it is now used as a rubbish tip for the local foresters, but it is still worth a look. It is situated in the woods that now cover the slopes and ridge and the quarry is now to your rear. Though it is difficult to tell with the trees, this structure would almost certainly have been able to support the previous redoubt. The track continues along the ridgeline but it is advisable to leave vehicles here and walk since it is extremely rough. A 4x4 vehicle would be preferable if you wish to explore in this direction and remember to carry sufficient water if you intend to walk. Using a telescope from various vantage points, there seem to be further forts along the line of this ridge if you have the time to seek them out.

FINAL POINTS

It is of course possible to save yourself time and effort by going on an organised coach tour to some of these locations. These are usually well organised and informative. However, those determined enough to undertake this kind of journey themselves should find it rewarding and far cheaper in comparison. With hindsight, an air-conditioned 4x4 vehicle is advisable for some areas and a week is only just long enough to visit this many locations. It is advisable to book hotels along the route well in advance and they are usually very good quality, but bear in mind that most travel agents will be unwilling to make this many bookings and you may have to do it yourself using the internet. Travelling over the ground still gives an insight into the problems Wellington and Massena faced, with several areas being unspoilt and a pleasure to photograph. Good quality optics and cameras are a must for this trip and, depending on the time of year, sufficient drinking water is imperative to prevent dehydration. Good luck to those with the courage to attempt such a venture!

Notes

CHAPTER 1 - THE PENINSULAR WAR

1. Glover, Michael, *The Peninsular War 1807-1814*, London, Penguin Books, 1974, 2001 edition, p22.
2. Stanhope, The Earl of, *Life of the Right Honourable William Pitt, Volume IV*, London, John Murray, 1867, p369. However, some sources dispute that the indomitable Pitt made this defeatist remark and Donald Grove Barnes claimed that if anything hastened his demise it was the disintegration of the Third Coalition, which had taken him so long to achieve. Grove Barnes, Donald, *George III and William Pitt, 1783-1806*, New York, Octagon Books, 1939, 1965 edition, p467.
3. For example Joseph Bonaparte was created King of Naples 1 April 1806 and Louis Bonaparte King of Holland 20 June 1806.
4. Glover, op.cit. p25. Lord Melville was the First Lord of the Admiralty in 1814.
5. Ibid. p24.
6. Chandler, David, *The Campaigns of Napoleon*, London, Weidenfeld and Nicolson, 1967, p598.
7. Ibid. p610.
8. *The Times*, 10 October 1808, p2.
9. Chandler, op.cit. p617.
10. Ibid. p620.
11. Ibid. p639.
12. *The Times*, 24 January 1809, p4.
13. Napier, Major-General W.F.P., *History of the War in the Peninsula and in the South of France, 1807-1814, Volume I*, London, Frederick Warne & Co., 1876, p311.
14. Fortescue, J.W., *A History of The British Army, Volume VI 1807-1809*, London, Macmillan & Co. Ltd, 1921, p351.
15. Curling, Henry (Ed.), *Recollections of Rifleman Harris*, London, Peter Davies Limited, 1929, p114.
16. Esdaile, Charles, *The Peninsular War*, London, Penguin Books Ltd, 2003, p155.
17. Fortescue, *Volume VI*, op.cit. p388.
18. *The Times*, 26 January 1809, p1.
19. *The Times*, 26 January 1809, p4.
20. Hibbert, Christopher, *Corunna*, London, B.T. Batsford Limited, 1961.
21. *The Times*, 24 January 1809, p4. This extract comprises part of a passage quoted in *The Times* from the French newspaper *Le Moniteur*.
22. Hibbert, op.cit. p199.

CHAPTER 2 - SON OF THE ARISTOCRACY

23. Guedalla, Philip, *The Duke*, London, Hodder and Stoughton Limited, 1933, p3.
24. Buchan, John Walter, *The Duke of Wellington*, London, Thomas Nelson & Sons, 1914, p10.
25. Keegan, John, *The Mask of Command*, Penguin Books Ltd, 1988.
26. Guedalla, op.cit. pp36-37.
27. Fortescue, J.W., *A History of the British Army Volume IV Part I 1789-1801*, London, Macmillan & Co. Ltd, 1915, p322. Walmoden, a Hanoverian General, wrote these remarks in a letter to the Duke of York, detailing the results of the retreat.
28. Guedalla, op.cit. p47.
29. Longford, Elizabeth, *The Years of the Sword*, London, World Books, 1971, p51.
30. Guedalla, op.cit. pp55-56.
31. Longford, op.cit. p61.
32. Ibid. p65.
33. Fortescue, J.W., *A History of the British Army Volume V 1803-1807*, London, Macmillan & Co. Ltd, 1921, pp32-33.
34. Maxwell, Herbert, *The Life of Wellington, Volume I*, London, Sampson Low, Marston & Company, 1900, pp59-60.
35. Longford, op.cit. p141.
36. Guedalla, op. cit. p125. In India the taking of salt symbolised a soldier's oath of loyalty and is the origin of phrases such as 'to be true to your salt' or 'to be worth your salt'.
37. *Wellington's Supplementary Dispatches, Volume V*, London, John Murray, 1860, p33.
38. Green, William, *Travels and Adventures of William Green (Late Rifle Brigade)*, Leicester, W.A. Hammond, 1858, p5.
39. Fortescue, *Volume IV*, op.cit. p73.
40. Green, op.cit. p6.
41. Fortescue, *Volume IV*, op.cit. p77.
42. Pool, Bernard (Ed.), *The Croker Papers 1808-1857*, London, B.T. Batsford Ltd, 1967, p11.
43. *Supplementary Dispatches, Volume VI*, p90.
44. Fortescue, *Volume VI*, op.cit. p212.
45. Ibid. p215.
46. Curling, Henry (Ed.), *Recollections of Rifleman Harris*, London, Peter Davies Limited, 1929, p33.
47. NAM 1964-04-76 Anonymous, *Journal of a Soldier of the 71st Regiment*.
48. *The Annual Register 1809*, London, G. Auld, 1811, p61. This is part of an extract from the Board of Inquiry conducted to examine the Convention of Cintra 1808.
49. NAM 1964-04-76, op.cit.
50. Esdaile, Charles, *The Peninsular War*, London, Penguin Books Ltd, 2003, p101.
51. NAM 7511-31 *Anonymous Captain in the British Army* – memoirs 24 August–16 September 1808.

52. In 1824 Harriette Wilson wrote her memoirs, which included lurid details about former lovers. Joseph Stockdale, her publisher, approached the then Duke of Wellington with the offer of excluding his name from the manuscript for a monetary consideration. His famous, if not fully corroborated, reply to this blackmail was to: 'Publish and be damned!' Wilson's subsequent revelations were embarrassing, occasionally inaccurate and almost certainly exaggerated.

53. Guedalla, op.cit. p184.

54. Thompson, W.F.K. (Ed.), *An Ensign in the Peninsular War*, London, Michael Joseph Ltd, 1981, pp51-52. Aitchison wrote this letter on 25 July 1809 from Talavera, before the battle.

55. Ibid. p57. Aitchison wrote this letter on 14 September 1809 at Belem weeks after the battle. The men were ordered to lie down to minimise the effect of the round shot that, bouncing over the ground, was likely to knock down more men if they were standing in line.

56. Stanhope, Philip, Henry, *Notes of Conversations with the Duke of Wellington, 1831-1851*, London, John Murray, 1889, p9.

57. *Supplementary Dispatches, Volume VI, July 1807-December 1810*, London, John Murray, 1860, p412. Letter from The Earl of Liverpool to Wellington, 20 October 1809.

58. Oman, Charles, *A History of the Peninsular War Volume III*, Oxford, Clarendon Press, 1908, p167.

59. Ibid. pp153-154.

60. Glover, Michael, *Wellington as Military Commander*, London, Penguin Books Ltd, 2001 – originally 1968, p67.

61. Oman, *Volume III*, op.cit. p169.

CHAPTER 3 - CHILD OF VICTORY

62. Marshal-Cornwall, James, *Marshal Massena*, London, Oxford University Press, 1965, p1. Due to his later ties with France, Massena favoured the French spelling of André rather than Andrea. Though many historians and some of his contemporaries spell his name with an accent (Masséna), his birth records refute this. Some sources claimed the family had Jewish origins and that his name was a corruption of 'Manasseh', but this assertion has no evidence to support it. The family hailed from a long line of peasant farmers and could trace their heritage back to the fifteenth century.

63. The French would often name armies after the areas they were intending to fight in. This was partially intended as a sign of revolutionary brotherhood implying that they wished to bring the benefits of their new political system to Italy rather than simply conquer the Italian states.

64. Butler, Arthur John (Ed. & trans.), *The Memoirs of Baron Thiebault, Volume I*, London, Smith, Elder & Co., 1896, pp282-283. Massena had a commanding presence but was slight in build and only 5ft 4in tall.

65. Marshal-Cornwall, op.cit. p48. This translates as the 'Sweet Child of Victory' but accounts differ over the exact wording. Berthier's report to the Directory recalled it as *'l'Enfant Gâté de la Victoire'* or 'Spoilt Child of Victory', which sounds less complimentary in English. It is notable that Wellington would later use this version of the epithet in the Peninsula.

66. Marshal-Cornwall, op.cit. pp57-58.

67. Ibid. pp86-87.

68. Butler, Arthur John, *The Memoirs of Baron De Marbot*, London, Cassell & Company Ltd, 1929, p41.

69. Ibid. p48.

70. Butler, Arthur John (Ed. & trans.), *The Memoirs of Baron Thiebault, Volume II*, op.cit. p42.

71. Chandler, David, *On the Napoleonic Wars*, London, Greenhill Books Ltd, 1999, p99.

72. Chandler, David (Ed.), *Napoleon's Marshals*, London, Weidenfeld and Nicolson, 1987, p282.

73. Butler, *Marbot*, op.cit. p215.

74. Ibid. p229.

75. Though Massena defended the village of Aspern rather than Essling during the battle, the French referred to the clash as the Battle of Essling at the time, which explains the title.

76. Marshal-Cornwall, op.cit. p13.

77. Butler, *Thiebault, Volume I*, op.cit. p308. Apparently Massena said this in a jovial, good-natured manner, although it may appear to be an arrogant statement.

78. Marshal-Cornwall, op.cit. p117.

79. Ibid. p118. Thiebault also spoke of the camaraderie that existed in Massena's division during the Italian campaigns: 'There was not one of us who was not proud of belonging to Massena's division, nor without pride in the part it was playing could the division have performed such prodigies.' Butler, Arthur John (Ed. & trans.), *The Memoirs of Baron Thiebault, Volume I*, London, Smith, Elder & Co., 1896, p318.

80. Butler, *Marbot*, op.cit. p237.

81. Bonaparte apparently told Massena: 'I love my brother Louis no less than you your son; but when he was my aide-de-camp in Italy he did his turn of duty like the others, and I should have been afraid of bringing him into discredit if I had sent one of his comrades into danger instead of him.' Butler, *Marbot*, op.cit. p239.

82. Butler, *Marbot*, op.cit. p39.

83. Koch, Général, *Mémoires de Massena, Volume II*, Paris, Paulin et Lechevalier, 1848-1850, p199.

84. Marshal-Cornwall, op.cit. pp120-121.

85. Lanfrey, P., *The History of Napoleon the First, Volume I*, London, Macmillan & Co., 1886, p62.

86. Butler, *Thiebault, Volume I*, op.cit. pp338-339.

87. Marshal-Cornwall, op.cit. pp67-68.

88. Chandler, David, *On the Napoleonic Wars*, op.cit. p105.

89. Marshal-Cornwall, op.cit. p149.

90. Butler, *Marbot*, op.cit. p246.

91. Marshal-Cornwall, op.cit. p272. Tortured by Josephine's infidelities, Bonaparte also played the adulterer in Egypt and later as the Emperor. His love for the Polish Countess Waleswska became common knowledge and he is said to have sired children by his mistresses.

CHAPTER 4 - THE KEY TO PORTUGAL

92. Junot, Laura, *Memoirs of Madame Junot Duchess of Abrantes Volume IV*, London, Richard Bentley & Son, 1893, pp182-183.

93. Ibid. p184.

94. Ibid. p184.

95. Oman, Charles, *A History of the Peninsular War Volume III*, Oxford, Clarendon Press, 1908, p208.

96. Ibid. pp208-209.

97. Marshal-Cornwall, James, *Marshal Massena*, London, Oxford University Press, 1965, p190.

98. Howard, Donald D., *Napoleon and Iberia – The Twin Sieges of Ciudad Rodrigo and Almeida, 1810*, London, Greenhill Books, 1994, p95.

99. Ibid. pp110-111.

100. Ibid. pp134-135.

101. Humble, Richard, *Napoleon's Peninsular Marshals*, London, Purcell Books Services Limited, 1974, pp130-131.

102. Howard, *Napoleon and Iberia*, op.cit. p148.

103. Butler, Arthur John, *The Memoirs of Bardon de Marbot*, London, Cassell & Company Ltd, 1929, p250. Marbot later claimed that Massena failed to thank him adequately for carrying him out of the line of fire, increasing his resentment of his commander.

104. Howard, Donald D. (Ed.), *The French Campaign in Portugal 1810-1811 – An Account by Jean Jacques Pelet*, Minneapolis, University of Minnesota Press, 1973, p74.

105. Howard, *Napoleon and Iberia*, op.cit. p181.

106. Howard, *Pelet*, op.cit. p81.

107. Ibid. p80.

108. Craufurd, Alexander Reverend, *General Craufurd and His Light Division*, Cambridge, Ken Trotman Ltd, 1987, pp123-124.

109. Brett-James, Antony (Ed.), *Edward Costello – The Peninsula and Waterloo Campaigns*, London, Longmans, Green & Co. Ltd, 1967, p33. Costello managed to crack his captor on the head with his rifle butt and flee but received a bullet in the leg shortly afterwards. With the help of his comrades he eventually managed to cross the bridge and find medical help but came very close to capture.

110. Fletcher, Ian, *Craufurd's Light Division*, Tunbridge Wells, Spellmount Ltd, 1991, p113.

111. NAM 6807-461 *Lieutenant Colonel Richard Brunton's papers*, then in the 43rd.

112. Leach, Lieutenant-Colonel J., *Rough Sketches of the Life of an Old Soldier*, London, 1831, pp149-150.

113. *Wellington's Supplementary Dispatches, Volume VI*, p563.

114. Ibid. p564.

115. Napier, Lieutenant-General Sir William, *The Life and Opinions of General Sir Charles James Napier*, London, John Murray, 1857, p139.

116. *The Times*, Wednesday 29 August 1810, p3.

117. Oman, *Volume III*, op.cit. p265.

118. Craufurd, op.cit. p39. Craufurd's entire letter appeared in *The Times*, 21 November 1810.

119. Fortescue, J.W., *Volume VII*, p484.

120. Howard, *Pelet*, op.cit. pp90-91.

CHAPTER 5 - THE THIRD INVASION

121. Howard, Donald D., *Napoleon and Iberia*, London, Greenhill Books, 1994, p253. Though British troops were occasionally used to force the peasantry from their lands, the bulk of such work was allotted to Portuguese troops and militia. Wellington knew full well that the Portuguese acceptance of their allies could swiftly evaporate if his troops became associated with such actions.

122. Ibid. p291.

123. Ibid. p253.

124. Ibid. p258.

125. Marshal-Cornwall, James, *Marshal Massena*, London, Oxford University Press, 1965, p193.

126. Howard, Donald D. (Ed.), *The French Campaign in Portugal 1810-1811 – An Account by Jean Jacques Pelet*, Minneapolis, University of Minnesota Press, 1973, pp110-111.

127. Ibid. p121.

128. Ibid. pp121-122.

129. Ibid. pp122-123.

130. Ibid. p306.

131. Butler, Arthur John, *The Memoirs of Baron de Marbot*, London, Cassell & Company Ltd, 1929, p252.

132. Fortescue *Volume VII*, p498.

133. *Wellington's Dispatches, Volume VI*, p588. Wellington believed that it might have been possible to extricate them without committing his army to a major engagement, though it would have been difficult to achieve.

134. NAM 7403-155 *Colonel John Elley, Assistant Adjutant General of Cavalry in Spain*, – personal letters and reports.

135. Butler, *Marbot*, op.cit. p253.

136. Howard, *Pelet*, op.cit. p136.

137. Ibid. p135.

138. Warre, Lieutenant-General Sir William, *Letters from the Peninsula 1808-1812*, London, John Murray, 1909, p145.

139. Fortescue, *Volume VII*, p504. Trant had enough men to overcome the escort, but their determined approach and disciplined fire unnerved the militiamen and they withdrew after destroying some artillery caissons and capturing prisoners. The rescue of the convoy was a lucky escape for the French and further proof of the ill-advised choice of their route.

140. Brindle, Rosemary (Ed.), *With Napoleon's Guns*, London, Greenhill Books, 2005, p95.

141. Butler, *Marbot*, op.cit. p254.

CHAPTER 6 - BUSAÇO RIDGE

142. Oman, Charles, *A History of the Peninsular War, Volume III*, Oxford, Clarendon Press, 1908, pp341-342. The majority of the *Ordenanza* dressed in civilian garb though some occasionally possessed militia uniforms.
143. Fortescue, J.W., *A History of the British Army, Volume VII*, London, Macmillan & Co. Ltd, 1912, p506.
144. Schaumann, A.L.F., (Ed. & trans. by Ludovici, Anthony), *On the Road with Wellington*, London, William Heinemann Ltd, 1924, p249.
145. Fortescue, *Volume VII*, p511.
146. Butler, Arthur John, *The Memoirs of Baron De Marbot*, London, Cassell & Company Ltd, 1929, p256.
147. Oman, *Volume III*, op.cit. p368. As a former member of the Army of Italy, Massena clearly still remembered the rivalry between the two armies.
148. Butler, *Marbot*, op.cit. p258. This tale of Marbot's should not be accepted without caution. Though no source directly questions his involvement, he seems to have possessed an uncanny knack for being in the right place and the right time on numerous occasions. Notwithstanding, it is a believable theory over why Massena was contented with such a poor reconnaissance.
149. Howard, Donald D. (Ed.), *The French Campaign in Portugal 1810-1811 – An Account by Jean Jacques Pelet*, Minneapolis, University of Minnesota Press, 1973, p175. Considering the rugged nature of the countryside it is likely that Ney's cavalry simply missed the road in question and since few locals had stayed in the vicinity to be questioned by the French this is understandable. However, Massena's supposed failure to order further checks to be sure of the ground does appear to be out of character with his reputation for amassing careful intelligence.
150. Howard, Donald D., *The Battle of Bussaco*, Florida, USA: The Florida State University, 1965, p81.
151. Brindle, Rosemary (Ed.), *With Napoleon's Guns*, London, Greenhill Books, 2005, p99.
152. Grattan, William, *Adventures with the Connaught Rangers 1809-1814*, Edinburgh, R&R Clark Ltd, 1902, p33.
153. Ibid. p37.
154. Girod de l'Ain, Maurice, *Grands Artilleurs: Drouot – Sénarmont – Eblé*, Paris, Berger-Laurault, 1895, p104.
155. Oman, *Volume III*, p380.
156. Ibid. p385.
157. Grattan, op.cit. p41.
158. Schaumann, A.L.F., (Ed. & trans. by Ludovici, Anthony), *On the Road with Wellington*, London, William Heinemann Ltd, 1924, p250. In contrast the Spanish and Portuguese did not share this professional attitude, with even their regular armies succumbing to a hatred of the French invaders. The French knew that those of their wounded left lying on the field were likely to be murdered by the peasantry to settle old scores.
159. Butler, *Marbot*, op.cit. p261.
160. Ibid. p262.

161. D'Urban, Sir Benjamin, Major General, (edited by Rousseau, I.J.), *The Peninsular Journal*, London, Longmans, Green & Co., 1930, p150.
162. Ibid. p150.
163. Grattan, op.cit. pp43-44.
164. Schaumann, op.cit. p254.

CHAPTER 7 - QUE DIABLE!

165. Howard, Donald D. (Ed.), *The French Campaign in Portugal 1810-1811 – An Account by Jean Jacques Pelet*, Minneapolis, University of Minnesota Press, 1973, p205.
166. Marshal-Cornwall, James, *Marshal Massena*, London, Oxford University Press, 1965, p210.
167. Butler, Arthur John, *The Memoirs of Baron De Marbot*, London, Cassell & Company Ltd, 1929, p264.
168. Marshal-Cornwall, op.cit. p218. The area north of Lisbon contains numerous large hills and ridges but Massena's reference to them as 'mountains' is an exaggeration, although perhaps pardonable under the circumstances.
169. Jones, John T., Colonel RE, *Memoranda Relative to the Lines Thrown up to Cover Lisbon in 1810*, East Sussex, The Naval & Military Press Ltd, 2004, p85.
170. Ibid. pp87-88.
171. Ibid. p82.
172. A flèche is an arrow-shaped earthwork open to the rear whereas redoubts are usually enclosed. Abbatis were obstacles formed by felled trees, often cut to present a hedge of sharpened branches and stakes to slow the progress of infantry.
173. Ibid. p103.
174. Oman, Charles, *A History of the Peninsular War, Volume III*, Oxford, Clarendon Press, 1908, pp177-178.
175. Jones, John T., op.cit. p100. The peasantry often had to provide their own farm carts to pull guns or transport food supplies into the lines. Even with the military road guns often had to be manhandled into redoubts by men alone due to their inaccessible locations.
176. *Wellington's Supplementary Dispatches, Volume VI*, p421.
177. Ibid. p404.
178. Oman, *Volume III*, op.cit. pp195-196.
179. *Wellington's Supplementary Dispatches, Volume VII* pp1-2.
180. NAM 7511-31 *Anonymous, Captain in the British Army* – memoirs 24 August–16 September 1808.
181. Fletcher, Ian, *The Lines of Torres Vedras*, Oxford, Osprey Publishing, 2003, pp25-26.
182. NAM 1964-04-76 *Anonymous, Journal of a Soldier of the 71st Regiment*.
183. Butler, *Marbot*, op.cit. p265.
184. Marshal-Cornwall, op.cit. pp220-221.
185. Grattan, William, *Adventures with the Connaught Rangers 1809-1814*, Edinburgh, R&R Clark Ltd, 1902, p48.

186. D'Urban, Sir Benjamin, Major-General, (Ed. Rousseau, I.J.), *The Peninsular Journal*, London, Longmans, Green & Co., 1930, p163.

CHAPTER 8 - THE RETREAT

187. Butler, Arthur John, *The Memoirs of Baron De Marbot*, London, Cassell & Company Ltd, 1929, p271. Marbot claims that this colourful character was later identified as a former smuggler hailing from around Dover who regularly spied for the British using disguise to aid his espionage.
188. Ibid. p272. In fairness to Soult, this was not just due to his dislike of Massena and a possible wish to see him fail. He could ill afford to spare 10,000 men and any such march would be opposed by the Portuguese fortress of Elvas, which would have to be taken or masked. They would be marching into unknown territory with two enemy held fortresses at their backs.
189. *The Times*, Tuesday 12 February 1811, p3.
190. Butler, *Marbot*, op.cit. p268.
191. *Wellington's Supplementary Dispatches, Volume VII*, p1. Indeed Wellington admitted that he would have encountered difficulty in feeding a division in such land under similar circumstances let alone an army.
192. Fortescue, J.W., *A History of the British Army*, in 13 volumes, London, Macmillan & Co. Ltd, 1917, p72.
193. Liddell Hart, B.H. (Ed.), *The Letters of Private Wheeler 1809–1828*, Gloucestershire, The Windrush Press, 1999, p51.
194. Grattan, William, *Adventures with the Connaught Rangers 1809–1814*, Edinburgh, R&R Clark Ltd, 1902, p56.
195. Liddell Hart, *Wheeler*, op.cit. pp51–52.
196. Fortescue, op.cit. p74.
197. Butler, *Marbot*, op.cit. p274.
198. Ibid. p275.
199. NAM 1964-04-76 *Anonymous, Journal of a Soldier of the 71st Regiment*.
200. Butler, *Marbot*, op.cit. p276.
201. Summerville, Christopher (Ed.), *The Exploits of Baron De Marbot*, New York, Caroll & Graf Publishers, 2000, p189.
202. Grattan, op.cit. p57–58.
203. Howard, Donald D. (Ed.), *The French Campaign in Portugal 1810–1811 – An Account by Jean Jacques Pelet*, Minneapolis, University of Minnesota Press, 1973, p492.
204. Ibid. p495.
205. Fortescue, op.cit. p96. This report was actually untrue with both towns possessing far greater resources. D'Erlon was presumably trying to discourage Massena's ambitions and save the army from further hardship. Napoleon had in fact made an order placing D'Erlon under Massena's direct command two weeks earlier though this information did not reach the army until it had withdrawn into Spain.
206. Grattan, op.cit. p61.
207. General Soult was the younger brother of Marshal Soult.
208. Grattan, op.cit. p62.

209. Butler, *Marbot*, op.cit. p279.
210. *The Times*, Thursday 2 May 1811, p3. Whilst established with the best of intent, these charities could not hope to deal with the scale of the destruction left in the wake of the three invasions. Portugal never truly recovered from the ravaging of her lands.
211. *Wellington's Supplementary Dispatches, Volume VII*, p102.
212. *The Times*, Tuesday 5 March 1811, p3.
213. *Wellington's Supplementary Dispatches, Volume VII*, p95.
214. Butler, Arthur John (Ed. & trans.), *The Memoirs of Baron Thiebault, Volume II*, London, Smith, Elder & Co., 1896, p330.

CHAPTER 9 - A LAST CHANCE

215. Moore-Smith, G.C. (Ed.), *The Autobiography of Sir Harry Smith 1787–1819*, London, John Murray, 1910, p47. Smith also questioned the abilities of Erskine commanding the Light Division, labelling him '...a short sighted old ass...' p45.
216. Kincaid, J. Captain, *Adventures in the Rifle Brigade*, London, Peter Davies Limited, 1929, p53.
217. Girod de l'Ain, Maurice, *Grand Artilleurs: Drouot – Sénarmont – Eblé*, Paris, Berger-Laurault, 1895, pp121–122.
218. Butler, Arthur John (Ed. & trans.), *The Memoirs of Baron Thiebault, Volume II*, London, Smith, Elder & Co., 1896, p320.
219. Ibid. p321. Shortly afterwards, exhausted by the rigours of campaigning, Henriette Leberton returned to France.
220. Ibid. p322.
221. Ibid. p322.
222. Koch, Général, *Mémoires de Massena, Volume VII*, Paris, Paulin et Lechevalier, 1848–1850, pp490–491.
223. Butler, Arthur John (Ed.), *The Memoirs of Baron De Marbot – Late Lieutenant-General in the French Army*, London, Cassell & Company Ltd, 1929, p282.
224. Butler, *Thiebault, Volume II*, op.cit. p323.
225. *The Times*, Monday 27 May 1811, p3.
226. D'Urban, Sir Benjamin, Major-General, (Ed. Rousseau, I.J.), *The Peninsular Journal*, London, Longmans, Green & Co., 1930, p204.
227. Kincaid, op.cit. pp53–54.
228. *Wellington's Dispatches, Volume VII*, p515.
229. *The Times*, Wednesday 29 May 1811, p2. Dated 7 May and written in his camp before Fuentes, Massena's letter to Napoleon was published in the French newspapers on 22 May and subsequently translated and printed by *The Times*.
230. *The Times*, Wednesday 29 May 1811, p2.
231. Ibid. p2.
232. Jones, B.T. (Ed.), *Napoleon's Army – The Military Memoirs of Charles Parquin*, London, Greenhill Books, 1989, p134.
233. Ibid. p134. Ney's enormous popularity amongst the army made Parquin's attitude commonplace and reveals why Massena tolerated his subordinate's intransigence for as long as he did.

234. NAM 6807-461 *Lieutenant Colonel Richard Brunton's (13th Light Dragoons) papers.*

235. Fortescue, J.W., *A History of the British Army, Volume VIII 1811–1812,* London, Macmillan & Co. Limited, 1917, pp158–159.

236. NAM 1964-04-76 *Anonymous, Journal of a Soldier of the 71st Regiment.*

237. Moore-Smith, op.cit. p49.

238. NAM 1964-04-76 op.cit.

239. Ibid.

240. *The Times,* Wednesday 29 May 1811, p2.

241. Ibid. p2.

242. Grattan, William, *Adventures with the Connaught Rangers 1809–1814,* Edinburgh, R&R Clark Ltd, 1902, p64.

243. Brett-James, Antony (Ed.), *Edward Costello – The Peninsula and Waterloo Campaigns,* London, Longmans, Green & Co. Ltd, 1967, p66. The Portuguese troops were referring to Craufurd's concern with supplies and, even though he punished looting severely, he was prepared to allow the occasional slaughter of livestock if the men were in severe want as long as some kind of restitution was made. In comparison, most officers in the Division were relieved to see the back of Erskine even though they had mixed views about Craufurd.

244. *Wellington's Dispatches, Volume VII,* p529.

245. Glover, Michael, *Wellington as Military Commander,* London, Penguin Books, 2001, p147.

CHAPTER 10 - THE MOST DANGEROUS HOUR OF THE WAR

246. Jones, B.T. (Ed.), *Napoleon's Army – The Military Memoirs of Charles Parquin,* London, Greenhill Books, 1989, p133. A colpack was a bearskin hat sometimes known as a 'busby' and some regiments had an ornamental pouch or bag that hung from it, usually red in colour.

247. NAM 1986-11-33 *The Account of Major Thomas, William, Brotherton, 14th Light Dragoons.*

248. Ibid.

249. Ibid.

250. Liddell Hart, B.H. (Ed.), *The Letters of Private Wheeler 1809–1828,* Gloucestershire, The Windrush Press, 1999, p54.

251. Ibid. p55. The 'Chasseurs Brittaniques' were a regiment largely composed of French exiles and deserters whose reputation was patchy and, for obvious reasons, were rarely trusted with outpost work. The battle of Fuentes de Oñoro was one of the few occasions where they distinguished themselves. The smoothbore musket was a weapon of dubious accuracy and firing over friendly troops was extremely risky even at close range. The fact that the Allies resorted to this tactic reveals how hard pressed they were at this point.

252. Brett-James, Antony (Ed.), *Edward Costello – The Peninsula and Waterloo Campaigns,* London, Longmans, Green & Co. Ltd, 1967, p67.

253. Jones, *Parquin*, op.cit. pp134–135. In the following charge, Parquin revealed how many in his regiment were unhorsed and how General Fournier had his horse shot from under him in the repeated attempts to halt the Allied withdrawal.
254. Liddell Hart, *Wheeler*, op.cit. p56.
255. Fortescue, J.W., *A History of the British Army, Volume VIII*, London, Macmillan & Co. Ltd, 1899–1930, p162. With the horrific prospect of battle, alcohol was sometimes issued to bolster courage, though not in amounts great enough to impair a soldier's abilities. However, it is quite possible that some soldiers may have obtained more than their official allowance.
256. Liddell Hart, *Wheeler*, op.cit. p55.
257. NAM 1986-11-33, op.cit.
258. Brett-James, Antony (Ed.), *Edward Costello – The Peninsula and Waterloo Campaigns*, op.cit. pp67-68.
259. Liddell Hart, *Wheeler*, op.cit. p56.
260. Napier, Major-General Sir W.F.P., *History of the War in the Peninsula and in the South of France, from the year 1807 to the year 1814, Volume III*, London, Frederick Warne & Co., 1851, p152.
261. Mockler-Ferryman, A.F., *The Life of a Regimental Officer During the Great War 1793–1815*, London, William Blackwood, 1913, pp166–167. Burning the colours was seen as a great shame to the 51st and Mainwaring received a severe reprimand from Wellington. The fact that he resorted to this measure reveals how close he thought his Regiment, and perhaps the Division, were to breaking. Shortly afterwards Mainwaring was wounded at Badajoz and Wellington had him invalided to Lisbon and replaced by Colonel Rice. He did not return to the 51st during its remaining time in the Peninsula.
262. Butler, Arthur John (Ed. & trans.), *The Memoirs of Baron Thiebault, Volume II*, London, Smith, Elder & Co., 1896, p327.
263. Schaumann, A.L.F., (Ed. & trans. by Ludovici, Anthony), *On the Road with Wellington*, London, William Heinemann Ltd, 1924, p303.
264. NAM 1964-04-76 *Anonymous, Journal of a Soldier of the 71st Regiment.*
265. NAM 6807-461 *Lieutenant Colonel Richard Brunton's (13th Light Dragoons) papers.*
266. *The Times*, Wednesday 29 May 1811, p2.
267. Koch, Général, *Mémoires de Massena, Volume VII*, Paris, Paulin et Lechevalier, 1848–1850, pp537–538. Many French historians cite Lepic's refusal to support the attack at this point as the reason for the French losing the battle.
268. Scarfe, Norman (Ed.), *Letters from the Peninsula – The Freer Family Correspondence 1807–1814*, Leicester, University College, 1953, p21.
269. NAM 6112-33 *The Account of Major William Stuart, 30th Regiment of Foot.*
270. Kincaid, J. Captain, *Adventures in the Rifle Brigade – in the Peninsula, France and the Netherlands from 1809 to 1815*, London, Peter Davies Limited, 1929 pp55–56.
271. Grattan, William, *Adventures with the Connaught Rangers 1809–1814*, Edinburgh, R&R Clark Ltd, 1902, p65.
272. Ibid. p67. Wallace's comment here is very revealing. The prospect of fighting in

the confined streets was horrific but a retreat over difficult ground with the barrier of a deep gorge to cross was even less appealing.

273. Ibid. p68.
274. Ibid. p69.
275. Ibid. p71.
276. Schaumann, op.cit. p303.
277. Fortescue, *Volume VIII*, p172.
278. Jones, *Parquin*, op.cit. p135.
279. Grattan, op.cit. p76.
280. Schaumann, op.cit. p302. Considering the paucity of supplies in the area and the enormous logistical difficulties the French were subjected to, this was almost certainly bravado on the part of the Colonel.
281. Butler, Arthur John (Ed. & trans.), *The Memoirs of Baron Thiebault, Volume II*, London, Smith, Elder & Co., 1896, p329.
282. *Wellington's Supplementary Dispatches, Volume VII*, p123.
283. Jones, *Parquin*, op.cit. p135.
284. Butler, *Thiebault, Volume II*, op.cit. p328.
285. Fortescue, *Volume VIII*, op.cit. p173.
286. Napier, *Volume III*, op.cit. pp154–155.
287. Fletcher, Ian (Ed.), *For King and Country – The Letters and Diaries of John Mills, Coldstream Guards, 1811–1814*, Staplehurst, Spellmount, 1995, p46.
288. Larpent, Seymour F., *The Private Journal of F.S. Larpent, Esq: Judge Advocate General of the British Forces in the Peninsula, attached to the head-quarters of Lord Wellington during the Peninsular War, from 1812 to its close*, London, Richard Bentley, 1854, p65.
289. *Wellington's Supplementary Dispatches, Volume VII*, pp176–177. Though the Government may have taken some inference from his failure to send a victory dispatch, the escape of Almeida's garrison stole some of the glory from Wellington's achievement.

CHAPTER 11 - THE END OF THE OLD FOX

290. Koch, Général, *Mémoires de Massena, Volume VII*, Paris, Paulin et Lechevalier, 1848–1850, p604.
291. Marshal-Cornwall, James, *Marshal Massena*, London, Oxford University Press, 1965, p251. Napoleon's greeting translates as: 'Ah, good! So Prince of Essling, it seems that you are no longer Massena!'
292. Stanhope, Philip Henry, *Notes of Conversations with the Duke of Wellington, 1831–1851*, London, John Murray, 1889, p90. Nevertheless, the lists of casualties appearing in *The Times* from Monday 3 June 1811 onwards spoke volumes.
293. *Wellington's Supplementary Dispatches, Volume VII*, p177.
294. *The Annual Register for the Year 1811*, p106.
295. Chandler, David, *On the Napoleonic Wars*, London, Greenhill Books Limited, 1999, originally 1994, p113.
296. Marshal-Cornwall, op.cit. p251. Massena still had his devoted supporters. Thiebault, hearing of his old chief's reappointment, immediately tried to gain a

command within the Army of Portugal, but desisted when he heard of Massena's illness – Butler, Arthur John (Ed. & trans.), *The Memoirs of Baron Thiebault, Volume II*, London, Smith, Elder & Co., 1896, p370.

297. Marshal-Cornwall, op.cit. p252.

298. Ibid. p254.

299. Stanhope, Philip Henry, *Notes of Conversations with the Duke of Wellington, 1831–1851*, London, John Murray, 1889, pp162–163.

300. Longford, Elizabeth, *The Years of the Sword*, London, World Books, 1971, pp440–441.

301. Marshal-Cornwall, op.cit. p256.

302. Koch, Général, *Mémoires de Massena, Volume I*, Paris, Paulin et Lechevalier, 1848–1850, pLXVI.

303. Marshal-Cornwall, op.cit. pp263–264.

304. Ibid. p264.

305. *The Gentleman's Magazine*, April 1817, p380.

306. Ibid. p380.

307. Junot, Laura, *Memoirs of Madame Junot Duchess of Abrantes Volume IV*, London, Richard Bentley & Son, 1893, p185.

308. Oman, Charles, *A History of the Peninsula War, Volume III*, Oxford, Clarendon Press, 1908, pp207–208.

309. Chandler, David, *On the Napoleonic Wars*, London, Greenhill Books Limited, 1999, originally 1994, p113.

310. Pool, Bernard (Ed.), *The Croker Papers 1808–1857*, London, B.T. Batsford Ltd, 1967, p174.

Bibliography

ARCHIVES CONSULTED
The British Library
Colindale Newspaper Archive
The National Army Museum
The University of Leicester

NATIONAL ARMY MUSEUM SOURCES
NAM 1986-11-33 *The Account of Major Thomas, William, Brotherton, 14th Light Dragoons.*

NAM 1964-04-76 *Anonymous, Journal of a Soldier of the 71st Regiment.*

NAM 7511-31 *The Memoirs of an Anonymous Captain in the British Army – 24 August – 16 September 1808.*

NAM 6807-461 *Lieutenant Colonel Richard Brunton's (13th Light Dragoons) papers.* Brunton served in several different regiments including the 43rd Light Infantry and the 3rd Caçadores.

NAM 7403-155 *Colonel John Elley, Assistant Adjutant General of Cavalry in Spain* – personal letters and reports.

NAM 6112-33 *The Account of Major William Stuart, 30th Regiment of Foot.*

NEWSPAPERS AND JOURNALS
The Annual Register
The Gentleman's Magazine
The Times

PUBLISHED CONTEMPORARY SOURCES
Brett-James, Antony (Ed.), *Edward Costello – The Peninsula and Waterloo Campaigns*, London, Longmans, Green & Co Ltd, 1967

Brindle, Rosemary (Ed.), *With Napoleon's Guns – The Military Memoirs of an Officer of the First Empire*, London, Greenhill Books, 2005

Butler, Arthur, John (Ed.), *The Memoirs of Baron De Marbot – Late Lieutenant-General in the French Army*, London, Cassell & Company Ltd, 1929

Butler, Arthur John (Ed. & trans.), *The Memoirs of Baron Thiebault*, in 2 volumes, London, Smith, Elder & Co., 1896

Curling, Henry, (Ed.), *Recollections of Rifleman Harris* London, Peter Davies Limited, 1929

D'Urban, Sir Benjamin, Major-General, (edited by Rousseau, I.J.), *The Peninsular Journal*, London, Longmans, Green & Co, 1930

Fletcher, Ian (Ed.), *For King and Country – The Letters and Diaries of John Mills, Coldstream Guards, 1811–1814*, Staplehurst, Spellmount, 1995

Foy, Maximilien Sébastien, *History of the War in the Peninsula*, in 2 volumes, London, Treuttel and Würtz, 1827

Girod de l'Ain, Maurice, *Grand Artilleurs: Drouot – Sénarmont – Eblé*, Paris, Berger-Laurault, 1895

Grattan, William, *Adventures with the Connaught Rangers 1809–1814* Edinburgh, R&R Clark Ltd, 1902

Green, William, *Travels and Adventures of William Green (Late Rifle Brigade)*, Leicester, W.A. Hammond, 1858

Hibbert, Christopher (Ed.), *A soldier of the Seventy-First* Gloucestershire, The Windrush Press, 1996, originally 1819

Howard, Donald D. (Ed.), *The French Campaign in Portugal 1810–1811 – An Account by Jean Jacques Pelet*, Minneapolis, University of Minnesota Press, 1973

Jones, B.T. (Ed.), *Napoleon's Army – The Military Memoirs of Charles Parquin*, London, Greenhill Books, 1989

Jones, John T., Colonel RE, *Memoranda Relative to the Lines Thrown up to Cover Lisbon in 1810*, East Sussex, The Naval & Military Press Ltd, 2004. A reprint of the 1829 edition

Junot, Laura, *Memoirs of Madame Junot Duchess of Abrantes*, in 4 volumes, London, Richard Bentley & Son, 1893

Kincaid, J. Captain, *Adventures in the Rifle Brigade – in the Peninsula, France and the Netherlands from 1809 to 1815*, London, Peter Davies Limited, 1929

Larpent, Seymour F., *The Private Journal of F.S. Larpent, Esq: Judge Advocate General of the British Forces in the Peninsula, attached to the head-quarters of Lord Wellington during the Peninsular War, from 1812 to its close*, in 3 volumes, London, Richard Bentley, 1854

Leach, Lieutenant Colonel J., *Rough Sketches of the Life of an Old*

Soldier: During a Service in the West Indies; at the Siege of Copenhagen in 1807; in the Peninsula and the South of France in the Campaigns 1808 to 1814, with the Light Division; in the Netherlands in 1815; including the Battles of Quatre Bras and Waterloo, London, 1831

Liddell Hart, B.H. (Ed.), *The Letters of Private Wheeler 1809–1828*, Gloucestershire, The Windrush Press, 1999

Mockler-Ferryman, A.F., *The Life of a Regimental Officer During the Great War 1793-1815 – based on the letters of Colonel Samuel Rice, 51st Light Infantry*, London, William Blackwood, 1913

Moore-Smith, G.C. (Ed.), *The Autobiography of Sir Harry Smith 1787–1819*, London, John Murray, 1910

Napier, Lieutenant-General Sir William, *The Life and Opinions of General Sir Charles James Napier*, London, John Murray, 1857

Pool, Bernard (Ed.), *The Croker Papers 1808–1857*, London, B.T. Batsford Ltd, 1967, originally 1884

Scarfe, Norman (Ed.), *Letters from the Peninsula – The Freer Family Correspondence 1807–1814*, Leicester, University College, 1953

Schaumann, A.L.F., (Ed. & trans. by Ludovici, Anthony), *On the Road with Wellington*, London, William Heinemann Ltd, 1924

Sommerset De Chair (Ed.), *Napoleon's Memoirs*, London, Faber and Faber Limited, 1948

Stanhope, Philip Henry, *Notes of Conversations with the Duke of Wellington, 1831–1851*, London, John Murray, 1889

Sturgis, Julian (Ed.), *A Boy in the Peninsular War – The Services, Adventures and Experiences of Robert Blakeney Subaltern in the 28th Regiment*, London, John Murray, 1899

Summerville, Christopher (Ed.), *The Exploits of Baron De Marbot*, New York, Caroll & Graf Publishers, 2000

Thompson, W. F. K. (Ed.), *An Ensign in the Peninsular War – The Letters of John Aitchison*, London, Michael Joseph Ltd, 1981

Warre, Lieutenant General Sir William, (Ed. by his nephew, Edward Warre), *Letters from the Peninsula 1808–1812*, London, John Murray, 1909

The Dispatches of Field Marshal the Duke of Wellington, 1799–1818, (compiled and edited by Lieutenant Colonel Gurwood) in 12 volumes, London, John Murray, 1834–1839

The Supplementary Dispatches and Memoranda of Field Marshal the Duke of Wellington, 1793–1827, (edited by the 2nd Duke of Wellington) in 15 volumes, London, John Murray, 1858–1872

SECONDARY SOURCES

Buchan, John Walter, *The Duke of Wellington*, London, Thomas Nelson & Sons, 1914

Chandler, David, *The Campaigns of Napoleon*, London, Weidenfeld and Nicolson, 1967

Chandler, David (Ed.), *Napoleon's Marshals*, London, Weidenfeld and Nicolson, 1987

Chandler, David, *On the Napoleonic Wars*, London, Greenhill Books Limited, 1999

Craufurd, Alexander Reverend, *General Craufurd and His Light Division*, Cambridge, Ken Trotman Ltd, 1987. Originally published 1898

Delderfield, R.F., *The March of the Twenty-Six*, London, Hodder & Stoughton, 1962

Esdaile, Charles, *The Peninsular War*, London, Penguin Books Ltd, 2002, 2003 edition

Fletcher, Ian, *Craufurd's Light Division*, Tunbridge Wells, Spellmount Ltd, 1991

Fletcher, Ian, *The Lines of Torres Vedras*, Oxford, Osprey Publishing, 2003

Fortescue, J.W., *A History of the British Army*, in 13 volumes, London, Macmillan & Co Ltd, 1899–1930

Girod de l'Ain, Maurice, *Grands Artilleurs; Drouot – Sénarmont – Eblé*, Paris, Berger-Laurault, 1895

Glover, Michael, *The Peninsular War 1807–1814*, London, Penguin Books, 1974, 2001 edition

Glover, Michael, *Wellington as Military Commander*, London, Penguin Books, 2001

Grehan, John, *The Lines of Torres Vedras*, Staplehurst, Kent, Spellmount Ltd, 2004

Grove Barnes, Donald, *George III and William Pitt, 1783–1806*, New York, Octagon Books, 1965

Guedalla, Philip, *The Duke*, London, Hodder and Stoughton Limited, 1933

Hibbert, Christopher, *Corunna*, London, B.T. Batsford Limited, 1961

Holmes, Richard, *Wellington the Iron Duke*, London, Harper Collins Publishers, 2003

Horne, Alistair, *How Far From Austerlitz?*, London, Macmillan Publishers Ltd, 1996, 1997 edition

Howard, Donald D., *The Battle of Bussaco*, Florida, USA, The Florida State University, 1965

Howard, Donald D., *Napoleon and Iberia – The Twin Sieges of Ciudad Rodrigo and Almeida, 1810*, London, Greenhill Books, 1994 – originally 1984

Humble, Richard, *Napoleon's Peninsula Marshals*, London, Purcell Books Services Limited, 1974 – originally 1973

Keegan, John, *The Mask of Command*, Penguin Books Limited, 1988

Koch, Général, *Mémoires de Massena*, in 7 volumes, Paris, Paulin et Lechevalier, 1848–1850

Lanfrey, P, *The History of Napoleon the First*, in 4 volumes, London, Macmillan & Co., 1886

Longford, Elizabeth, *The Years of the Sword*, London, World Books, 1971

Lynn, John A., *The Bayonets of the Republic*, Urbana & Chicago USA, University of Illinois Press, 1984

MacDonell, A.G., *Napoleon and his Marshals*, London, Prion, 1996, originally published by Macmillan & Co., 1934

Marshall-Cornwall, James, *Marshal Massena*, London, Oxford University Press, 1965

Index